RAN AARONSOHN

ROTHSCHILD AND EARLY JEWISH COLONIZATION IN PALESTINE

Geographic Perspectives on the Human Past
Series Editor: Robert D. Mitchell

American Environment: Interpretations of Past Geographies
    edited by Lary M. Dilsaver and Craig E. Colten
In the Absence of Towns: Settlement and Country Trade in Southside Virginia, 1730–1800
    by Charles J. Farmer
Common Ground: The Struggle for Ownership of the Black Hills National Forest
    by Martha Geores
Upstate Arcadia: Landscape, Aesthetics and the Triumph of Social Differentiation in America
    by Peter J. Hugill
Derelict Landscapes: The Wasting of America's Built Environment
    by John A. Jakle and David Wilson
Nationalism and Territory: Constructing Group Identity in Southeastern Europe
    by George W. White

RAN AARONSOHN

ROTHSCHILD AND EARLY JEWISH COLONIZATION IN PALESTINE

ROWMAN & LITTLEFIELD PUBLISHERS, INC.
Lanham · Boulder · New York
THE HEBREW UNIVERSITY MAGNES PRESS, JERUSALEM

ROWMAN & LITTLEFIELD PUBLISHERS, INC.

Published in the United States of America
by Rowman & Littlefield Publishers, Inc.
4720 Boston Way, Lanham, Maryland 20706
http://www.rowmanlittlefield.com

Copyright © 2000 by The Hebrew University Magnes Press, Jerusalem

All rights reserved. No part of this publication may be reproduced, stored in a retrieval system, or transmitted in any form or by any means, electronic, mechanical, photocopying, recording, or otherwise, without the prior permission of the publisher.

ISBN 0-7425-0914-1

Printed in Israel

The paper used in this publication meets the minimum requirements of American National Standard for information Sciences—Permanence of Paper for Printed Library Materials, ANSI 239.48-1992.

CONTENTS

List of tables	7
List of maps	8
List of figures	9
Preface	11
Introduction: On colonization: Some Theoretical and Practical Aspects	15

PART ONE

BARON ROTHSCHILD AND THE JEWISH COLONIES: STAGES OF INVOLVEMENT

Introduction: The Pre-Rothschild Years — Sporadic Settlement	49
Chapter one: First Overtures, 1882–1883	53
Chapter two: Deepening Ties, 1883–1887	68
Chapter three: A Relationship Solidified, 1887–1890	87

PART TWO

THE ROTHSCHILD ADMINISTRATION: HIERARCHY, ACTION AND IMPACT

Introduction: Responsibilities of the Administration	119
Chapter four: Administrators and Clerks	122
Chapter five: Agronomists and Technicians	134
Chapter six: Communal Workers	146
Chapter seven: Other Employees	154

PART THREE
THE JEWISH COLONIES IN 1890: THE MARK OF THE BARON

Introduction: The End of a Decade	175
Chapter eight: Layout and Architecture	176
Chapter nine: Farm and Economy	210
Chapter ten: Society and Culture	236
Epilogue: Early Jewish Colonization: Figures and Features	257
Bibliography	300
Index	319

LIST OF MAPS

1. Zikhron Ya'akov, 1884 — 72
2. The lands of Zikhron Ya'akov and daughter colonies, 1887 — 77
3. Route and outcome of Rothschild's visit to Eretz Israel, 1887 — 89
4. Lands of Castina (Be'er Tuviya), 1896 — 103
5. Plan of colony of Be'er Tuviya, 1896 — 145
6. Zikhron Ya'akov in 1890 (reconstruction) — 178
7. Yesud ha-Ma'ala in 1890 (reconstruction) — 181
8. Gedera in 1890 — 182
9. Petah Tikva in 1890 — 184
10. Rishon le-Zion in 1890 — 185
11. Rosh Pinna in 1890 — 186
12. Rishon le-Zion winery — 197
13. Jewish settlement in Eretz Israel, 1882–1890 — 230
14. Rothschild's projects outside "his" colonies — 263

LIST OF TABLES

1. The Rothschild colonies in the 1880s: A chronology of establishment and patronage — 112
2. Spatial and functional hierarchy: The colonies and Rothschild officials — 131
3. Direct aid from Rothschild to settlers, 1890 — 167
4. Population of Jewish colonies circa 1890 — 237
5. Demographic development of Petah Tikva, 1882–1890 — 239
6. Mortality rates in Rosh Pinna, 1883–1890 — 240
7. Inventory of the Jewish Colonies circa 1890 — 255
8. Rothschild colonies and other rural Jewish settlements, 1890 and 1900 — 276

LIST OF FIGURES

Founders of Zikhron Ya'akov, 1889	50
Settlers in Mazkeret Bayta (Ekron), 1898	57
Rishon le-Zion in its early days (1883?)	63
Early private home in Rishon le-Zion, built in 1883	65
Cultivated land and community buildings in Rosh Pinna, c. 1898	71
Some of the houses and huts in Zikhron Ya'akov (1885?)	75
Vineyards and wine cellar in Rishon le-Zion, c. 1898	79
The colony of Ekron, 1892	82
Yahud (Petah Tikva) with its wind-operated pump, c. 1898	86
Gedera and its settlers, 1892	93
One of the administration buildings, Rishon le-Zion, c. 1899	94
Bat Shlomo, c. 1898	100
The colony of Shefeya, 1898	107
Yesud ha-Ma'ala, 1898	110
Baron Edmond de Rothschild	120
Administrator and settlers in the main street of Zikhron Ya'akov (1886?)	126
Members of the Baron's administration (E. Scheid in the center), Zikhron Ya'akov, c. 1897	129
A young colonist as a pupil in Mikveh Israel, c. 1898	137
First water tower, built in Zikhron Ya'akov 1891	141
Rishon le-Zion wine cellar and some of its technical workers, 1898	143
The medical staff of Rishon le-Zion, c. 1890	147

Rosh Pinna's school headmaster with family, 1887	150
Rothschild's aides: M. Erlanger, S. Hirsch, C. Netter	156
Some of the first administration buildings, Zikhron Ya'akov, c. 1899	162
Standard single-family dwelling unit in the Rothschild colonies	188
One of the first dwelling huts in Zikhron Ya'akov	190
Rishon le-Zion synagogue, c. 1899	191
The first well of Rishon le-Zion (1910)	199
"The administrators' street" in Zikhron Ya'akov (aerial photo, c. 1947)	203
"The vineyards' street" in Rosh Pinna, c. 1898	208
Vineyards in Gedera, 1898	214
Rishon le-Zion and its fields (aerial photo, 1917)	217
Agricultural implements in Castina, 1898	227
The wineries of Zikhron Ya'akov, c. 1895	234
A local committee, Rishon le-Zion, 1897	241
School gymnastics in Rishon le-Zion, 1897	244
Synagogue and the agronomist's house, Zikhron Ya'akov c. 1899	249
The entrance to Rosh Pinna (1918)	259

PREFACE

This volume probes the beginnings of modern Jewish colonization in Palestine during the late nineteenth century, through its institutional setting: Baron Edmond de Rothschild and his agents.

Beyond a careful reconstruction of the major developmental trends and phenomena of this case study, we have considered the efforts of the Jewish settlers in Palestine from the broad vantage point, in the context of colonization enterprises in other regions of the world. Our basic premise is that in spite of the geographical, historical and ideological uniqueness of the Jews' return to their ancient homeland, their establishment of agricultural settlements was part of a global phenomenon that literally reshaped the world in the nineteenth century.

The extent to which colonization in Palestine was similar to such ventures in the "New World" is the pivotal question and point of departure in the current work, whereas the Hebrew edition, published in 1990, is narrower in theme, dealing with colonization in Palestine per se. This earlier study examines the development of the Jewish colonies only in light of the assistance of Baron de Rothschild and his administration. Indeed, the Baron's indelible imprint on the early Jewish settlements in Palestine is a leitmotif which runs throughout both works; but the canvas is now larger and the theme of colonization has been added. In consequence, the history of individual colonies and the precise nature of the assistance rendered by Rothschild and his officials are less detailed (interested readers may consult the Hebrew edition for more particulars and references).

In terms of structure, the historical-geographic approach of the Hebrew volume remains largely intact. However, the shift in focus has led to two important additions. One is a lengthy introduction that establishes colonization and colonialism as two distinct terms (despite the tendency to link them in common usage), and analyzes selected examples of European colonization in various parts of the world, with special emphasis on the Mediterranean. French and Italian colonization in North Africa are therefore discussed in greater length because of the basic similarities with Palestine, where German Templer colonization is also presented. Another addition is the epilogue, which positions the Jewish colonies in their rightful place among the other colonizing endeavors of the nineteenth century and answers the thematic questions that inspired the writing of this work.

Both volumes limit themselves, in their discussion of the case study, to the first eight years of modern Jewish colonization in Palestine, 1882–1890, on the grounds that within this brief span of time, the colonies were cast in the mold they were to follow for many years to come. Through an understanding of the functioning of the early colonies and the factors that influenced them during this formative period, it is hoped that the reader will gain new insights into the Jewish settlement enterprise as a whole.

In other words, the present work is therefore a reworking of my Hebrew volume, which places the theme of colonization in Palestine within the context of similar developments elsewhere.

Finally, one semantic comment — with contemporary overtones — is in order. "Palestine" in this volume refers to that territory located along the eastern Mediterranean shore which is also known as "The Land of Israel" or "The Holy Land," to which the Jews returned to settle in it once again, and where they established their colonies. Notwithstanding the fact that they always referred to it as "Eretz Israel" (The Land of Israel), and despite political-ideological connotations, we have preferred occasionally to use "Palestine." Since this was generally the name given to that than-undefinated territory in neutral contemporary sources, whether by its rulers — the Ottomans, and later the British — or by European and other foreign elements, we believe this term to be suitable for an academic study dealing with the late nineteenth and early twentieth centuries.

The publication of this volume was made possible through the generous support of the Faculty of Humanities of the Hebrew University of Jerusalem, The James Amzalak Fund for Research in Historical Geography, at the Hebrew University of Jerusalem, the Institute for the Research on the History of JNF, Land and Settlement, The Amos Fund for Encouraging Scholars and Writers, founded by the President of Israel.

Research in France was enabled by funds placed at my disposal by the Bureau for Cultural Relations of the French Foreign Ministry.

Thanks are also due to Rowman and Littlefield Publishers for accepting my book in their "Geographic Perspectives on the Human Past" series.

I am most grateful to Mrs. Gila Brand who undertook the enormous endeavor of translating the Hebrew text into English, to Mr. Yohai Goell for his faithful efforts in style-editing, and to Mrs. Tamar Sofer for her accurate cartographic work.

It gives me great pleasure to thank my many teachers, colleagues and students who contributed their thoughtful comments throughout the various phases of this work. Special thanks are due to Professor Paul Claval of the Université de Paris IV — Sorbonne, and to Professor Robert D. Mitchell of the University of Maryland. Finally, I would like to express my heartfelt gratitude to Mr. Dan Benovici, director of the Hebrew University Magnes Press, for his consistent and gracious support, and to Professor Yehoshua Ben-Arieh of the Hebrew University of Jerusalem, who continuously enlightened me with his comments and assistance throughout the years.

Ran Aaronsohn
Jerusalem

INTRODUCTION

ON COLONIZATION: SOME THEORETICAL AND PRACTICAL ASPECTS

Defining Colonization

Colonization is basically a two-step process that begins with migration and ends with the development of new settlements.[1] Judging by the visible changes colonization has introduced on the map, it would seem to be a primarily geographic phenomenon. However, it rarely occurs in a vacuum. In modern times, especially during the era discussed here (the second half of the nineteenth and the early twentieth centuries), it has mainly gone hand in hand with colonialism, the policy adopted by the world powers who speedily extended their authority over foreign territories. The global processes that stimulated colonialism, i.e., population growth, commercial and industrial development, and competing interests in the New World, also set the stage for a series of colonization enterprises that led many Europeans to leave their homes and settle wherever a European flag was flown — in the Americas, Africa, Australia, and sometimes in Asia.

Colonialism or the forceful occupation of foreign territory was thus perceived at the end of the nineteenth century as an inseparable partner of colonization, with the government of the occupying power as the third side of this new triangle. In the research on colonies and colonization that proliferated between the two world wars, the role of the government

---

1   In French there is also a linguistic distinction between settlement, which is done anywhere, and colonization, which takes place in a foreign country. See Librarie Larousse: *Dictionnaire moderne Français–Anglais*, p. 141.

as a conquering force was virtually taken for granted.[2] Thus, the term "colonization" gravitated from a purely geographical designation to a political concept harboring economic and social overtones. The substance of "decolonization" has also drifted away from its original meaning, now connoting what should have actually been defined as "decolonialism."

Confronted with the primarily political-historical and socio-economic approach to colonization and the absence of geographical studies,[3] Chaim Arlosoroff declared that his own writings on the history of colonization would analyze "the colonization process itself."[4] Even to this very day it would seem that the few scholars purporting to study the geographical perspective have failed to accomplish their aim. Their arguments have tended to become overly caught up in the political relations between occupiers and the conquered rather than the relationship between the colonists and their land, i.e., the impact of human beings on the landscape or the role of the new environment in the development of settlements.

In his classic study on "Geography and Colonization," G. Hardy defined colonization in two senses, which he termed narrow and wide:

> Dans son sens restreint, qui est en même temps le plus ancien, il exprime la mise en valeurs du sol par des colons européens installes à demeure...
> Dans son sens large... il designe alors le developpement méthodique des resources et l'amelioration de la vie indigene dans un pays place sous la domination ou la tutelle d'une nation moderne.[5]

For Hardy, colonization in both senses mirrored a specific relationship between whites and non-whites or between mother countries and dependencies. He did not address such sweeping aspects as Europe versus the New World or of people forging ties with a new land. His work is geographical in that it discusses colonization enterprises on different

---

2   Tartakower, p.11. Tartakower devotes an entire chapter to colonialism and colonization. See: ibid., pp. 103–139, and references cited in footnotes, pp. 139–147.
3   See bibliographical lists in Hardy, Tartakower, and Church; also nn. 8–10 in Griffin. The term "colony" itself has lost its geographical connotation, and is more often associated with international relations.
4   Arlosoroff, pp. 10, 19. This work was completed only up to the mid-nineteenth century.
5   Hardy, p. 25.

continents, in a variety of physical surroundings. Yet these enterprises are grouped and characterized by form of government, using terminology clearly associated with colonialism. Furthermore, in his assertion that the European colonies were worthy of praise because they improved the lot of the natives and brought development to the conquered territories Hardy demonstrated that he, too, embraced the anthropo-political view common among his contemporaries that white supremacy was fundamental to colonization.[6]

Renowned geographer Harrison Church structured his study of "Modern Colonization" along similar lines. He divided the colonies into two major and two minor groups by type of government and its declared aims.[7] In a geographical survey of the French colonies in the Chèlif plains of Algeria, X. Yacono defined colonization as the phenomenon arising when migrants from an advanced society settle in regions where the population is techonologically inferior.[8] Thus we see that geographers have also tended to emphasize the aspects of occupation and to view the phenomenon of colonization through the prism of politics.

Even today, a clear differentiation between colonization and colonialism is lacking. Even in the most recent editions of many reference books little, if any, distinction is made between these terms. *Encyclopaedia Britannica* and the *International Encyclopedia of Social Sciences* define colonialism only.[9] The entry on colonialism in the *Encyclopedia*

---

6   Hardy later reaches the conclusion that "la colonisation apparait essentiellement comme la transformation d'une region attardée ou negligée dans le sens des intérêts humains." See ibid., p. 203.
7   Church, p. ix.
8   Yacono, I, p. 63. I have cited several works in English and French, but the phenomenon has also been explored by researchers writing in other languages. The German geographer Gottfried Zöpfl, for example, distinguishes between four types of colonization determined by the relationship between the colony and the occupying country; see: Tartakower, p. 11, and p. 23, n. 5.
9   *Encylopaedia Britannica* (1951), VI; *International Encyclopedia of Social Sciences* (1968), III. The *Encyclopedia of Social Sciences* discusses colonialism only, from a political and economic perspective. The *Britannica* offers two definitions for colonization: "(a) the settlement of the subjects of a state in an area outside its geographical boundaries, but within its administrative sphere; or (b) a territorial unit outside the limits of a state, but closely associated with it by the ties of nationality, administration, economic interest or sentiment." The second could be an acceptable definition, but the material that follows is inapplicable and corresponds only with the

Americana is followed by a section on the "history of colonization" which relates to the phenomenon as a modern one and speaks of colonization in the same breath as imperialism.[10] Even in cases where colonization and colonialism merit separate entries, the distinction between them remains unclear. *La Grande Encylopédie Larousse*, for example, attempts to define both terms. Colonialism is described as "doctrine qui tend a legitimer par des raisons politiques ou morales, l'occupation et l'administration d'un territoire, voire d'une nation, par le gouvernment d'un Etat étranger," while colonization is defined as "constitution, à une assez grand distance d'une métropole, d'un établissement permanent, échappant à l'autorité des populations indigène et demeurant dans la dépendance de la métropole d'origine."[11] However, this definition of colonization is followed in the same entry by an elaboration on *colonial* expansion, and almost all the references in the bibliography are to studies of a historical-political nature.

The *Encyclopaedia Hebraica* explains that colonialism is a broad phenomenon in which individuals (or groups) settle in a new region for personal reasons such as self-betterment, whereas colonization is more specific and involves "the deliberate takeover of a portion of land outside the geographical borders of a country in order to establish a basis for the economic, political or military activity of the entire society, or the seizure of additional land for the creation of a new economy and society."[12] Colonization is further defined as the settlement of groups dispatched by an organization, movement or government with the aim of creating (or reinforcing) new residential, agricultural or social entities. However, once again, the rest of the essay is an exposé on *colonialism*. The features and inner mechanisms of colonization are scarcely touched upon, apart from the brief mention of three obstacles typically faced by colonization enterprises. Instead, the authors offer a lengthy historical review that skims the surface structure of colonization, i.e., the political

---

first definition, which is purely political. (A more recent edition of the *Britannica*, published in 1985, contains no entries at all on colonization or colonies.)
10 *Encyclopedia Americana* (1970), VII, p. 302.
11 *La Grande Encylopédie Larousse* (1973), X, pp. 3063, 3065.
12 *Encyclopaedia Hebraica* (1962), XV, col. 646 (Hebrew).

and economic framework, and develops into a discussion of imperialism, colonialism and even anti-colonialism.[13]

Associated so often with colonialism and imperialism, it is small wonder that colonization has become laden with negative connotations and conjures up images of racial inequality, oppression and exploitation. The question to be asked is to what extent colonization and colonialism are indeed synonymous, and whether they always go hand in hand. G. Wakefield was aware of this problem when he wrote:

> ...What do we mean by settlement? If French Canada became a British colony after its conquest, then it is the occupation and rule by a foreign people that is called colonization. But this cannot be... Does colonization also mean government, or does it refer only to the migration of people from their homeland to a new country without the desire to govern their new country?[14]

From a geographical standpoint, we suggest that every effort should be made to keep these two terms distinct. Our assumption is that colonization (the act of migrating and founding new settlements in a foreign land) and colonialism (the act of conquering a foreign territory or population and plundering its resources) do not necessarily coincide. Without ignoring the governmental, political and economic factors associated with colonization, our goal is to explore the subject from a geographical perspective. In this light, colonization becomes the reshaping of the landscape following the migration and settlement of a foreign entity.

The question of whether colonialism was part and parcel of modern Jewish colonization in Palestine is a valid one. However, our interest as geographers focuses on the development of the new body of settlement and how it changed the landscape of the country, namely: colonization processes. The added value of such an approach is that Jewish colonization can be studied in depth without being too greatly Zionocentric or Palestinocentric, and without becoming entangled in political arguments, often generated by hazy semantics and failure to distinguish between colonialism and colonization.

Before addressing the specific case of modern Jewish colonization in

---

13   Ibid., cols. 648–666.
14   G. Wakefield, translation into Hebrew in Arlosoroff, pp. 12–13.

Palestine, we shall glance briefly at a number of colonization enterprises in other parts of the world, all of them chosen with an eye to illustration and subsequent comparison with Palestine. Each of the examples dealt with here involves the migration and resettlement of Europeans in a country of temperate climate during the second half of the nineteenth and the early twentieth centuries.

An outstanding example, which we shall discuss below at length, is European — primarily French and Italian — settlement in North Africa, a region partly ruled by the settlers' home countries, and partly not. We shall also deal with the settlement of East European Jews in Argentina by the Jewish Colonisation Association, and of Protestant German members of the Temple Society in Palestine. All these were more or less contemporaneous with the beginnings of modern Jewish colonization in Palestine, upon which this volume focuses. The object is to maintain some kind of chronological, cultural and geophysical common denominator as a basis for comparison, thereby excluding all other kinds of examples — no matter how interesting they may be: colonization in earlier times (studied for instance by Arlosoroff), or recent endeavors such as European colonization in southern Brazil (studied by Waibel); the colonization of whites in the tropics (studied by Grenfell) or colonization by colored peoples in non-European cultures, such as the Chinese in the Far East.

Other noteworthy examples, which will not be discussed here, are cases of government-initiated, domestic colonization, such as those on the Canadian prairies, in the eastern provinces of Germany, and the settlement of Siberia and many other frontier areas of Russia during the period under discussion (see, e.g., England; Reichman–Hasson). It should also be noted that our comparisons do not encompass the colonization process as a whole, a topic too extensive for the framework of the present work, but focus on the institutional and intellectual contexts within which colonization was implemented in the late nineteenth century, since our discussion focuses on the contribution of Baron Edmond de Rothschild and his officials to modern Jewish settlement in Palestine.

By contrasting Jewish colonization in Palestine to comparable ventures in other parts of the world, the processes at work can be viewed from a global vantage point and the efforts of the Jewish colonists can be placed in a broader context.

Colonization in the Mediterranean: The French in Algeria

French colonization in North Africa, especially Algeria, has often been compared with Jewish colonization in Palestine. The resemblance has been noted in a variety of sources, from letters written in the 1880s to modern day research.[15] At first glance, the geophysical and governmental-legal features seem similar enough, both cases involving the settlement of Europeans in a Mediterranean, Muslim-Ottoman country. A review of the literature will enable us to ascertain whether this assertion is correct.

In a collection of essays marking the centennial of French rule in Algeria (1830–1930), G. Yver established a direct link between colonization and occupation.[16] Most of his attention focuses on France's military victory and the administrative mechanism developed to run the country after its conquest. He also challenges the conclusions reached in some of the important studies on colonization in Algeria, and outlines four sub-periods in the development of the French colonies:

a) The first decade, 1830–1840, known as the "heroic" period, marked by free and spontaneous colonization outside the large cities or in fortified outposts near French military installations in the plains of Algeria, particularly in the Mitidja Valley, not far from the city of Algiers.

b) The period of "official" colonization (1841–1860), during which large areas were settled with the assistance of the authorities. For the first ten years, colonization activity was carried out mainly on a small, private basis in colonies established and supervised by the French government; over the next ten years (the 1850s), most of the initiative came from capitalists, who built farms and villages on land offered as a free government concession.

c) The period of relative inactivity (1860–1870), during which the policies of Napoleon III and military authorities in Algeria impeded further development.

d) The resumption of free, government-aided colonization (1871 onwards). Throughout the 1870s, there was small-scale private settlement

---

15 Among the studies that compare Jewish colonization in Palestine to colonization in North Africa, see: Aaronsohn, Colonisation; Straus, p. 331; Church, p. 55; Zemach, p. 83.
16 Yver, p. 299.

in new colonies established with government loans. Over the next two decades, huge farms were set up by private capitalists who by the end of the century virtually controlled the fertile regions outside the large cities, in the Mitidja Valley and the Sahel Plains east of the city of Oran. Around 1880, extensive vineyards were planted by farmers who immigrated to North Africa from southern France after their crops had been destroyed by phyloxera. Bringing with them capital and agricultural expertise, they purchased farms both from the natives and from Europeans who had settled in the country in the previous decades with government assistance.[17]

In sum, Yver regards French settlement in Algeria as a combination of "official" colonization sponsored by the government for political and security reasons (populating the region with Frenchmen would ensure its control) and "free" colonization by private individuals in search of a livelihood or personal gain through exploitation of Algeria's resources. Official colonization entailed the establishment of small farms overseen by government administrators which were successful if enough funding was made available. Free colonization was largely dependent upon private capital, though the government often played a role in the acquisition of land (through the concession, lease or sale of land in its possession).

Julien examines the history of colonization in Algeria through the prism of the manner in which the French administration functioned.[18] He believes, the so-called "heroic" period of the first decade of occupation to have been a "period of anarchy" due to the disorganized colonization efforts pursued at the time, the indeterminate state of land ownership, and land speculation that caused prices to spiral, adversely affecting the Arabs, whom he considers the "real workers." A law passed in 1834 encouraged European investment in rural Algeria and officially sanctioned colonization. The few foreigners, mostly from Germany and Switzerland, who took up the challenge, were subjected to harassment by the local population and prevented from buying or selling their goods on the market. The small farmers soon found themselves on the verge of economic collapse, but several private investors prospered, particularly

---

17   Ibid., pp. 298–306.
18   Julien, pp. 540–685.

those who purchased land in the Sahel Plains, which was almost entirely owned by Europeans.

Two of the investors were Baron de Vialar and General Clauzel. Baron de Vialar was a pioneer of French colonization in Algeria. Following his arrival in 1832, he acquired large tracts of land upon which he built farms and villages. General Clauzel, operating in civilian capacity, founded an investment company that financed colonization schemes. His major contribution was the establishment in 1832 of a model farm, Ha'ouz-Hassan Pacha, on ten thousand dunams of land leased from the French government in the eastern part of the Mitidja Valley for the unrealistic nominal fee of one franc per ten dunams. However, the farm was plagued by security problems and illness, and during its ten years of existence never became fully productive. Poor hygienic conditions in the colonies caused the death of as many as one-third of the settlers within a period of five years.[19]

Piquet's survey of one hundred years of French settlement in Algeria describes Clauzel's colonization scheme in the western Mitidja Valley. In 1836, Clauzel bought up the lands of Boufarik and distributed small plots of forty dunams (!) to settlers who undertook to build houses and farm the land within a period of three years. Seventy-six farms were established and eighty-three homes completed by the end of the year, forming the basis for a village that was to flourish in the coming decades.[20]

As the French occupation of Algeria entered its second decade, twelve European colonies with a population of 2,500 had gained a foothold in the country (of a total of 25,000 Europeans resident in Algeria). Some 80,000 dunams of land were under cultivation, the major sources of income being wheat and livestock. Hundreds of thousands of trees had been planted, along with 87,000 mulberry, 64,000 olive, and 240,000 other varieties, including an unspecified number of grapevines. All this was terminated by the "Massacre of Mitidja" on November 20, 1839, when the soldiers of the emir, Abdul-Kadr, stormed the valley and murdered most of the colonists.[21]

---

19 Ibid, pp. 647–649.
20 Piquet, p. 74. For a more detailed discussion of colonization in Boufarik, see below, p. 27.
21 Julien, p. 649. The settlements established by the Europeans are referred to in

Piquet's study provides us with an in-depth account of the next two decades of French settlement, i.e., the years of "official" colonization. From 1840, France followed a plan devised by Comte Guyot to enhance European presence in Algeria.[22] Throughout the 1840s and 1850s, the government sent over settlers, mostly Frenchmen but others, too, providing each one with a small piece of land, a house (or building materials), seeds, saplings and work animals. The army prepared the infrastructure for the new colonies and was responsible for apportioning land, paving roads, and so on. In the 1840s, prospective colonists went through a screening process and only those who possessed some private capital (at least 1,200–1,500 francs) were accepted. Government assistance, as noted above, was granted on a one-time basis. In the 1850s, the screening stopped and aid was increased. The colonists were supported by the government for three years, the maximum allotment of land being raised from 120 to 200 dunams. The first decade of "official" colonization resulted in the establishment of thirty-eight colonies, and the second decade in another forty-two, with a population of 13,500. In addition, eighty-one farms were established on 6,000 dunams of land granted to European investors as personal concessions.[23]

Who were these early colonists? L. Beaudicour contends that the majority were not farmers, although over half the population of France was then engaged in agriculture. Usually they were impoverished laborers or craftsmen, or middle-class shopkeepers with a small amount of private capital. Most of the settlers of the "heroic" and "official" periods belonged to the second group. Members of the working class became the dominant element at the end of the 1840s when riots and labor unrest in Paris in 1848 spurred the government to relocate workers in Algeria. With

---

the literature as "villages," "colonies," "settlement centers" (Piquet) and "camps" (Julien).

22 Many colonies founded during the years of official colonization, 1846–1869, were inhabited by immigrants from other countries, such as Italy, Spain and Ireland. Clusters of Swiss colonies were prominent in the Mitidja Valley and around the city of Algiers, as were German colonies near Oran. See Grandadir, p. 19.

23 Piquet, pp. 71–79. For additional material on the stages of official settlement and authorized data on the number, area and population of the colonies by decade, see *Colonisation en Algérie*, especially the chart on p. 47.

free tracts of land, government credit and administrative supervision, the colonies established by these lower-class laborers proved more successful than those of the middle-class shopkeepers that were soon on the brink of collapse.[24]

The early colonists also included a number of wealthy capitalists who established farms and villages (populated, of course, by laborers and artisans) and a group of demobilized soldiers who founded a colony on lands owned by the military administration, under the leadership of General Bugeaud.[25]

In his study of the major colonizing companies operating in North Africa, R. E. Passron differentiates between *petite colonisation* and *grande colonisation*: the colonization of numerous middle-class capitalists which created a network of many small farm units, as opposed to colonization sponsored by wealthy capitalists or companies who purchased extensive, contiguous tracts of land and established colonies and adjoining farms as one large unit. *Petite colonisation* was almost wholly dependent upon the government and therefore frequently synonymous with "official" colonization, whereas *grande colonisation*, even when assisted by government concessions, was always autonomous.[26]

Among the public settlement companies active in Algeria by permission of the French government were:

a) Compagnie Genevoise which began to operate in the Setif region near Constantine in 1853. To comply with the terms of the government concession, efforts were made to organize large-scale settlement. When this proved unsuccessful, the company reneged on its commitments and after 1858, ran its affairs on a simple, profit-seeking basis.

b) La Société de l'Habra et de la Macta, established in 1864 to carry out drainage work and improve agricultural technology. Most of its efforts in the French colonies in Algeria were devoted to irrigation.

c) La Société General Algérienne et la Compagnie Algérienne, established in 1865 with the dual purpose of creating infrastructure for French colonization and cultivating farmland. This society built roads and railways throughout Algeria, and cultivated over one million dunams

---

24 Beaudicour, pp. 146–158.
25 Julien, p. 655; Yver, p. 301.
26 Passron, throughout the work.

(chiefly in the Constantine area) which yielded bountiful crops and high profits.[27]

Passron shows that the large settlement companies in Algeria operated in two directions. As capitalist business ventures they were interested in making a profit; as beneficiaries of the French government, from which they received land and other means of production, they were committed to the objective of expanding French settlement. At the outset, these companies made great efforts to fulfil their obligations to the government, but as time went on and the obstacles mounted, the profit motive took priority. In the long run, the difference between them and ordinary capitalist enterprises was very small.

While the above studies explore colonization as a broad, national-political phenomenon, a few researchers have studied the French colonies in Algeria from a localized or regional perspective, dwelling on some of the more technical aspects. One example is the work of J. Franc, who accompanies his discussion of settlement in the Mitidja Valley with maps, photographs and detailed diagrams. He describes a less known form of colonization pursued by middle-class capitalists between 1848 and 1860, and concludes that 218 farms covering an area of 25,000 hectares were established in the valley during this period (with approximately 7,000 hectares or 350 dunams devoted to agriculture on each 1,260-dunam farm).[28]

One French farm in the Mitidja Valley is studied more in depth. It covered 11,000 dunams of land, of which 1,100 dunams were planted with wheat and 450 with tobacco. Livestock holdings totalled 160 head of cattle, and 11 camels that were used for conveyance in the absence of a carriage road. In addition to farm buildings, the owner built two family residences and four houses to accommodate the seven families of laborers in his employ, a total of thirty-eight persons. Until the 1880s, wheat and tobacco continued to be the major crops. Following the phyloxera epidemic that destroyed vineyards in southern France, grapevines were planted, eventually accounting for one-quarter of all the cultivated area.[29]

27 Ibid.
28 Franc, p. 489.
29 Ibid., p. 660.

Although Franc's approach is essentially geographic, he, too, upholds the traditional historiographic association between colonization processes and government. His breakdown of French colonization in Algeria into the "heroic" stage (1830–1841), the "military" stage (1842–1858) and the "victory" stage (after 1858) is highly reminiscent of the historians cited above. Franc, however, perceives a direct relationship between the form and extent of colonization, and the government in power. In his view, the colonization ventures embarked upon during the "heroic" stage, for example, were closely linked to the procession of military governors who came and went during the decade in question.

X. Yacono studies colonization in the Chèlif, a major valley that stretches 200 kilometers across Algeria from east to west and spills into the Mediterranean near the city of Oran.[30] Two of his five parts are based on the traditional classifications. One part deals with colonizing endeavors in the Chèlif in political terms, with chapters on "military-inspired" colonization (1843–1848), "politically-inspired" colonization (1848–1857), "commencement of ordinary colonization" (1857–1870), and so on. Another part dwells on "colonization and the natives," emphasizing demography (three million people occupied an area of 300,000 square kilometers, which works out to ten persons per kilometer),[31] and the economic and social impact of colonization.

The other three parts employ a different perspective. The first one describes the state of affairs in Algeria in 1830, when the early pioneers arrived. Particular attention in this cross-section is devoted to the system of land ownership. *Melk* land was privately owned by the head of a family; *sabega* was cooperatively owned by an entire tribe; *habou* was controlled by religious endowments; and *beylik* was government land, now owned by France.[32]

The second one explores what Yacono considers to be the two main aspects of colonization: land acquisition and the development of the human component. He argues that because colonization in the Chèlif

---

30 X. Yacono, "La colonisation des pleines du Chèlif," Ph.D. thesis, Université de Paris, 1955–6, 2 vols.; also published as a book: see Yacono.
31 Ibid., I, p. 207. Yacono notes that this is his own estimate, there being no conclusive figures for the number of native Algerians in 1830. The estimates range from 400,000 to 10 million.
32 Ibid., I, pp. 217–227.

commenced on *habou* and *beylik* land seized by the French government, the land ownership issue determined the location of the first French colonies along the eastern and western borders of the valley. Over a period of thirty-three years, the government expropriated nearly 300,000 dunams, mainly along the outer rim of the valley, and established nine "colonial centers" ranging in size from 9,000 to 45,000 dunams. This colonization process came to an end when the rights to those lands was restored to the local tribes in April 1863 by the Senatus Consulte law, which declared that those who had traditionally farmed them were the rightful owners.[33]

The last part dwells on the "agents of change": security, sanitation, transportation, water supply, and capital resources. In all these areas, the crucial role of government is readily apparent. The roads and railways built by the French authorities were instrumental in determining both the location of villages and their degree of prosperity. The bridges and overpasses erected by the authorities enabled cultivation of formerly inaccessible lands on the other side of the valley.[34] Nearly four million francs — almost one-quarter of all French investment in the region — was spent on digging wells, constructing dams, developing water sources and building conduits that often carried water over many kilometers. Some efforts in this sphere, such as the drilling carried out in 1885-1886 in search of artesian wells, proved unsuccessful.[35] For the first time, attention was paid to improving security and health. From the 1840s onward, the government took steps to combat malaria by draining swamps, planting trees, and building hospitals, even though the pace and efficiency of these programs left much to be desired.

Of all the spheres connected with colonization, the government was least attentive to the need for agricultural credit. As a result, the 2,000 middle-class farmers (whose assets amounted to an average of 11,200 francs per family) found themselves in desperate financial straits, caught between loan sharks and the expansion of wealthy capitalists. Indeed,

---

33 Ibid., I, pp. 283–307. In the following years, tracts of land for settlement were acquired through barter agreements (the method preferred by the villagers) and purchase (mainly from local capitalists with private property). Expropriation of land also continued.
34 Ibid., I, pp. 416–419.
35 Ibid., II, pp. 17–27.

the two major obstacles facing the settlers in the Chèlif, according to Yacono, were the shortage of water and the lack of capital.[36]

In a micro-level study marking fifty years of French occupation, *Un siècle de colonisation*, E. F. Gautier distinguishes between the "actors" (i.e., settlers, intellectuals, soldiers, natives, clergy) and the "stage" (i.e., Algeria, mines, railroads, plains). Special attention is focused on colonization in the village of Boufarik in the eastern Mitidja Valley. The Boufarik venture is carefully scrutinized and held up as a model of French colonization in Algeria as a whole.[37] Gautier employs the classic geographical-historical method of juxtaposing two time periods (1830 and 1930), carrying out a step-by-step comparison between them.

Gautier describes the hardships faced by the pioneers of Boufarik when the colony was founded in 1836. Despite poor security, scarce capital resources and threat of malaria, the population grew from 150 to over 500 by the end of the decade. After the "Massacre of Mitidja," the number of inhabitants dropped to 400 (142 families), but was back to 500 two years later. As Boufarik entered its third decade, a period of rapid growth ensued, population figures climbing to 2,000. By 1866, some 8,000 persons, nearly half of them Europeans, had settled in the village.[38]

An interesting demographic finding is that 55 of the 560 residents of Boufarik in 1842 were "servants and laborers." The following year, the population totalled 846 and comprised 105 "natives," 149 "foreigners," and 592 Frenchmen. Gautier also sheds light on two social and economic phenomena: the launching of private and public financial enterprises that stimulated non-agricultural settlement (such as a market and a well-drilling cooperative) and the establishment of public institutions. The only institutions in 1841 were a school, a church and a court of justice; in 1844, a pharmacy and fire department were opened. By 1847, Boufarik had its own municipality and was on its way to becoming a rural center along the lines of the French *bourg*.

---

36 Ibid., I, pp. 388–394; II, pp. 40–63.
37 Gautier, p. 76.
38 Ibid., pp. 61–65. Today Boufarik is one of the large satellite cities in the ring of urban settlements around Algiers.

European Colonization in Other Parts of North Africa

During the nineteenth and early twentieth centuries, Europeans settled in other North African countries. Two examples are the government-sponsored colonization of Italians in Libya after its occupation in 1911, and the colonization of Europeans in Tunisia, which became a French protectorate in 1881 but retained autonomy in internal affairs.[39] French settlement in Tunisia was partially sponsored by the French government, whereas the settlement of Italians and other European nationals in the country after 1881 did not enjoy sponsorship.[40]

Italian colonization in Libya after 1921 is the subject of a study by Despois. He distinguishes between two periods of settlement, both colored by the policy of the Italian government. The occupation of Libya was originally perceived as an economic move and colonization during this period was minimal. In 1933, after twelve years of rule, a total of 2,000 Italian families, numbering 7,000 persons, were living on 10,000 hectares (nearly 110,000 Turkish dunams) of government land, chiefly in the Tripoli region. After 1933, during what was characterized by Despois as the second period, the Italian government recognized the potential of colonization in Libya as a demographic solution for its domestic problems and took various measures to encourage the relocation in Libya of destitute Italian laborers, particularly from Sicily.[41]

The most important contribution of the Italian government was a series of agrarian reforms by which the property of rebels and uncultivated land were expropriated and resold to Italian colonists at very low rates. Settlers were exempt from taxes for twenty-five years, and the government took

---

39 French colonization in Morocco was similar, but it commenced in 1912 after the Fez Treaty and assumed sizeable proportions only after World War I. Because it was fairly recent and almost uniquely urban in character, we have not included it in our study.

40 French and Italian colonization in Tunisia have also been compared to Palestine. See Church, pp. 56–61, for a comparison with Italian settlement in Libya; Aaronsohn A., Colonisation, pp. 353–359, for a comparison with French settlement in Tunisia.

41 Despois, pp. 48–51, 94–98.

charge of parcelling out the land, developing the water supply, paving roads, and granting loans.[42]

Despois contends that the Italians were influenced by the French colonies in Algeria and Tunisia. Like the French farmers who settled in the Sfax province of southern Tunisia, the Italians in the Tripoli region planted olive trees rather than grapevines as the latter were disease-prone, their produce more difficult to market, and better suited to the coastal plains. The cultivation of olives proved successful in Libya and with the help of the Italian government literally changed the face of Tripolitania.[43] Colonization in Cyrenaica was also dependent upon government aid. The funds channeled into the colonies by the large settlement corporations were in fact governmental in origin, the Italian authorities assuming responsibility for laying infrastructure and solving the water problem that plagued farmers in this arid region.[44]

J. Poncet's macro-level study of European colonization and farming in Tunisia from 1881 is noteworthy for its comprehensive data on crop yields, commercial activity, etc., on a national scale. D. V. McKay's account of French settlement in Tunisia is less useful because although he acknowledges the importance of geography and physiography in the history of Tunisia, this theme is not developed. Instead, he offers a lengthy historical review of French occupation from a political and economic perspective.[45]

P. Ficaya analyses the economic changes which Italian immigrants brought to North Africa. He focuses on population growth, the proportion of farmers among them and the extent of their land holdings.[46] According to Ficaya, Italians represented the largest immigrant community in Tunisia at the end of the nineteenth century, far outnumbering the French. On the whole, the settlers were poor farmers from southern Italy;

---

42 Ibid., pp. 52–54, 125. When the Facists came to power in 1928, government aid was augmented by reimbursement for buildings, equipment, etc. (ibid., p. 60).
43 Ibid., pp. 66–86, 130–134.
44 Ibid., pp. 105–125.
45 Poncet; also see McKay.
46 Ficaya. In contrast to other studies utilized here, Ficaya's work is marred by a reliance on secondary sources and lack of accurate references. His was the only available study of Italian colonization in Tunisia apart from Poncet, which addresses all European settlement in the country, and Loth, which was unobtainable.

the majority were Sicilians, but there were also Napoliteans, Tuscans and Lombards. Their chief problem was the lack of private capital and the minimal, insufficient assistance provided by the Italian government. As a result, farms were very small, usually comprising no more than ten hectares (approximately 110 dunams), and many of the Italian colonists were compelled to work as hired laborers or tenant farmers in the French colonies. Living standards were low even among those who owned land.[47]

The proportion of Italians, who numbered over 4,000 in the 1850s and constituted virtually the only foreigners in the country, decreased in the 1880s after Tunisia was declared a French protectorate. The Italian population increased from 11,200 to 21,000 between 1881 and 1891, whereas the French population swelled from 700 to 10,000 (the ratio of Frenchmen to Italians increasing from 6 to 48 percent). The French community expanded rapidly over the next decade, reaching a total of 24,200 persons by 1901, but the growth rate of the Italians was even higher, their numbers totalling 71,600 that year (reducing the ratio of Frenchmen to Italians to 34 percent). In addition to Frenchmen and Italians, Tunisia became home to thousands of newcomers from other European countries. who numbered 7,000 in 1881, 11,700 in 1891, and 15,300 in 1901.[48]

The rural landscape of Tunisia underwent a transformation in the 1890s as the Italians began to purchase farmland and establish their own colonies ("agricultural centers"). Although the proportion of landowners was not high compared with the overall size of the Italian community, the number of Italian farms increased steadily, from 346 encompassing 18,000 hectares in 1895, to 740 encompassing 36,500 hectares in 1902 (an average of 540 dunams per farmstead).[49] Some of these new settlements were founded by Italians who had been working in the French colonies.

---

[47] These conclusions based on Ficaya, pp. 20, 41, 50–52, 55–56. Near the city of Sousse on the Tunisian coast, the Italian farms were no larger than six or seven hectares (less than eighty dunams). See ibid., p. 49.

[48] Official data published by the local government (Direction Général de l'Agriculture et du Commerce) in Ficaya, p. 44. Another source states that the Italian colonies in Tunisia in 1900 were comprised of 64 percent male — a typical feature of immigrant populations (ibid., p. 45).

[49] Ibid., p. 52.

No figures are offered for the population of the Italian colonies, the number of laborers and tenant farmers, or the body of Italians who continued to be employed on French and other farms.

Many of the Italian farms were on the outskirts of the large cities and specialized in supplying their markets with fresh produce. They were often near main highways or railroad lines traversing the coastal plain as these locations were advantageous for marketing. Grapes were the most important crop, followed by grain and vegetables. In 1902, the vineyards of the Italian settlers spread over 4,200 hectares (over 46,000 dunams). They made no effort to adapt the farming methods they had used in Italy to local conditions. They omitted deep plowing, planted densely (270–400 vines per dunam), disregarded soil type, and mixed different strains. While harvests were abundant, between thirty and fifty hecoliters per hectare (300–500 liters per dunam), the grapes were of poor quality and could not compete with the produce of the French colonies.[50]

Despite their low income, the Italian settlers managed to make ends meet. They subsisted on the profits of previous years, adopting a frugal lifestyle. Some assistance was obtained from a settlement corporation in which the Italian government invested 7.5 million francs. After the passage of the Enzel Law they took advantage of the long-term lease of land belonging to religious endowments, which was offered to European settlers on easy terms. The Italians also founded cooperative land societies that bought up large tracts of land and parcelled out plots to their members for a small deposit. After settling on the land, the remaining sum was repaid annually at low rates of interest.[51]

Sethom offers a valuable regional study of European settlement in Tunisia that focuses on agricultural colonization on the Cape of Bon, a large, fertile peninsula situated east of the capital city of Tunis. The Cape of Bon experienced a serious decline in the nineteenth century after much of the population was wiped out by epidemics, especially cholera. Large, old settlements dwindled in size until they were abandoned altogether,

---

50 Ibid., pp. 56–63.
51 Ibid., pp. 53–54. Ficaya mentions a colony of seventy farms, ten hectares each (a total of 7,700 dunams), established by a cooperative society under the leadership of a silversmith from Trapani. Colonists paid the society a quarter of the price upon receiving their land and the remainder, over a period of ten years at five-six percent interest.

and much of the land came into the hands of absentee landlords and religious endowments.[52]

When Europeans began to settle on the Cape of Bon in 1881, they found a population of 52,000 residing in an area of 3,000 square kilometers (seventeen persons per kilometer). Most of the cultivated land was in the fertile plains of Grombalia and owned by a handful of urban capitalists who reaped large profits from the region's flourishing olive groves. The unfarmed land was used by the Bedouin to grow wheat and graze their herds. Only the less profitable tracts were sold to foreigners.[53] The colonization of Europeans thus occurred in regions where the owners of large estates were prepared to relinguish a portion of their land. A small number of Europeans purchased citrus groves in the Grombalia plains or established small plantations of their own.

The bulk of Sethom's work is devoted to official colonization on the Cape of Bon after 1904, when legislation passed by the French government enabled state-owned land to be apportioned and sold to Europeans at subsidized rates.[54] Our interest lies in the semi-official and unsponsored colonization that took place between 1881 and 1904. Most of the Frenchmen who purchased property in the Cape during Tunisia's first two decades as a French protectorate were not farmers. Some leased their land to local residents, while others were speculators who planned to re-sell it later for a profit. Those who did settle on the land found it neglected and difficult to farm. Many years of toil were necessary before these early colonies became productive, and few actually succeeded.[55]

Sethom makes special mention of the Italian immigrants who were employed on French farms in Tunisia, living modestly and putting their money into savings. In 1903, the 106 French settlers on the Cape of Bon owned nearly 42,000 hectares of land (an average of 4,500 dunams per settler!), whereas the 89 Italian settlers owned only 3,000 hectares (340 hectares per settler). When the Italians later secured government credit and loans from settlement companies, they began to purchase more land

---

52 Sethom, I, pp. 98–101.
53 Ibid., I, pp. 101–111; III, p. 877.
54 Ibid., I, pp. 114–115, 121–123.
55 Ibid., I, pp. 113; III, p. 878.

(or obtain leases on French land) and hundreds of Italian families settled in colonies and villages of their own.[56]

Viticulture on the Cape of Bon is also explored at length in Sethom's study. Before 1881, grapes were no more than a traditional Mediterranean crop of minor importance. With the exception of the vineyards belonging to former Italian consul who lived in a small village on the eastern part of the Cape, all grapes in the region were grown for local consumption or the raisin industry. The pursuit of viticulture on a large, marketable scale was a totally European innovation — "a creation of the colonies" in Sethom's words.[57]

From the moment the French settlers planted their first vineyards, the race was on: by the mid-1880s, vineyards covered an area of 5,000 dunams, by 1895 — 65,000 dunams, within another decade — 150,000 dunams. Plant infestations and diseases were problematic at first, but the farmers soon overcame them. Phyloxera, the greatest threat to winegrowers, was not to hit the Cape of Bon until 1936. As viticulture expanded, Italians began to work in French vineyards in growing numbers, thereby stimulating Italian immigration and settlement in this part of Tunisia. Furthermore, because grapes were planted along the coast (up to twenty kilometers from the shore), Sethom claims that viticulture played an important role in dispersing European settlement across the Cape.[58]

Jewish Colonization in Argentina

The efforts of Baron de Hirsch and the Jewish Colonisation Association (JCA) in Argentina merit special attention because of their relevance, as a Jewish settlement scheme financed by private capital, to that in Palestine.[59]

---

56 Ibid., I, pp. 115–117; III, pp. 878–889.
57 Ibid., II, p. 487; I, p. 121. The most common grape varieties raised on the Cape of Bon were those used to produce red wines, chiefly Carignan, Alicant, Grenach, Muscat, Sultanine and Clairette. Carignan accounted for forty-five percent of the vineyards in Tunisia, and Alicante — twenty three percent. See ibid., III, p. 513.
58 Ibid., III, pp. 487–501; I, pp. 115, 121.
59 Most of the work on this subject has been published in Yiddish or Spanish. In

In 1891, Baron Maurice de Hirsch of London founded the JCA and contributed 50 million francs towards the mass resettlement of Jews in South America. He envisaged large-scale agricultural colonization as a solution to the social and political predicament of the Jews, and chose Argentina because of its cheap arable land, plentiful rainfall, and relatively well-developed transportation system. However, the owners of the "humid pampas," the fertile land in central Argentina, especially around the capital city of Buenos Aires, were reluctant to sell, so the JCA purchased most of its land in outlying regions that were much less suited to farming. Only one-quarter of the two million dunams acquired by the association in 1896 were in the humid pampas, and the additional 1.5 million dunams purchased over the next decade were situated in areas where soil and precipitation were poor. The Jewish colonies in Argentina were hard hit by natural disasters such as locust plagues and alternating years of flooding and drought, while their physical remoteness from urban centers prevented the cultivation of crops which required direct marketing.[60] The JCA thus opted for extensive monoculture farms of 50–150 hectares (approx. 550 to 1,700 Turkish dunams) based on grain or cattle. Clustered settlement was difficult due to the size of the farms, and the JCA's initial efforts to establish colonies of 25–50 families proved unsuccessful because the farmhouses were too far from the fields.

By 1896, the JCA had brought over 6,760 Jewish settlers and established 910 farms. There were now four major colonies, each consisting of a series of small villages with homes and farms extending over hundreds of thousands of dunams. At its peak, Moisesville, the largest colony, measured over one million dunams.[61] However, only two-thirds of the colonists remained farmers within five years of their arrival, and many resettled in the cities. At this point, the JCA realized that its comprehensive programs were not succeeding and adopted measures to improve productivity. That same year marked the death of Baron

---

English, see Grünwald; Winsburg; and lately: Avni, *Argentina*. The most detailed work is Avni, *Promised Land*.

60   Avni, *Promised Land*, pp. 319–320; idem, Jewish Agriculture, pp. 313–320.
61   Ibid., pp. 314, 324, 328–329. According to another source, some 10,500 Jews entered Argentina during the first decade of colonization (1891–1900). See Gartner, p. 360.

de Hirsch, who had personally overseen the colonization enterprise in Argentina from its outset.

The JCA's steadfast adherence to the operational principles adopted in the early days proved to be an obstacle in the future. With its rigid hierarchy, insistence on weekly reports, and cold, patronizing attitude toward the colonists, friction was inevitable. In some colonies, relations between the farmers and JCA administrators became so strained that the colonists staged an outright rebellion. While the dispute was sometimes personal, there was an obvious conflict of interest between the colonists, who were attracted by economic opportunities outside the agricultural sector, and the JCA, which was intent on productivization. Among the tactics employed by the JCA to ensure cooperation was a contract signed by the colonists upon receipt of their land. This document, binding for twenty years, prohibited the colonist from leasing his land or hiring outside labor until all debts had been repaid.[62]

Numerous errors of judgment in the spheres of administration, settlement procedure and interpersonal relations plagued the colonization enterprise in Argentina. The outcome was an unwieldy bureaucracy, mistrust between administrators and colonists, insufficient income during the first agricultural seasons, inadequate farm planning, marketing failures, faulty screening of candidates, and financial mismanagement — all of which weakened those with ambition and goodwill and strengthened the hold of negative elements seeking philanthropy.

However, no factor contributed more to the success or failure of the Jewish colonies in Argentina than geographic-economic and sociopolitical conditions. With market prices and profitability dictated by events unfolding in other parts of the world, it was soon apparent that basing the economy of the colonies on the production of grain and beef for export was a serious mistake. Despite the JCA's efforts to remedy the problem through experimentation with crops such as sunflowers, the introduction of dairy farming, and the establishment of cooperatives to reduce dependence on middlemen and improve efficiency, the colonists were affected by the low esteem with which farming was regarded in Argentina. This hindered the development of a strong ideological

---

[62] Avni, *Promised Land*, pp. 90–95, 121–129, 278–280; Avni, Jewish Agriculture, pp. 314, 326–327.

foundation in the colonies and the farmers' children, who were sent to continue their education in the cities, often found employment in the urban sector and remained there.[63]

German Templer Colonization in Palestine

A public colonization venture in the second half of the nineteenth century was that of the "German Temple Society" (Der Deutsche Tempelgesellschaft), whose members' religious beliefs inspired them to settle in Palestine. Our survey shall be selective, concentrating on several central developments and basic historical facts concerning the Templers' settlement in Palestine which have relevance to the overall context of colonization processes throughout the world. We shall not attempt to summarize all aspects of Templer colonization, but rather to concentrate on the early development of these colonies: the first decade (the 1870s) and the next one (which was contemporaneous with the beginnings of modern Jewish agricultural settlement in Palestine), with special emphasis on the financial support extended by a wealthy private individual.

The beginnings of the German Temple Society can be traced back to the establishment in Württemberg of "The Society for the Gathering of the People of God in Jerusalem" in 1854, which seceded from the Evangelical Church in 1861. Believing that they were the true "People of God" who were to inherit the Holy Land at the Coming of the Messiah, in 1867 the Templers decided to emigrate to Palestine and establish colonies there.

In that year, a spontaneous attempt, unauthorized by the sect's leadership, was made by some thirty young members to settle a barren piece of land in the north of Palestine. It failed within a year after many of them died of malaria. Organized Templer settlement began with the visit to Palestine late in 1868 of the sect's two leaders, Georg David Hardegg and Christoph Hoffmann.[64] Four settlements were established during the first decade, but — as we shall see — many of these efforts, too, began

---

63 Ibid., pp. 322–324, 329, 331–332; Avni, *Promised Land*, pp. 279–282.
64 Carmel, pp. 4–12, 13, 16–19. For a recent more detailed description of the Templers'

without prior planning. Two temporary outposts were first established in 1869 in the port cities of Haifa and Jaffa, speedily becoming permanent colonies. Their location on the seashore was consciously chosen to facilitate communication and provide security for the European settlers. They, in turn, gave birth to two additional Templer settlements.

The first colony, founded on land adjoining Haifa in 1869, developed rapidly. The number of buildings increased from ten (including a communal hall and a school) at the end of the first year to eighty-five (including a hospital, a hotel and two flour mills) when the colony was five years old. Simultaneously, population increased from 120 at the end of 1870 to 311 in 1875. The area of the colony's agricultural land — farming being the chief economic occupation of the colonists — expanded accordingly as the settlers purchased or leased additional tracts. By 1875, the Haifa colony cultivated 3,100 dunams (ca. 800 acres) of farm land, most of which had been planted with cereal crops, while the rest was devoted to orchards and vineyards. From the early 1870s, the colonists were also actively involved in transportation: they built a dock, laid a carriageway to Nazareth (the first such road in northern Palestine!) and ran a carriage service between Haifa and Acre.[65]

The Haifa colony expanded more rapidly than planned, at a rate that in fact displeased the Temple Society's leadership. They opposed non-selective mass immigration, trying to meticulously choose the settlers they sent to Palestine according to their capabilites, but were unsuccessful in their attempts to prevent others from joining the ranks.

Speedy development of the colony resulted in a massive deficit which within four years amounted to 100,000 French francs. A fund-raising tour of Germany and Sweden by Hardegg, chairman of the Haifa colony, failed. Similarly unsuccessful were the steps adopted by the colony's local committee, which tried to control the transfer of land to new settlers and levied a compulsory loan upon them. When the central organs of the Temple Society in Germany refused to cover the deficit incurred in

---

    inception, by a member of the Society itself, see: Sauer, pp. 17–48 (and references there).

65 Carmel, pp. 19–27 (data for 1875 hereafter based on the P.E.F.'s Survey of Western Palestine).

Haifa, Hardegg resigned. In 1874, together with about one-third of the colonists, he left the Society.

The foundations of the split in the Templer community in Palestine were laid almost from the outset, when the second leader of the Society, Christoph Hoffmann, arrived in Palestine, bought five houses in Jaffa, and turned them into the nucleus of a second Templer colony.[66] Like its counterpart in Haifa, the Jaffa colony developed very quickly in the early 1870s. Additional lands and houses were acquired in Jaffa and the vicinity, a hospital (with the first European-trained doctor in the city), a hotel (considered to be the finest in the country) and a school were soon established. Population doubled from 110 in 1870 to 220 in 1875.

The Jaffa colonists, like their brethren in Haifa, were the first to develop transportation services in the area. From the outset, however, the character of the Jaffa colony was less of an agricultural nature and more like an urban suburb. Consequently, most of the colonists were employed in trade and crafts, which accounted for the greater part of their income. Three shops, a flour mill and various small workshops established in the early 1870s provided the region's inhabitants with modern services.[67]

Another urban colony began to develop in 1873 on empty plots of land privately acquired by a member of the Templer Society near Jerusalem. Within two years, the settlement consisted of seven buildings and with a population of some 100 persons. This unplanned suburban Templer enterprise received official recognition in 1875 when the Society's leadership decided to move its center to Jerusalem. However, when Hoffmann's fundraising mission to Germany and Switzerland failed, the transfer to Jerusalem was delayed for three years due to lack of financial resources.

A second agricultural colony had been established in 1871 to the north of Jaffa and was named Sarona. Within a year it counted seven buildings and fourteen families, and a communal hall was under construction. Sarona's development, however, was curbed by disease and an outbreak of malaria, from which many died. Though the plague was overcome, the terrible impression left by the tragedy stifled Sarona's development for many years to come, and also reduced the extent of Templer emigration

---

66 Ibid., pp. 27–28.
67 Ibid., pp. 29–30.

to Palestine in general. In 1875 there were eighty residents in Sarona, all of them making a bare living from the mixed farming (which included some viticulture) of the farms they established on the limited land of the colony. Even though its land resources had tripled, Sarona's area in 1875 totalled no more than 1,500 dunams (less than 400 acres). Out of necessity, some of the colonists made a living by supplying transport services, as members of the transportation cooperative which they ran together with a few members of the Jaffa colony.[68]

In brief, at this stage the Templer colonies in Jaffa and Jerusalem developed as urban neighborhoods which specialized in supplying modern services, in contemporary terms. The colony at Haifa also underwent a transformation away from its original agricultural character, following diseases that attacked its vineyards and the failure of commercial orange growing. By 1889, only twenty-five of the seventy-six owners of farms still made their living in agriculture. Only in Sarona did farming continue to be the main source of income, though it was not very profitable. About thirty of its families were farmers, most of them specializing in viniculture. A side-product of the changeover to viniculture, in the mid-1880s, was the establishment of a large wine-cellar whose products were exported.

From a statistical survey conducted in 1889, after twenty years of Templer settlement in Palestine, we know that the total Templer population was 1,343 persons (ca. 250 families), of which 59 families, comprising 269 individuals, lived in Sarona, the only remaining agricultural colony.[69]

A less-known episode concerning the Templer colonies in Palestine is connected with Baron Joseph Freiherr von Ellrichshausen and the society he established to aid the German colonies in Palestine. Ellrichshausen, a former member of the Reichstag and a pious Evanglical Protestant from Swabia, was a member of Kaiser Wilhelm II's entourage during the imperial tour of Palestine in 1898. Following the visit to the German colonies, which had by then been in existence for almost thirty years, he founded "The Company for the Promotion of the German Colonies in

---

68 Ben-Arieh, *Jerusalem*, pp. 127–137; Carmel, pp. 31–34, 36–38.
69 Ibid., pp. 39–45 (1889 data derived from the Templers' periodical "Die Warte des Temples").

Palestine," whose prime objective was the acquisition of additonal land for second-generation Templers in the colonies.[70]

The society was established in Stuttgart in October 1899 as a private, all-German organization, but its activities were in effect limited to Württemberg. Its capital, raised by selling bonds, was much less than the one to two million marks that Ellrichshausen had envisaged; in ten years only about one-third of a million had been raised. These funds were used to acquire over 17,000 dunams of land that served to establish three new agricultural colonies. Furthermore, the baron's society was unable to stop colonists from leaving the veteran agricultural settlement of Sarona, both due to a lack of funds and political difficulties — reservations expressed by the imperial Foreign Ministry, which feared that the Ottoman authorities would oppose the society's activites, and the hesitant, unofficial support which the government of Württemberg was willing to extend. The great blow suffered by the Society for the Advancement of the German Colonies in Palestine in 1910, when several families sold their farms in Sarona and emigrated to German East Africa, apparently brought about the cessation of its activities and final liquidation.[71]

In later years, there was almost no increase in Templer settlement in Palestine. The number of their colonies remained constant at seven and their overall population was stabilized at about 1,700 persons, though their economic condition improved, until they were closed down by the British Mandate authorities after the outbreak of World War II.

Conclusion: Colonization Characterized

In the literature, colonization enterprises are commonly ascribed to one of two categories, "colonization of dominion" or "colonization of settlement," depending on the major goal of the bodies involved. The former, often called "exploitative" or "captive" colonization (*colonisation d'exploitation, colonisation d'encadrement*), is always associated with the takeover by one country of another territory and the use of

---

70 Sauer, pp. 74–76.
71 Ibid., pp. 74–76; Carmel, pp. 55–57, 59–60.

local resources to benefit the occupier.[72] Among the first steps taken by a government intent on "colonization of dominion" is to initiate legislative action that will facilitate the pursuit of its political, strategic and economic aims (through the introduction of laws, taxes, customs duties, expropriation of land, etc.). "Colonization of dominion" does not necessarily entail the establishment of permanent foreign colonies in the occupied country. If such colonies are established, they are merely a means of achieving the occupier's exploitative goals. Most of the colonization in the tropics falls into this category, which as we see from the efforts of Leopold II in the Congo, is more akin to colonialism.[73]

"Colonization of settlement," also known as "peopling" or "root" colonization (*colonisation de peuplement, colonisation d'enracinement*), always involves a genuine relationship with the land. In this type, the colonists leave their home country and establish points of settlement, usually agricultural colonies, in a new region. "Colonization of settlement" may occur in a colonial context, sponsored directly by the settlers' country of origin and resulting in a "layered" colonial-colonization process (illustrated by French colonization in Algeria or Italian colonization in Libya). It may also occur in cases of indirect or partial sponsorship by the country of origin (such as French colonization in the protectorate of Tunisia), without any government sponsorship at all, or even in opposition to the government (as in many instances of "flagless" or *sans drapeaux* colonization).

Geographical research employs similar categories. Harrison Church, for example, differentiates between *colonisation de peuplement* or *colonisation d'enracinement*, which involve permanent settlement, and *colonisation d'exploitation* or *colonisation d'encadrement* which are motivated by the desire for political and economic control. He also refers

---

72 The broad category of "colonization of dominion" includes "colonisation commerciale," "colonisation de plantation," and "colonisation stratégique" or "de position."

73 A. Belgian scholar, C. Manheim, totally confuses the terms colonization and colonialism. He defines the former as an authoritative act on the part of one nation vis-à-vis another, less-developed nation, with the object of accelerating its social and ethical development for the benefit of the entire human race (Manheim, p. 15). Despite the title of his book, which refers to colonization, he mainly discusses colonialism and the history of colonial imperialism. See Manheim, pp. 22 to end. For another work purporting to study colonization but dealing entirely with colonialism, see Doucet.

parenthetically to "strategic colonies" (*colonies de position*) and "settler colonies in alien lands," by which he seems to mean private, spontaneous colonization judging from the example he brings of German and Italian settlement in Brazil.[74]

Some geographers, such as George Hardy, relate to the physiographic environment of the colonies in question and categorize them on the basis of geographical location, topography, soil, and especially climate. Hardy discusses colonization in the prairies, evergreen forests, deltas, mountains, deserts and antarctic countries.[75] However, at a later stage he regroups these enterprises in the customary manner and discusses "strategic" as opposed to "root" colonization (which parallel the "dominion" and "settlement" categories cited above).

Colonization can be characterized in yet another way. Aside from the varying measures of political sanction enjoyed by colonization enterprises, they also differ in their ability to mobilize economic resources (capital, but also manpower, knowhow and technology) to their advantage. Four possible configurations are colonization lacking in economic and political support, colonization founded on economic support only, colonization founded on political support only, and colonization enjoying both political and economic support.

The colonization of Italians in Tunisia at the end of the nineteenth century, which was wholly dependent on the colonists and whatever resources they mustered on their own (a typical "grass-roots" endeavor), belong to the first category. The colonization of Italians in Libya and the French in Algeria belong to the last category, in which national, economic and political support combine and resources flow freely.

Up to this point, we have characterized the phenomenon of colonization from a national-political, geographical, and economic perspective. For a complete typology, we must also consider two additional factors associated with the social and cultural-ideological dimension. The first is the nature of the settlers themselves and their motives for colonizing —

---

74 Church, p. IX. The last fall into the "colonization of settlement" category, while the first into that the "colonization of dominion."
75 Hardy, pp. 25–27, 91–201. Church also devotes a chapter of his book to physical geography (pp. 26–42), adopting an almost deterministic attitude on the impact of the environment, particularly soil and climatic conditions.

for example, the push and pull factors that inspired them to leave their homeland and settle elsewhere.[76] The second is the structure of the new social entity and especially its relations with the local, native populace. In this respect, studies of immigration and settlement commonly refer to four types of colonization: a new society that replaces the former (by destroying it or evicting the inhabitants); a new society that integrates with the former after gaining control; a new society that co-exists with the former; and a new society that emerges where none existed before. This approach has also influenced the writing of geographers studying colonization.[77]

To summarize, colonization as a world-wide phenomenon can be characterized by the role and policies of the government, the geography of the region, the availability of financial resources, the goals of the settlers, and the relations between settlers and local inhabitants. In this light we shall examine the beginnings of modern Jewish settlement in Palestine, to which the term colonization is applied.

---

76 A similar approach is taken by E. Cohen, who characterizes settlement in new regions by the type of social organization behind it. See Cohen.

77 Tartakower, pp. 15–19. Hardy devotes the entire first part of his work to a study of four types of *colonisation d'enracinement*, determined by the relationship between the settlers and the native population. See Hardy, pp. 33–90.

PART ONE

BARON ROTHSCHILD AND THE
JEWISH COLONIES:
STAGES OF INVOLVEMENT

Introduction: The Pre-Rothschild Years — Sporadic Settlement

With the resurgence of Jewish settlement in Eretz Israel in 1882, the pioneers of the First Aliya banded together and established three colonies in the once barren hills of the Holy Land: Rishon le-Zion, Rosh Pinna and Zikhron Ya'akov. Another group of newcomers made possible the rebirth of a fourth colony, Petah Tikva, which had been abandoned shortly after its establishment in the 1870s.[1]

The first of these, Rishon le-Zion, was founded on 31 July 1882 by Jews who had immigrated from southern Russia, followed by Rosh Pinna and Zikhron Ya'akov, founded on 17 September and 6 December 1882 by separate groups of Jews from Rumania. On 8 October 1882, several of the founding fathers of Petah Tikva returned to the deserted site and succeeded in reviving the colony with the help of a reinforcement of Russian immigrants who arrived in 1883.

The driving force behind these early colonization efforts was the Hovevei Zion organization ("Lovers of Zion") whose various branches in Eastern Europe operated as full-fledged, financially independent settlement societies responsible for the planning and implementation of their own colonies. Each society drew up a charter, investigated settlement opportunities, sent out emissaries to find land, and screened potential settlers. After the colony was established, these societies continued to exercise control by retaining ownership of the land, distributing funds as necessary, and in the case of Zikhron Ya'akov, stationing officials in the colony to oversee its progress.[2]

All the land in question had belonged to Arab landlords or effendis, although much of it, notably the lands of Petah Tikva and Rosh Pinna, had been in Jewish hands since the 1870s.[3] Large tracts were cultivated by Arab tenants, whose approach to farming was extensive and old-fashioned; the lands of Rishon le-Zion had never been farmed at all.

---

1 See the detailed bibliographies on the First Aliya colonies: Bassin, *Jewish Yishuv*, and Bassin, *Selected*.
2 On the societies that founded the first colonies, see Aaronsohn, Establishment.
3 The lands of Rosh Pinna were purchased by Jews from Safed who endeavored to establish the colony of Ge-Oni in 1878, several weeks before the first attempt in Petah Tikva. On this episode, see Harosen, pp. 38–56, and references to primary sources.

Founders of Zikhron Ya'akov, 1889

Colonization took place in stages, with the men camping on site and the families living in nearby towns. The Rishon le-Zion settlers based themselves in the Jaffa area, those of Rosh Pinna near Safed, and of Zikhron Ya'akov near Haifa. Eventually, the families moved to the colonies, where their first accommodations were either temporary, as in Gedera and Yesud ha-Ma'ala, or permanent, as in Rishon le-Zion.

At the outset, the colonies operated along the lines of a commune: land was not parcelled out and work followed a centralized plan, using common funds.[4] Before farming commenced, approach roads were levelled, a water source was developed and the fields were cleared of rocks and brush. Tents, wooden shacks or other temporary shelters were constructed, sometimes utilizing old structures acquired with the land (such as the mud-huts, *hushot*, in Zikhron Ya'akov). Only in Rishon le-Zion was permanent European-style housing of wood or stone available within the first year of settlement. Even if the camping site of

---

4   This work arrangement was instituted in three colonies in 1882. Petah Tikva began to operate as a commune only the following year, when immigrants from Bialystok arrived.

the early pioneers was elsewhere, it was during this stage of colonization that the permanent location of each colony was determined (see Maps 1, 2).

While not all the land at the colonists' disposal was utilized during the first season, the quantity of farmland increased greatly. In addition to the traditional dry farming, vineyards were planted and the colonists ran auxiliary farms, raising livestock and vegetables in the yard next to their homes for their own consumption.[5] By one estimate, the new colonies encompassed over 22,530 dunams (with a population of 480) by the end of the first year; another source cites 31,827 dunams.[6]

The majority of the colonists were middle-aged religious Orthodox Jews with only basic schooling and few personal assets. In Europe they had made a living as shopkeepers, tradesmen or low-ranking civil servants and had no agricultural experience whatsoever. They usually brought their wives and children, and often younger siblings and elderly parents, too. With the exception of two minority groups — the few young enlightened liberals who founded Rishon le-Zion and the small group of unmarried, non-religious, socialist Bilu pioneers who established Gedera in 1884 — the cultural background and national origins of the early colonists were similar. The Jerusalem Jews who founded Petah Tikva originally came from Hungary, and the colonists who joined them in 1883 were from Bialystok (Lithuania) and its environs. However, socio-economic differences often led to conflict over pragmatic issues such as money, which was in short supply. In those colonies where leadership was non-existent or ineffective, the problem was resolved through the intervention of a certain wealthy outsider, whom we shall soon discuss.

The preliminary financial planning for each colony was carried out by the Hovevei Zion society which had established it. There were variations from one colony to the next, but the underlying assumptions were the same: that the colonists would be self-supporting from their second year of colonization; that founding and living expenses would

---

5   Aaronsohn, Establishment, pp. 60–72, 123–130.
6   Gurevich and Gertz, pp. 31, 46; Yavne'eli, II, p. 35. A metric ("square") dunam equals 1,000 m^2 (2.5 acres or 1 hectar); henceforth, a "dunam" refers to the Turkish dunam which was used in Palestine at the time and equalled 919m^2.

be paid by the settlement association until that time; and that the total expenditure for land purchase, travel expenses, housing, farm equipment, and upkeep during the first year, could be calculated in advance.[7] These assumptions failed to meet the test of reality: income was lower than anticipated and expenses were immeasurably higher. When the colonists failed to honor their financial commitments, the settlement societies, which were dependent on Jewish philanthropy and private capital from their membership, refused to send the promised funding to the colonies. On the other hand, problems in land registration and securing building permits necessitated an enormous outlay for legal fees and the payment of bribes, a widespread practice in the Ottoman Empire. In addition, tapping water resources was more costly than envisaged, and the establishment of public services such as education and health care, which were not provided by the government, demanded a sizeable portion of the budget.

With so many expenses within the first few months, the shortage of funds was felt immediately, especially in Rishon le-Zion, where work advanced at a faster pace than elsewhere. One of the founding members, Joseph Feinberg, was sent to Europe to secure a loan which would enable the colony's continued development. In October 1882, he met a wealthy Parisian Jew who agreed to put up the sum: Baron Edmond de Rothschild. Thus, long before the end of the first year of Jewish colonization, an external element was introduced through the initiative of the colonists themselves.

However, this was not the first commitment in Baron de Rothschild's lengthy history of involvement in the Jewish colonies. As we shall see, he had already been persuaded to support the establishment of another model colony in Palestine by Rabbi Samuel Mohilewer, a leading figure in the Hovevei Zion movement in Europe.[8]

---

[7] See, for instance, "Expenditures for Colonization" drawn up by Levontin for the Yesud ha-Ma'ala Committee which founded Rishon le-Zion, *Ha-shahar* 10 (1882), p. 660.

[8] On the reasons for Rothschild's involvement, see Aaronsohn, Establishment, pp. 9–14.

CHAPTER ONE

FIRST OVERTURES, 1882–1883

The Rothschild-Netter Colonization Plan

Baron Edmond James de Rothschild (1845–1934) of Paris, scion of the famous Rothschild family, was more attracted to art, science and modern technology than to banking. When James Jacob de Rothschild died in 1868, the financial affairs and management of the family bank were taken over by his eldest son, Alphonse; Edmond, the youngest son, and his brother Gustave were appointed advisors. It was Alphonse who was most active in Jewish philanthropy, including support to Eretz Israel.[1] Edmond showed less interest in his Jewish brethren, although he was a member of the Jewish Consistory of Paris (Consistoire Central) and on a modest scale, carried on the longstanding family tradition of involvement in Jewish affairs. When he married his cousin Adelaide Ada in 1877, a daughter of the Frankfurt Rothschilds known for their religiosity and patronage of Jewish causes, Edmond was appointed chairman of the Jewish Charity Committee of Paris (Comité de Bienfaisance de Paris) which contributed vast sums to the needy Jews of France.[2]

1   Edmond de Rothschild left a lasting mark on two important cultural institutions in Paris: the Louvre, which consulted him as an art expert and to which he later donated his collection of rare etchings and drawings, and the National Institute of Biochemistry, which was financed and supported by him from the 1890s. His elder brother Alphonse is remembered by the French as the banker who acted as guarantor for the five billion francs in reparations that France was forced to pay Germany in 1871 after its defeat in the Franco-Prussian War. For Edmond's peripheral role in the family bank, see Bouvier, an economist who wrote about the business affairs of the House of Rothschild.
2   The Rothschilds' philanthropy among the Jews of Paris increased in the 1880s, reaching 150,000 francs in 1886 (see Schama, p. 51). Documents in Rothschild Family Archives in Paris show that as of the 1870s, the family also contributed

Edmond's work on behalf of the Jewish community gathered momentum at the end of 1881, when pogroms against the Jews in the Ukraine spread rapidly and brought about a mass exodus of Jews from the Russian Empire. Together with his brother Alphonse, Edmond was among the founders of the *Comité Général de Secours* established to aid Jewish refugees. Although the sources contain only veiled references to a pivotal phase in Edmond's life at the time, his activities from this point on seem to have assumed a broader radius, extending beyond French Jewry to involvement with Jewish affairs on a global scale.³

The Rothschilds were also known for their support of the "Old Yishuv" in Eretz Israel (the Orthodox urban Jewish community). Their representative, Dr. Albert Cohn (who had been the young Edmond's tutor) was sent there in 1854 to supervise the establishment of medical and educational institutions which were funded by the Rothschilds for many decades. The family archives contain documents which indicate that the Rothschilds were responsive to many direct appeals for assistance from the old Jewish communities in the Holy Land.⁴

Edmond's interest in Jewish colonization seems to have been influenced from the outset by three factors: his contacts with the Alliance Israélite Universelle (AIU), the leading international Jewish organization of the time; his support of the Mikve Israel agricultural school, the first Jewish agricultural settlement in Eretz Israel established by the AIU in 1870; and his relationship with its founder Carl (Ya'akov) Netter, who presided over the school during its first twelve years. Netter, another distinguished member of the French Jewish elite, probably met Edmond de Rothschild in early 1882, when he was appointed secretary of the

---

close to 500,000 francs a year to the Alliance Israélite Universelle on behalf of Eastern Jewry (Archives Nationals Françaises, 132AQ: Rothschild). By comparison, the 21,000 dues-paying members of the AIU donated a total of 160,000 francs in 1881 (see Ever-Hadani, PICA, p. 14).

3   On Edmond de Rothschild as philanthropist and Jewish activist, see Aaronsohn, *Baron*; Bouvier; Druck; Schama, p. 336.

4   The family archives (see note 2, above) contain receipts for the transfer of tens of thousands of francs contributed by the Rothschilds to Palestinian Jewish communities (mainly in Jerusalem and Hebron) in the 1880s. For 1882, see Rothschild Archives, France, vol. 1069–1070 13L; for the remainder of the 1880s, see ibid., correspondence 26L17, and cables 16L8–17 (dépeches).

Comité Général de Secours.[5] In his correspondence with Samuel Hirsch, headmaster of Mikve Israel from 1879 to 1891, Rothschild mentions his talks with Carl Netter in the summer of 1882, prior to Netter's departure for Eretz Israel on 8 August 1882.[6] Contrary to popular belief, these talks were more than theoretical; they gave birth to a plan for settling Russian Jewish refugees in Eretz Israel which was soon to be implemented.

With financial support from the baron, Netter and the AIU planned the establishment of a small experimental farm project in which 50-100 Russian Jews would spend several months training as farmers at Mikve Israel; those found suitable would be provided with land for permanent settlement. Among the details discussed by Rothschild and Netter were infrastructure (buildings, water supply), farming (dry farming, green fodder, orchards), manpower (screening and training of prospective settlers), and administration (farming instructors and managers).

The Founding of Ekron

On 28 September 1882, during the holiday of Sukkot, Baron de Rothschild met with a leader of the Hovevei Zion movement, Rabbi Samuel Mohilewer, who sought his help in resettling Russian Jews in Eretz Israel. Rothschild's immediate response was to link this appeal with the enterprise envisaged by Carl Netter, thereby combining the resettlement of refugees with the establishment of a model colony run by qualified farmers.[7] Although Netter died on 2 October, only four days later, the project was not abandoned. Samuel Hirsch agreed to act as supervisor in Netter's stead, and a group of settlers was readied for the journey to Eretz Israel.

5   Druck, p. 15; Klausner, *Nation*, p. 135.
6   On the Netter–Rothschild talks, see Yavne'eli, I, pp. 78–79; Klausner, *Nation*, pp. 264–266; and Kellner, *Zion's Sake*, pp. 165–172.
7   Much has been written about the influence of the chief rabbi of Paris, Rabbi Zadoc Kahn, and Michael Erlanger, a leader of the AIU and vice president of the Consistoire, on the young Rothschild's interest in Jewish colonization in Eretz Israel. Kahn and Erlanger continued to encourage this interest and promote the cause of Jewish colonization, both in his name and their own. On Rabbi Kahn see Weil; on Erlanger, see Idelovich, pp. 148–149.

On 19 October 1882, a team of ten experienced farmers from the Jewish colony of Novo Peblovka was assembled by the Hovevei Zion society in Rozhany, Lithuania. Yehiel Brill, editor of the Hebrew newspaper *Halevanon* and a former resident of Jerusalem, was selected to accompany them and maintain correspondence with their families, as the farmers themselves were illiterate. Prior to their departure, Brill drew up a contract restating the major points of the plan: groups of pioneers would be trained at Mikve Israel for two to three months under an agronomist (*jardinier*) hired by Baron de Rothschild, after which land would be purchased, housing constructed, and the families brought over. The cost of transportation was to be borne by the farmers, whereas expenditures for land, equipment and upkeep during the first year would be granted as a loan.

On 21 November 1882, the "Radom pioneers," as they were known, set out on a harrowing, twenty-day journey to Eretz Israel.[8] On 14 December they occupied a building at the Mikve Israel agricultural school and began to work in its fields. All the while, Baron de Rothschild supported their families in Russia and paid for their upkeep at the school (first channeling the money through the AIU, and then paying the settlers directly). On 21 October 1883, after a ten-month search for an appropriate site for permanent settlement, 3,600 dunams of land were purchased in Akir, an Arab village south-east of Ramla.[9] At the price of 70,000 francs, this worked out to less than 19.5 francs per dunam. In practice, however, there were only 2,800 dunams, raising the cost to over 25 francs per dunam. In a move proposed by Samuel Hirsch, the land was registered in the name of Michael Erlanger, a Hovevei Zion leader in Paris and administrator of charities of the French Rothschilds.[10]

Cultivation began as soon as the bureaucratic procedures were complete, if not earlier. The moving spirit seems to have been Hirsch, who cabled Erlanger on 5 November urging that sowing be commenced

---

8 Brill, pp. 19–29.
9 *Ha-maggid* 28 (1884), no. 46; Aaronsohn, *Baron*, pp. 17–19.
10 Ibid., pp. 19–20; other sources provide different data, see Aaronsohn, Jewish Colonies, p. 67.

Settlers in Mazkeret Batya (Ekron), 1898

immediately to prevent the loss of an agricultural season.[11] Baron de Rothschild instructed the farmers to proceed accordingly, and contributed 28,000 francs towards the general expenses of the new colony of Ekron. The eleven colonists took up residence in a building which apparently came with the land, and used the money to acquire fifteen pairs of oxen for plowing, fourteen draft animals (mules, horses, donkeys and camels), and two calves. The first crops to be planted were winter wheat, barley and a small quantity of lentils. Judging by the number of oxen, between 1,800 and 2,250 dunams were cultivated. Seven colonists and eight hired Arab laborers carried out the plowing and sowing; the four remaining colonists laid fertilizer and assembled building materials. That winter, a trench was dug around the land and prickly pear was planted to designate the boundaries.[12]

---

11 Erlanger's letter to Hirsch on 11 November 1883, in: Yavne'eli, II, p. 241. Presumably, the purchase was rushed because of the agricultural timetable: winter wheat, the main crop, had to be planted at a specific time, in conjunction with the first rain.
12 Erlanger associated Akir with the Biblical city of Ekron in a letter to Hirsch on 23 November 1883. Thus the colony became known as Ekron, although its name was officially changed to Mazkeret Batya in 1887. Modern research has shown that the two are not identical.

During the first agricultural season, Rothschild's officials played a very minor role. Samuel Hirsch was no longer directly involved, and no resident administrator had been appointed, although Abraham Moyal, a representative of the baron, assisted the colonists in a general, non-defined capacity from his seat in Jaffa. This was the arrangement which was considered ideal by Erlanger, who recommended in March 1883 that the Radom pioneers manage their own affairs, and later reaffirmed by Baron de Rothschild.[13] Moyal helped with the purchase of land in the early days, and continued to visit the colony and monitor the work progress at unspecified intervals. His major function seems to have been dispensing the baron's monthly allowance of one franc per colonist per day. Both this allowance and the funding for general expenditures were figured into the list of "Total Estimated Expenses" which Hirsch calculated at a maximum of 5,000 francs per family (i.e., a total of 55,000 francs for the entire colony). Founding costs included basics such as housing, draft animals, farm equipment and subsistence until harvest time, assuming that the colonists would be self-sufficient after the first agricultural season. Not included was the baron's investment of at least 78,000 francs prior to November 1883.[14]

First Aid to Rishon le-Zion

Baron de Rothschild's efforts on behalf of Jewish colonization thus commenced with the Netter-Rothschild plan which culminated in the establishment of Ekron. However, his first practical assistance to the colonies preceded the arrival of the Radom pioneers. On 18 October 1882, some three weeks after his meeting with Mohilewer, Baron de Rothschild met Joseph Feinberg, one of the leading pioneers of Rishon le-Zion, sent to Europe on 15 August after the colony found its resources depleted

---

13 In Rothschild's correspondence with Hirsch throughout 1883 no administrative problem is mentioned, which strengthens our belief that Rothschild was confident in the ability of the Radom pioneers to manage without outside assistance. See letters of Erlanger to Hirsch, 3 March, 9 November and 28 December 1883, and 4 January 1884 in Yavne'eli, II, pp. 233, 241, 242, 244.
14 Financial data from Rothschild's letter of Hirsch, dated 6 April 1883, ibid., p. 81.

within the span of two weeks.[15] Feinberg was seeking a loan which would allow the pioneers to complete the digging of a well, as well as a private sponsor to support six needy families. After traveling to Vienna and Berlin, he proceeded to Paris where he succeeded in interesting the AIU. Michael Erlanger and Rabbi Zadoc Kahn, the chief rabbi of Paris, helped to arrange the meeting with Rothschild. Some sources claim that Feinberg was also assisted by a letter of recommendation from Carl Netter, establishing a link between the Baron's aid to Rishon le-Zion and the colonization plan collaborated upon with Netter.[16]

Feinberg's telegram to Rishon le-Zion on the day of his meeting with Rothschild is revealing on two issues: first, the appointment of Samuel Hirsch as overseer and treasurer of the colony, and second, the Baron's desire to remain anonymous:

> Hirsch choisi par un personnage comme inspecteur et caissier de Rishon Lezion. Je lui porte des documents.

The information omitted from the telegram, namely the amount and terms of the financial aid to Rishon le-Zion, appeared in Rothschild's letter to Hirsch two days later: a maximum of 25,000 francs would be granted as

> concours partiel... à la construction de quelques habitations et à des travaux pour la recherche de l'eau — selon le desir de ces pauvres gens — que je voudrais que cet argent fut exclusivement employé.[17]

In his next letter, he stipulates that the money be distributed by Hirsch, that J. Dugourd serve as the colony's technical director, and that the colony accept Bilu members ("the Biluim"). A contemporary source mentions additional demands: that the colony open its doors to ten to fifteen new families, that assistance be sought from no one else, and that his name remain secret (hence the epithets *Ha-nadiv ha-yadu'a*

---

15 Freiman, p. 10. On the founding of Rishon le-Zion, see Levontin, pp. 31–79; and Aaronsohn, Establishment (various chapters and references).
16 Various letters in Yavne'eli, II, pp. 35–36, 51, 57; Aaronsohn, *Baron*, pp. 22–23.
17 First quote in Margalith, p. 79; second quote in Rothschild's letter to Hirsch, 20 October 1882, in Yavne'eli, II, pp. 68–69.

and *Ha-baron ha-neʻelam*, i.e., the "Well-Known Benefactor" or the "Anonymous Baron"). According to this source, Rothschild transferred the sum of 30,000 francs and promised to send more if the need arose.[18] He also pledged to finance the excavation of an artesian well and to engage an agronomist.

This transaction illuminates the major problems faced by Rishon le-Zion: the shortage of funding for public infrastructure, the regulation of the water supply, the poverty of individual families, and the lack of farming experience. With the help of Rothschild and his representatives (Dugourd and the Biluim from Mikve Israel who were brought in as laborers), public works such as the digging of a well, securing building supplies for the needy families and the construction of a communal hut, were carried out at the end of 1882. The Biluim also transported water from Mikve Israel, hauled stones and lumber for building, and purchased food supplies in Jaffa.[19]

The first crisis during this period of assistance occurred in December 1882. Taking no chances, the colonists had divided up their land three days before Dugourd's arrival. However, as they prepared to plant their winter wheat crop, the needy families found themselves without seeds, plows or draft animals. With the money loaned by Rothschild, two pairs of horses were purchased for these families and a weekly allowance was distributed by the leaders of the colony, Levontin and Feinberg, to all those who requested it.[20] The money was also used to pay the wages of Dugourd and cover the expenses of his laborers who received one franc per day and a pair of horses to draw their loads.

It should be emphasized that this was not a period of *patronage*, as it is so often described in the literature on early colonization in Eretz Israel and the philanthropic efforts of Baron de Rothschild. Rishon le-Zion continued to be run as in the past, by a committee elected by the colonists themselves, representing their interests alone. As witnessed by a variety of sources, especially the committee's minutes book, of

18   Rothschild to Hirsch, 23 November 1882, ibid., p. 69; Levontin, p. 67.
19   Hissin, *Diary*, p. 46; Brill, p. 176.
20   Levontin, pp. 84, 86–87; V. Dubnow to S. Dubnow, 27 December 1882, in Druyanow and Laskov, I, p. 564. On the internal discord in the colony connected with the arrival, expulsion and conditional reacceptance of the Bilu pioneers, see Aaronsohn, Establishment, pp. 104–105.

which a copy still exists, this body convened and reached decisions in an independent manner, with no intervention on the part of Rothschild's officials.[21] The Bilu members were accepted as residents by vote, after the loan was received and Dugourd and Hirsch were active in the colony. Among the duties of the committee were parcelling out farmland and building lots, approving or rejecting real-estate transactions, and accepting new members. The colonists continued, then, to exercise control over means of production and land ownership, and could freely transfer right of possession. At this stage, Baron de Rothschild's involvement was restricted to one facet of life in Rishon le-Zion: the funding of public works.

The Turning Point: From Credit to Patronage

Rothschild's aid to Rishon le-Zion's public works revolved at that stage around farming and what was necessary for the development of an agricultural settlement. Water supply was apparently a major concern. Dugourd's notification on being transferred to Rishon le-Zion said nothing about the nature of his duties in the colony apart from supervising the drilling of artesian wells.[22]

When the baron offered his assistance in November 1882, there were two dry, partially excavated wells in Rishon le-Zion — one at the top of the hill and another at its foot. Dugourd and his laborers, the Biluim, proceeded with the excavation of the lower well using traditional methods, shovelling earth into baskets and elevating them by pulley. After reaching a depth of some thirty meters, newer techniques were introduced. A narrow drill bit was purchased in Jaffa and Rothschild sent a special drill (eighty meters long) from Paris. Jacob Papo, who had trained under a French hydraulic engineer by the name of Lippman, supervised the drilling, and tests were conducted to ascertain the best method of drawing out the water, from waterwheels to steam pumps. On

---

21 Minutes of meetings no. 15–20 dated 16 November 1882 to 5 January 1883, Minutes Book, CZA A192/217/2.
22 Dugourd to Hirsch, 11 November 1882, French manuscripts, CZA J41/51.

23 February 1883, two weeks after the drill arrived from France, water was discovered at a depth of forty-two meters.[23]

Thanks to the loan extended by Rothschild, important strides were also made in the spheres of farming, housing and population growth. The twelve-dunam field on the outskirts of the colony, which had been used for growing vegetables before the well became operative, was planted with grapes, lemons and oranges at the beginning of 1883.[24] The work was carried out by the Bilu members under the supervision of the baron's agronomist, Dugourd, who also beautified the colony by planting rows of mulberry trees along the central lane. No less than one thousand trees were planted in Rishon le-Zion during that first winter season.

At the end of December, the Bilu members built a communal hut on the hilltop as a shelter for themselves and the colony's six horses. By April, four stone houses had been completed and another four, to accommodate the needy families, were under way. The building financed by Rothschild, while not innovative in any way, was more "disciplined and orderly" and imparted a more uniform appearance than the haphazard efforts of individual colonists who undertook to build their own homes at this time. Five such homes had been erected by the spring of 1883, and another three or four were in various stages of construction.[25]

The baron's actions were instrumental in increasing and diversifying the population of Rishon le-Zion. At his insistence, the Biluim, who differed from the founders from a socio-economic standpoint, were brought in and employed as laborers and an agricultural expert (Dugourd) was sent to Rishon le-Zion to live and work there as Rothschild's first official representative. Thus, two new socio-economic elements were added to the colony.

Rothschild's involvement in Rishon le-Zion took another step forward in April 1883 when his one-time dispensation ran out and he agreed

---

23 Various letters in Yavne'eli, II, pp. 64–65, 69–71, 77, 234; Aaronsohn, *Baron*, p. 30.
24 Levontin's letter to *Ha-maggid*, 25 February 1883 in Levontin p. 91. Also see additional letter cited there and more details on pp. 66, 73, 84; Druyanov and Laskov, I, p. 546.
25 Undated letter from Levontin, in Levontin, p. 90; also Hissin, *Diary*, pp. 46, 50; Freiman, I, p. 9; V. Dubnow to S. Dubnow, 16 November 1882, in Druyanow and Laskov, I, p. 530.

First Overtures, 1882–1883

Rishon le-Zion in its early days (1883?)

to double the sum to 50,000 francs.[26] The relationship was clinched, however, by another crisis which emerged at this time: payment had become due on a mortgage taken out in the summer of 1882 to finance the purchase of land. Frutiger's Bank, a branch of the Ottoman Bank in Jerusalem, threatened to repossess the land if Rishon le-Zion's debt of 12,000 francs (10,000 francs at twenty percent interest) was not paid in full.[27] By harvest time, the colonists realized that the winter wheat upon which their hopes rested barely covered planting costs.[28] Of all the crops, only the vineyard was successful, though it would be three years before

26 Rothschild confirmed this in a letter to Hirsch, 6 April 1883, in Yavne'eli, II, p. 79. Also see Hissin, *Diary*, p. 53, who writes that the sum of 30,000 francs was almost gone by the end of April, and makes no mention of the supplementary loan.
27 Freiman, I, p. 13; Brill, p. 162; Levontin, p. 71. According to these sources, the land, previously registered under the name of Haim Amzalak, was mortgaged by Zvi Levontin, who put up most of the money towards its purchase. Another source claims the land was mortgaged only in the autumn, after Feinberg's trip to Europe, to secure "funding for daily needs" (Hissin, *Diary*, p. 42). This discrepancy remains unexplained. Nevertheless, the colony had only forty-eight francs to its name that winter. See receipt in Levontin, p. 87.
28 See Scheid, p. 182, who claims that no more than "forty percent of the seeds planted" reached harvest. Also see Hissin, *Diary*, pp. 45, 53; Raab, p. 90; Freiman, I, p. 173. The first summer crops also failed. It should be emphasized that the colonization budget for Rishon le-Zion was founded on the assumption that the income from crops would enable the settlers to fend for themselves after the first agricultural season. See "Colonization Expense Account" of Z. D. Levontin, *Ha-shahar* 10, no. 12 (1882), p. 660.

the fruit could be marketed. Their hopes of immediate self-sufficiency dashed, the colonists seized upon their only remaining option: financial patronage, including repayment of the mortgage, in exchange for their most valuable asset — land.

Naturally, they appealed to Baron de Rothschild, who had come to their aid before and proved willing to do so again. Through his representative, Michael Erlanger, who met with the colonists on 10 June 1883, Rothschild promised to repay the mortgage and to augment his investment in the colony as needed. No figures were quoted, but it was agreed that the baron would finance the completion of housing for the needy families, furnish them with farm equipment, cover all public expenditures (including the building of a school, employment of a ritual slaughterer and health care), and purchase more land to be divided among those colonists who had none.[29]

This heralded a turning point in the development of Rishon le-Zion and had immediate implications for the baron's involvement in Jewish colonization on a larger scale. The two conditions he set for this massive aid were responsible for altering the entire decision-making apparatus in the colony, his relationship with the colonists, and the shape of the colony in the years to come.

Rothschild's major stipulation was the transfer of land ownership so that the title deed bore the name of his representative, Michael Erlanger.[30] This step served a triple purpose: Rothschild could hold the land as collateral in the sense of an ordinary mortgage, the colonists could not sell it and profit at his expense, and most importantly, he could maintain a watchful eye over the colonists' spending, effectively taking charge of the administration and eliminating the basis for autonomous decision-making.[31] The colonists were also obligated to comply with

---

29   Hissin, *Diary*, p. 54. Rothschild ordered the transfer of 12,000 francs to repay the mortgage on 22 June 1883. See Yavne'eli, II, p. 84.

30   The official transfer of land ownership and receipt of the *kushan* (deed) took place on 12 July 1883. See Freiman, I, p. 14. Also see copy of reapportionment of land between Rishon le-Zion and Erlanger as the baron's representative, French manuscripts, Jaffa, 18 October 1883, in CZA A192/217/2.

31   This arrangement was appealed by three of the wealthier colonists who had paid for their land in full and were able to repay their share of the mortgage. These three demanded and received separate title deeds.

Early private home in Rishon le-Zion, built in 1883

Rothschild's second condition — the appointment of his agronomist, Dugourd, as supervisor of all internal aid.[32]

First Stage: A Process Set in Motion

At the end of 1882, Baron de Rothschild's endeavors in the sphere of Jewish colonization in Eretz Israel took two separate directions: the establishment of a new colony, later known as Ekron, and the support of an existing colony — Rishon le-Zion. From the standpoint of financial investment and the number of people involved, both were small-scale projects. The funding constituted a loan which was expected to be

---

32   See Freiman, I, p. 14, who also states that the "community record books, stamp, etc." were given to Hirsch after the transfer of land ownership. A document signed by Hirsch on 9 July 1883 attests to this (Hebrew manuscripts, CZA A197/217/2). The colony's minute books thus made their way from Rishon le-Zion to Mikve Israel and, finally, to the Central Zionist Archives in Jerusalem.

66   *Chapter One*

repaid,[33] and all parties agreed that aid would not extend beyond the first year on the assumption that self-sufficiency would be attained by that time. In short, Rothschild's initial undertakings involved two specific geographical locations and branched out no farther.

Baron de Rothschild's chief objectives at this point seem to have been the economic and social rehabilitation of Jewish refugees from Russia. Combatting Christian missionary activity in the Holy Land and refuting the antisemitic arguments that Jews were unproductive may have also played a role,[34] but were of secondary importance compared with the humanitarian-philanthropic goal of resettling homeless Jews. With this cause in mind, he promoted a variety of schemes in Eretz Israel, including the encouragement of small businesses. All these early projects were in the category of experiments designed to solve the problem of Jewish emigrés. They were part of a broader plan of action which was not necessarily connected with the Holy Land, as demonstrated by Rothschild's willingness to consider Jewish colonization in Santo Domingo or the United States, and even the resettlement of Jews in Russia.[35]

The basically experimental nature of Rothschild's projects that first year was pointed out even in his own times. Less attention, however, has been devoted to the turning point towards the end of 1883, when Rishon le-Zion was given into the baron's hands and his activities in Palestine entered a new stage, known as the "period of patronage." This was also the moment when Rothschild's endeavors shifted from the humanitarian-philanthropic sphere, concerned chiefly with the Jews of Eastern Europe, to the spatial-national sphere, in which Eretz Israel as a territorial base assumed prime importance. Henceforth, Rothschild

---

33   In his correspondence, Rothschild reiterates that this financial aid was a loan. See letter to Hirsch dated 6 April 1833 (Yavne'eli, II, p. 79) and unpublished letter dated 19 October 1885 (French manuscript, CZA J41/72). In the former, he writes that the repaid sums would be used to assist new colonists. In effect, the Bilu pioneers never anticipated more than a year of financial aid.

34   On Rothschild's desire to prove that the Jews could be farmers, see his first letter to Hirsch, dated 20 October 1882 (Yavne'eli, II, p. 69); on missionary activity in the Holy Land and his desire to provide the Jews with a means of livelihood, be it farming, crafts or industry, see letter of 1 February 1883 (ibid., p. 76) and elsewhere.

35   Klausner, *Nation*, p. 264.

ceased to investigate possibilities for Jewish settlement in other regions of the world and concentrated exclusively on Eretz Israel, where his efforts now reached beyond the two existing settlements of Mikve Israel and Rishon le-Zion and the newly-founded colony of Ekron, to the country as a whole.

CHAPTER TWO

DEEPENING TIES, 1883–1887

Relationship with the Northern Colonies

Taking over the lands of Rishon le-Zion changed more than Baron de Rothschild's relationship with a particular colony; it signified a new depth of personal involvement in Jewish settlement all over Palestine. Rothschild's conscious resolve to become a leading force in this sphere was demonstrated during the second half of August 1883 when he agreed to support the northern colonies of Rosh Pinna and Zikhron Ya'akov, and later Petah Tikva, under an arrangement similar to the one reached in Rishon le-Zion.[1] In addition to widening the circle of colonies that depended upon him for financial assistance, Rothschild now stood at the helm of a bureaucratic mechanism that would supervise further development and lead the colonies toward economic independence.[2]

Rothschild's relationship with the northern colonies did not materialize from thin air. The settlers of Zikhron Ya'akov and Rosh Pinna were aware that aid from an anonymous source was being channeled to the colonies through Hirsch and the AIU, and appealed to Hirsch to consider them as their financial condition deteriorated.[3] When approached, Rothschild agreed to take these colonies under his wing and engaged the services of Elie Scheid of Alsace, secretary of the Jewish Charity Committee of Paris, to assist in their reorganization. On 10 October 1883, Scheid travelled to Palestine to settle matters in Rosh Pinna only, but during

---

1   Letters of Erlanger to Hirsch, 3 August–5 October 1883, in Yavne'eli, II, pp. 235–240. Also see Ever-Hadani, PICA, p. 51.
2   On the poverty of the northern colonies in 1883, a year after their establishment, see Aaronsohn, Establishment, pp. 74, 132–135.
3   Aaronsohn, *Baron*, pp. 39–42.

his three-month stay he successfully negotiated agreements in both Rosh Pinna and Zikhron Ya'akov, and laid the necessary groundwork for future reforms.[4]

Strictly speaking, there was no need for Scheid to discuss the transfer of land with the colonists of Zikhron Ya'akov. All the property had been registered in the name of the chairman of the Central Committee in Galatz, Rumania, whose son and heir was in Paris and prepared to sign over the land in bulk. However, Scheid feared the colonists might refuse to cooperate and he sought their written consent. The day after his arrival in Haifa, he sat down with them and drafted a letter to Rothschild in which they declared:

> We place ourselves in your hands, and proclaim in this letter our willingness to rely on your judgment in all that pertains to the organization of the colony. We accept without any reservations the administrator you choose as our guide.[5]

His next stop was Rosh Pinna, where the colonists also signed such an agreement and agreed to its publication in a newspaper soon afterwards.[6] This document is highly illuminating with regard to Rothschild's initial involvement with Jewish colonization. As in Ekron and Rishon le-Zion, he accepted full financial responsibility in exchange for the transfer of property rights and the colonists' pledge to obey his administrators, and he maintained his policy of limiting monetary support to a period of nine months, i.e., until harvest time. However, in his dealings with the northern colonies three new elements were introduced: the settlers' committee was explicitly recognized as a decision-making body, the settlers promised to comply with the "comprehensive laws binding colonists in France," and committed themselves to accepting French citizenship.

These last two items seem to indicate that Scheid and Rothschild were interested in imparting a French character to Jewish colonization

---

4   Scheid's mission is first mentioned in Rothschild's letter to Hirsch, 30 September 1883, in Yavne'eli II, p. 88; Erlanger's letter to Hirsch, 5 October 1883, ibid., p. 239.
5   Letter to Rothschild signed by fifty-three farmers of Zikhron Ya'akov, 24 October 1883, in Samsonov, pp. 88–89. Further details in Aaronsohn, *Baron*, pp. 42–43.
6   The agreement was published in *Ha-melitz* 23, (1883) no. 101 (reprinted in Yavne'eli II, p. 142); *Der Colonist* 1 (1883), no. 49; *Ha-maggid* 28 (1883), no. 50. More details and discussion in Rogel.

in Palestine, although there is no other written proof that Rothschild subscribed to such an approach. Unfortunately, the phrasing of this document is unclear. None of the literature on French colonization mentions laws that applied specifically to French colonists, and in the absence of the original document, probably in French or German, it is difficult to know whether the reference was to owners of French farms in North Africa or southern France, or to another type of French colonization. On the other hand, the requirement to become French citizens was not necessarily connected with a desire to disseminate French culture. It may have been a means of circumventing the legal obstacles that the Turks imposed to hinder Jewish settlement. Whatever the purpose, this stipulation was never fulfilled. Due to some prior commitment to the government or legal impediment in obtaining French citizenship, the colonists of Rosh Pinna became subjects of the Ottoman Empire instead.[7]

No major changes in the number of colonists or the administrative network took place in Rosh Pinna during this stage of Rothschild's involvement (November 1883–July 1884). However, the change in the physical landscape was unmistakable. Now that the colonists were relieved of the mortgage on their land and their personal debts, and received a regular monthly stipend of ten francs per person, they began to increase their livestock holdings and build more barns and animal pens. New public buildings such as a synagogue, school and bathhouse, were constructed.[8] Work commenced on previously untilled land, putting to use the seeds, draft animals and plows purchased in November 1883, and a health service was set up with regular visits from a Safed physician.

Under Rothschild, Rosh Pinna was greatly transformed. Housing and farm buildings were erected, the needy families were provided with living quarters, and a large communal stable was built. By the summer of 1885, four community services functioned in public buildings: a secretariat, a synagogue with a women's section, a school conducted in

---

7   Reported by M. Taubenhaus, *Ha-zefirah* 4 March 1884. Turkish citizenship was received on 3 February 1884, i.e., before Scheid left the country.
8   Scheid, p. 31, claims that all three public services were housed in the same building, Also see Gordon, who reports the construction of a water pipeline to the colony.

Cultivated land and community buildings in Rosh Pinna, c. 1898

both Hebrew and French, and a bathhouse which served also as a ritual bath. Farmland was redistributed according to family size, and each colonist was given two oxen, a milking cow, a donkey, and several goats and sheep. Separate areas were set aside for the three chief agricultural crops: wheat, grapes and vegetables,[9] and three teachers — the colonist M. D. Shub and two outsiders — were hired by Rothschild to work in the school. Access to the colony was improved by a carriage road that was built by order of the governor of Safed, again with funding from Rothschild.

The shift to patronage was more pronounced in Zikhron Ya'akov. In Rosh Pinna, the settlers' committee had supervised the continuation of agricultural work without a break, but Zikhron Ya'akov had begun to stagnate and decline before Rothschild stepped in, and the presence of his administrators in Haifa and the colony itself set the colonists working again at a brisk pace. During 1884, Zikhron Ya'akov was conducted temporarily as a commune. The land was not parcelled out to individual farmers, the male settlers lived 5–10 to a room, and meals were eaten in a communal dining hall. Their families remained in Haifa, where schooling and health services were provided by the AIU and paid for by Baron de Rothschild. Meanwhile, the men cleared the hilltop site of stones and brush, and planted wheat, barley and vetch. After the winter rains, a nursery was set up next to the spring and the surrounding

---

9   Frumkin, p. 174.

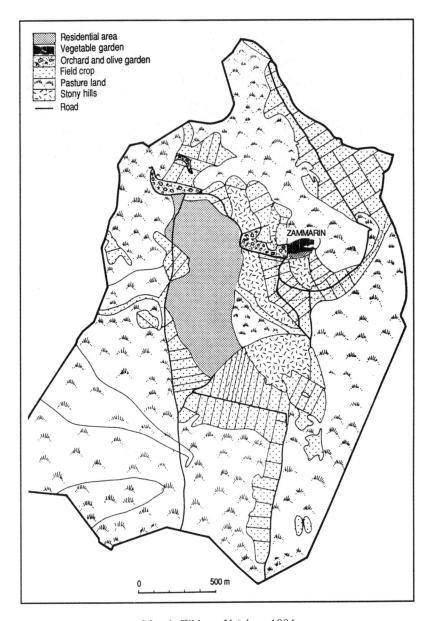

Map 1: Zikhron Ya'akov, 1884
Source: Lubman, Plan of Sde Shomron, 1884 (in Samsonov, between pp. 56–57)

slopes were planted with olive trees from a nearby Arab village. The route leading from the spring was repaired and intensive construction work commenced to provide housing, farm facilities and services.[10]

Land Ownership and Diplomacy

As the development of the colonies proceeded, the problem of land ownership became a source of concern. The Ottoman ban on Jewish immigration and land purchase made it difficult for the early pioneers to obtain a *kushan* (deed) from the authorities, and as long as the land was classified as *miri* (state-owned), they could not get a *rukasiyye* (legal permit) to build on it or dig wells. Among the strategies they devised to circumvent this obstacle was to register the land in the name of an acceptable Ottoman citizen or apply for a license to build "farm structures" which could be obtained relatively easily from local authorities.

Initially, Rothschild and his officials followed their lead. In Rishon le-Zion, Rosh Pinna and Zikhron Ya'akov, building activities were pursued on the basis of permits received prior to the baron's intervention. In Ekron, where Rothschild was involved from the very start, inquiries about a license commenced in January 1884. After months of correspondence, a permit was issued on 5 April 1884 for the construction of farm buildings only.[11] Legally, the colonists of Ekron could build shelters for farm animals on an area of two dunams. Consequently, the four large buildings completed at the end of 1884 housed both the colonists and their livestock.

Around this time, a major dispute arose over the lands of Zikhron Ya'akov which were registered in the name of the chairman of the Central Committee in Galatz, Rumania. After his death in May 1883, arrangements had been made to transfer the property to Rothschild.

---

10 Data on work in Zikhron Ya'akov derived from Scheid, pp. 59–69; Samsonov, p. 103. See Map 1.
11 Erlanger's letters to Hirsch, 11 January, 8 February, 7 March, 14 March and 21 March 1884, in Yavne'eli, II, pp. 244–246.

However, the Turkish government contested the heirs' rights and expropriated the land. For six months, from May to November 1884, Elie Scheid travelled throughout the Levant and fought this decision in every Ottoman court in Haifa, Acre, Beirut and Constantinople until he was awarded a kushan in Erlanger's name. The permit was received on 11 November 1884 and became official eleven days later.[12]

This battle over the lands of Zikhron Ya'akov had an important effect on Rothschild's modus operandi While the matter was in the courts, he channeled greater sums than ever before into the colonization effort, some of it openly used to bribe officials, as was customary at the time. In addition, he and his representatives exploited their contacts with French consular agents, Turkish Jewry (primarily Isaac Fernandez, president of the AIU in Constantinople), and the Hovevei Zion societies in Rumania.[13]

This episode also marked Rothschild's first foray into diplomacy. Until then, he had consciously avoided confrontation with the Ottoman authorities because he knew European activity in the region was a sensitive issue and liable to be detrimental to the colonization effort. In his earliest correspondence with Hirsch in January 1883, he recommended that the Radom pioneers take out Turkish citizenship in view of the obstacles imposed by the government on land purchase for Jewish settlement. He also advocated that colonies not be established along the route to Jerusalem so as not to irritate those in power:

> J'ai encore une recommendation à vous faire relativement à l'achet de ces terres, ce serait de choisir de préférence un endroit qui ne serait pas sur la route de Jérusalem, pour ne pas grouper ces colonies toujours dans la même direction et eviter de donner bien à certaines suspicions.[14]

12 On this episode in detail, see Scheid, pp. 72–78. Also see interesting data on the legal problems of Zikhron Ya'akov in the letters of the French Foreign Minister, 9 March 1884 and 4 August 1885, in Margalith, pp. 185–190; letter of Wormser to Hirsch, 2 May 1884, ibid., pp. 208–209; CZA, J15/5003, J15/5978.
13 On the appeal to the French consular agents, see letters in Margalith, pp. 185–190; on Fernandez's subsequent efforts in Constantinople on the baron's behalf, see Citron, p. 248; on the continued ties between Rothschild's representative and Hovevei Zion in Rumania, see Klausner, *Hibbat Zion*, p. 248.
14 Letter of Rothschild to Hirsch, 3 January 1883, CZA J15/7058. Rothschild broaches the issue again the following month, explaining that "...pour ne pas eveiller des

Throughout the decade, Rothschild kept his activities in the Holy Land as inconspicuous as possible, and Elie Scheid was careful to use the Jewish Charity Committee of Paris as a cover. However, when it became clear that only direct contacts with officials in the local and central government would produce the permits needed to further work in the colonies, Rothschild changed his strategy accordingly.

The Zikhron Ya'akov case was vivid proof that owning the land was crucial to Jewish colonization. Under Ottoman rule, the colonists were restricted in their land use and required to apply for permits each step of the way. When the land was expropriated and put up for sale, work came to a standstill and it was feared that all the investment had been for naught. Only when the title deed came into Jewish hands did life return to normal and the colonists began to build at an accelerated pace, no longer restricted to the hilltop site where the first pioneers had settled.

Some of the houses and huts in Zikhron Ya'akov (1885?)

---

susceptibilités politiques des Turcs ou au moins leur suspicions, de ne pas grouper toutes ces colonies sur le route de Jérusalem" (letter of 1 February 1883, ibid.).

In December 1884, tracts of land to the west of the original site were apportioned by lottery and readied for the arrival of sixty prefabricated wooden homes from Rumania. Foundations were also laid for four stone buildings to be used by the entire community. By 1885, there were close to seventy buildings in the colony, which was officially named Zikhron Ya'akov in memory of James Jacob Rothschild, the baron's father, during the cornerstone laying for the new synagogue on 1 June 1885.[15]

In addition to the upswing in building, the legal dispute over the lands of Zikhron Ya'akov led Rothschild to step up the acquisition of property on the outskirts of his colonies. Over the next two years, he purchased 9,000 dunams, including vast tracts of land west and east of Zikhron Ya'akov (Map 2), outside Rishon le-Zion, near Ekron, and in the vicinity of Rosh Pinna. Rishon le-Zion was the first colony in which Rothschild promoted independent private settlement. Most of the newly-acquired land, which totalled 3,500 dunams, was sold at cost price to a group of twenty-four new colonists, who were expected to farm the land using Jewish labor only (at Rothschild's request!) and to manage on their own, without loans or administrative assistance. In consequence, both the area and population of Rishon le-Zion had doubled by 1886.[16]

Did these extensive land purchases signify a broader, more nationally-oriented approach to colonization on Rothschild's part? There seems to be no evidence of this, at least from a geographical point of view. All the land acquired at this stage was associated with the expansion of the existing colonies rather than with the creation of new areas of settlement. If any conscious decision was made in 1884–1885, it was to maintain the status quo in the defined spatial zone of the four colonies. Over the next four years, no land was purchased outside the boundaries delimited in 1884.

---

15 Brill, p. 179; letter of Wissotsky to Erlanger, 9 June 1885, in Wissotsky, pp. 166–168; also see Map 1–2.

16 Bibliographical references in Aaronsohn, *Baron*, p. 51, nn. 48–49.

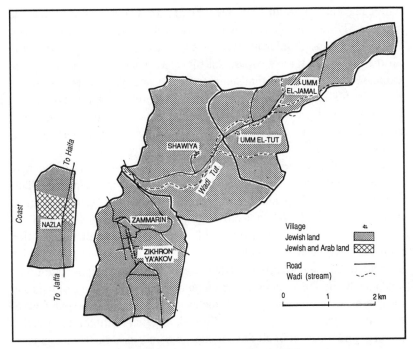

Map 2: The lands of Zikhron Ya'akov and daughter colonies, 1887
Source: Schumacher, Plan de la colonie Zicron-Jacob et ses environs, 1887
(in Samsonov, between pp. 138–139)

Perpetuation and Change in Farming Patterns

The purchase of additional land around the four colonies served a double purpose: on the one hand, the absorption of new settlers and the increase in the number of persons employed in agriculture; and on the other, the provision of a more solid agricultural basis by raising land quotas and enabling farmers with little land to branch out. Although there are no figures for this phenomenon, it was no less important than the first and helped to solve the problem of land shortage that threatened the colonization effort from the start. It was also related to another issue which became central in 1885: the type of farm which was most likely to succeed. By the end of two growing seasons under Rothschild's auspices, it was clear that grain crops were not the answer. The poor harvests in all the colonies in 1884 came as a blow, especially after the optimism expressed by the farmers that summer. The meager yields were disastrous not only for individual colonists but for the future of the colonies as a whole. There was no longer any doubt that farms producing wheat on 75–200 dunams were incapable of providing even the most minimal living standards.[17]

Rothschild had envisaged between one and three years of involvement in the colonies prior to their achieving economic independence. This required a plan of operation and a decision as to what type of farming would be pursued. When Rothschild purchased property around the colonies and allocated land to those whose farms were small, his intention seems to have been to provide more farmland for wheat-growing, which continued to be the major crop. He had not planned to acquire additional lands for Rishon le-Zion until Hirsch reported on the shortage of land and meager harvest in January 1884, which led him to approve the purchase of the adjacent lands of Ayūn Qāra.[18] Considering that Rothschild proceeded to take similar action in all the colonies, we may assume that his general policy was to maintain wheat as the main branch of agriculture but make it more profitable by adding to the size of the farms.

At the same time, new approaches began to materialize; there were those who believed that a more variegated farm economy was necessary, with an emphasis on plantations. During this period, both the baron's administrators and the colonists drew up ideas and conducted trial and error experiments that eventually led them in the right direction. Whereas wheat was sown at the advice of Dugourd in 1883–1884, another of the baron's agronomists urged the colonists of Rishon le-Zion to plant vineyards the following year, testing Arab varieties in addition to the simple French strains provided by Mikve Israel.[19]

---

17   The yields for 1884 are predicted in Dugourd's letter to Hirsch, 10 June 1884, in Margalith, pp. 207–208.
18   Erlanger's letters to Hirsch dated 11 January, 4 April, 9 May 1884 in Yavne'eli II, pp. 244, 247, 249.
19   Freiman, I, p. 17; II, p. 246. More on the shift to viticulture below.

Vineyards and wine cellar in Rishon le-Zion, c. 1898

When Joshua Ossowetzky, one of Rothschild's officials, presented his plan to replant the wheat fields of Rishon le-Zion with grapes in early 1884, most of the settlers were opposed. Their idea was to purchase land on the outskirts of the colony and sow more wheat. By the end of that year, however, they realized that the prospects for wheat growing were poor. On the other hand, the grapevines planted by three colonists had done well, prompting many of their colleagues to follow in their footsteps in 1885. Menaché Meerovitch, a Bilu member who settled in Rishon le-Zion, also drew up a plan which shifted the agricultural emphasis to plantations.[20] The extent to which Rothschild and his officials were responsible for changing the type of farm economy is an issue that has been dealt with elsewhere. At any rate, the planting of vineyards was one of Rothschild's conditions for the sale of the Ayūn Qāra lands to new settlers, and the fact remains that by 1886, close to 400 dunams of grapes (100,000 seedlings) were being cultivated in Rishon le-Zion.[21]

The other Rothschild colonies were also in the throes of change. At the insistence of Elie Scheid, the northern colonies abandoned dry farming in favor of traditional unirrigated plantations such as olives,

---

20 Letter of Z. Dubnow, 22 June 1884, in Druyanow and Laskov, II, p. 425; Smilansky, *History*, p. 134; Meerovitch, *Advice*, p. 235.
21 *Ha-havazzelet* 15 (1885), no. 13.

grapes, almonds, mulberries and figs. At the end of 1884, Scheid claimed that ninety dunams of olives per family could supply a Galilee farm with sufficient income. In 1886, Rothschild's agronomist in Rosh Pinna supervised the planting of vineyards and fruit orchards in addition to a fertilized, irrigated garden equipped with glassed-in greenhouses.[22]

In 1885, Rothschild provided each family in Ekron with the means to plant two dunams of grapes and about one hundred olive and citrus trees (citrons, lemons and oranges), and the following year, a pump was added to the newly-excavated well in order to irrigate them. Nevertheless, Ekron remained the only Rothschild colony where wheat continued to be a major crop in the coming years. In this respect it lagged behind Rishon le-Zion, Zikhron Ya'akov and Rosh Pinna which rapidly adapted to the introduction of new farming schemes.

Rothschild's administrative network, which played a crucial role during this period, grew steadily over the course of three years in response to changing needs. In addition to the administrators who remained in Zikhron Ya'akov and Rosh Pinna after Scheid's return to Paris in early February 1884, and the newly-appointed administrators of the Judean colonies, the baron's team was widened to incorporate agronomists and, later, a class of professionals referred to as community workers: physicians, teachers and religious functionaries. The second part of this work is devoted to a more thorough examination of the administration, but it should be remembered that its operational methods were shaped between 1884 and 1887. Rothschild initially authorized a variety of management techniques for the sake of experiment. However, his personal preference, voiced as early as 1884, was for a centralized hierarchy.[23] The final form taken by the administration was developed in response to serious problems that emerged over the years, such as the colonists' revolt against the administration in Rishon le-Zion at the end of 1883 and a similar uprising in Rosh Pinna in mid-1885 (see below, pp. 87ff.).

The growing dimensions and diversity of the baron's administrative mechanism and his choice of management tactics were an interplay of cause and effect. Without his officials, Rothschild's involvement in the colonies would have remained superficial, and only with the help

22 Aaronsohn, *Baron*, p. 54.
23 Letter of Erlanger to Hirsch, 19 September 1884, in Idelovich, p. 131.

of a large number of administrators specializing in different fields and powerful enough to carry out their plans could the colonies make the strides in housing, infrastructure and agriculture that would hasten their economic independence.

At this stage, the policy in all three spheres was a combination of perpetuation and change. In construction, for example, Rothschild's officials supervised the implementation of plans which had been drawn up previously for housing and farm buildings, while moving ahead from 1884 with new plans for synagogues, schools and offices. The first colony to have such public buildings was Ekron: by 1886, the colony gained an office building and a three-story structure that housed a synagogue and a school. Throughout the period, the colonists continued clearing the land, building roads and developing the water supply. A new element was the introduction of public services in the areas of religion, education and health. Catering to the colonists' religious and educational needs was discussed in mid-1884, but such services were not provided immediately because Rothschild was ambivalent about them. He feared that schooling, for example, might stand in the way of raising a new generation of hardy, unpretentious farmers capable of achieving economic self-sufficiency.

In agriculture, too, the period was characterized by both perpetuation and change. Alongside efforts to supply the colonists with equipment and basic instruction in farming, experiments were carried out with new crops, a more variegated farm economy and modern technology. Rothschild's hiring policies were also in a state of flux. At first, he was prepared to employ Arab gardeners. Within two years, however, he insisted on utilizing European methods and expertise, with implements and instructors brought over from France. The baron's agronomist in Rosh Pinna introduced fertilized, irrigated gardens and greenhouses in the summer of 1886. That autumn, the land was prepared for planting vines and fruit trees, and the wheat fields were fertilized and tilled with European farm machinery instead of the traditional Arab pin plough.[24]

It was this process of change in all the colonies, together with the shift to plantations, that inaugurated the next phase of Rothschild's

---

24 For primary sources in Hebrew and French on these three issues, see Aaronsohn, *Baron*, p. 56, nn. 61–63.

The colony of Ekron, 1892

involvement in the Jewish colonies — a phase marked by embracing agrarian reforms.

Second Stage — Important Strides

The second stage of Rothschild's alliance with the colonies was a period of deepening ties. First of all, the time limit for financial support was extended beyond the nine to twelve months which formed part of the original agreement. From the colonists' perspective, this meant the conversion of all their short-term private debts to individuals and institutions into one lump debt to Baron de Rothschild. Repayment was thus flexible and could be postponed until the colonies were capable of operating on their own.

In the hope of promoting economic independence within a shorter span of time, Rothschild initiated the construction of public buildings, the development of local community services, and above all, the purchase of more land and the introduction of new farming methods. In the sphere of agriculture, the baron operated on two planes: on the one hand, he continued to support the traditional farm structure in which wheat was predominant by providing the means for larger crops, and on the other, he advocated new models of farming based on European technology and an emphasis on plantations. As a result, more thought had to be invested in the as yet amorphous administrative system. From the standpoint of production and income subsidies, Rothschild assumed full responsibility, yet the colonists continued to play a role in decision-making. At this stage, the baron not only allowed private farms to be run alongside those managed by his officials, but extended aid to them and encouraged the trend on a broad scale in Ayūn Qāra, outside Rishon le-Zion. In addition, settlers' committees and welfare societies were organized in the colonies under Rothschild's auspices and in cooperation with his officials.

During the period in question, Rothschild extended his patronage to two additional colonies, although his main interest continued to lie in the settlements he had nurtured from the start. Support of colonization enterprises elsewhere in the country was left to other bodies operative at the time. Among the smaller associations promoting Jewish settlement was the Bnei Yehuda society formed by a group of Jews from Safed in the summer of 1884. At the end of 1885, members of the society purchased land in Rumthaniyya in the Golan (east of the Upper Jordan Valley) and made an unsuccessful attempt to found a colony there.[25] (See below pp. 98–99).

The most prominent of the Jewish colonization organizations was Hovevei Zion, whose various societies in Eastern Europe were brought together under one roof during the Kattowitz Convention on 6–12 November 1884. Among the resolutions of this conference were the establishment of a new colony for the Bilu pioneers in Qatra and the support of Petah Tikva and Yesud ha-Ma'ala. After the first pioneers of Petah Tikva abandoned the colony in 1881 and returned to Jerusalem, they asked Yechiel Michal Pines, a representative of the Sir Moses Montefiore Testimonial Fund, to help them find a buyer for the land among the settlement societies whose emissaries were then in the country. When this proved unsuccessful, they sent an emissary overseas and the property, spanning 13,000 dunams, was sold to Hovevei Zion groups in

---

25 Sources in English: *Jewish Chronicle*, no. 805, 29 August 1884, p. 16; ibid., no. 816, 14 November 1884, p. 7; ibid., no. 899, 18 June 1886, p. 6; in Hebrew: Klausner, *Ascending*, pp. 57–63; Ilan, pp. 54–75.

Lithuania, principally Bialystok and its environs. At the beginning of 1882, another 150 dunams of land were purchased in Yahud, an hour's walk from the old site. This became the new nucleus of the colony, to which several of the original founders returned on 8 October 1882. In 1883, they were joined by newcomers from Bialystok and the population of Petah Tikva reached thirty-nine families and a total of 170 persons by the end of 1884.[26]

However, their requests for the kushan and rukasiyye permits that were necessary for construction were held up by the Ottoman authorities and the pioneers soon depleted their funds. Only a dozen homes had been built on the site in Yahud when the Turkish governor ordered the work to stop at the end of 1883 and took the colonists to court. Most of the Petah Tikva pioneers thus found themselves living in overcrowded Arab buildings acquired with the land, and some families continued to live in Jaffa for another two years.[27] In this respect, the problems of Petah Tikva were very similar to those of other colonies founded in the 1880s.

Another Hovevei Zion society founded the colony of Yesud ha-Ma'ala. The majority of its twenty-four members hailed from Mezhirech, Poland and the remainder from Brisk, Lithuania. Delegates of the society were sent to Eretz Israel in the spring of 1883 to purchase land. On 18 August 2,500 dunams were acquired in a village in the Upper Galilee near Lake Hula.[28] The former Jewish owners, the distinguished Abu family of Safed, had renamed the site and employed Arab tenants to farm the land under a Jewish foreman. The Mezhirech society planned to send over a small number of colonists to plant fruit trees with the help of hired laborers, and the rest of the group was to follow after the first harvest.

The ten founding members of Yesud ha-Ma'ala arrived in March 1884 and took up residence in Safed. Anticipating the arrival of their

---

26 This separate piece of land was purchased because the proximity to the Yarkon River caused many cases of malaria among the early pioneers. See Aaronsohn, Building, p. 241, n. 12.
27 Goldman, General View, pp. 136–137; report on the history of Petah Tikva (undated — end of 1891?) in Raab, pp. 55–57. See summary of Pines in *Mevasseret Zion* (1884), pp. 9–13, continued in ibid., 2, pp. 45–49.
28 Harisman, pp. 46–49. See interesting documents on the establishment of Yesud ha-Ma'ala in the archives of the Jewish National and University Library, Jerusalem, file no. V55; and in CZA A109/24.

colleagues, they postponed the organization of a settlers' committee and did not draw up a charter, leaving the handling of their affairs to the settlement societies in Mezhirech and Lithuania. These societies occasionally sent small sums of money to cover expenses, but none of the remaining landowners ever moved to Palestine, which seriously impeded the colony's development. Furthermore, the long delay in receiving a kushan prevented the colonists from building even the flimsiest housing.[29]

Much of the land of Qatra, which became Gedera on 12 December 1884, was owned by Hovevei Zion. At the request of this organization, Yechiel Michal Pines arranged for the settlement in Qatra of nine Bilu pioneers who had been working at Mikve Israel. The colony consisted of two tracts of land purchased from a Christian resident of Jaffa: 1,000 dunams of land north of a small valley which had been cultivated by tenant farmers from the village of Qatra, and 2,000 dunams of barren, rocky terrain to the south. The former was to be used to raise wheat, and continued to be worked by the peasants during the colony's first year. A small wooden cabin with a red-tiled roof was erected on the second tract, and thirty-five dunams of land were cleared for planting.[30]

Gedera was beset with problems from the very start. The quality of the soil was poor, water was scarce, agricultural knowhow and manpower were limited and private capital was non-existent. The colonists lived in isolation and suffered constant harassment from their Arab neighbors. They received monthly wages and a meager subsidy from Hovevei Zion, and were obligated to report to a supervisor who lived outside the colony. However, the Bilu pioneers and their mentor, Pines, were a special breed. Despite the hardships, they elected a settlers' committee, convened regularly and reached decisions on crucial topics such as farm management, crops, division of labor, the choice of a permanent site, and even social and religious practices, which was one sphere in which Gedera differed from the other colonies.[31]

In the summer of 1885, one of Hovevei Zion's wealthiest activists, K. W. Wissotsky, was sent to Eretz Israel to organize a coordinating branch in Jaffa. In addition to the projects already under way, i.e., three

---

29 Druyanow, *Documents*, I, pp. 220–223, 584–597, 787–788.
30 Ariel, pp. 27–30.
31 Laskov, pp. 223ff; Salmon, pp. 133–137.

Hovevei Zion-sponsored colonies and several private farms, the country was scouted for new sites. In this respect, Hovevei Zion seemed to be more active than Rothschild. However, its plans to purchase land and establish more colonies were not successful, and the financial support it was able to extend to those colonies it had already founded was far from sufficient. Moreover, at the Kattowitz Convention, the society voted that all its funding to the colonies be routed through the Rothschild administration. Michael Erlanger was appointed to transfer the money to Samuel Hirsch in Palestine, who was to exercise control over its use in the colonies, and the latter, who headed the Hovevei Zion office in Jaffa together with Joshua Ossowetzky, did not hesitate to approach Rothschild on Hovevei Zion's behalf in the event of any difficulty.[32]

Rothschild was reluctant to become involved in the activities of Hovevei Zion and to overstep the physical boundaries of his own four colonies. Despite their entreaties, he refused to assume financial responsibility for the colonies established by Hovevei Zion with the exception of a small amount of aid to Gedera in later years, a one-time grant to Yesud ha-Ma'ala, and more substantial support to Petah Tikva as it struggled for survival in the early days.[33]

Yahud (Petah Tikva) with its wind-operated pump, c. 1898

---

32 Wissotsky (throughout most of the book); Klausner, *Kattowitz*, I, pp. 55–95, 140–177; protocols of the Executive Committee in: Druyanow, *Documents*, I.
33 For more information on Rothschild's aid to the Hovevei Zion colonies and references to source material, see Aaronsohn, *Baron*, pp. 58–63, 89–93.

CHAPTER THREE

A RELATIONSHIP SOLIDIFIED, 1887–1890

The Events of 1887

Historiographic studies commonly denote 1887 as a pivotal year in the ventures of Baron de Rothschild in the Holy Land.[1] Indeed, three developments in 1887 forged yet another link in the chain of events which, one by one, strengthened Rothschild's ties with the colonies. These were the settlers' revolt in Rishon le-Zion, Rothschild's journey to Eretz Israel, and the Druskieniki Conference followed by the Pinsker–Rothschild meeting.

When the farmers of Rishon le-Zion rose up against the colony administrator, Joshua Ossowetzky, in February 1887, the incident was widely reported in the Hebrew press and figured prominently in the correspondence of Hovevei Zion leaders. Modern studies have analyzed the episode from different angles, scrutinizing contemporary sources.[2] Ultimately, the revolt in Rishon le-Zion was a power struggle between the colonists who balked at taking orders, and the administrators who insisted on being obeyed.

The conflict was seemingly resolved at the end of April, when Rothschild made his first journey to the Holy Land. On 22 April 1887, Rothschild disembarked in Jaffa and after a brief stop at Mikve Israel, continued directly to Jerusalem. He spent five days visiting the sites (synagogues, the Wailing Wall, the Church of the Holy Sepulchre,

---

1   This is evident in two perceptive studies on Rothschild and the colonies. Both authors begin new chapters with the year 1887 but do not explore their reasons for doing so. A brief explanation is offered by Margalith, but Schama overlooks the issue altogether. See Margalith, pp. 109–110; Schama, pp. 88ff.

2   For primary and secondary sources, and further elaboration on the settlers' revolt, see Aaronsohn, *Baron*, pp. 64–66.

welfare institutions and schools) and meeting with prominent members of the Jewish, European-Christian and Turkish communities. With his guide, Nissim Behar, he also spent some time touring Jericho (including an adjacent area on both sides of the Jordan Valley), and made short visits to Rachel's Tomb and Solomon's Pools (see Map 3).

On 27 April Rothschild arrived at Rishon le-Zion, whose fields, vineyards and homes he was taken to see the following day.[3] That afternoon, he called a meeting with the colonists and threatened to withdraw financial support from any who persisted in their rebellious actions. Many hours were spent in separate talks with the farmers and administrative personnel. On his third and last day at Rishon le-Zion, he announced that Ossowetzky would be removed from his post. He also extended a pardon to all the rebels except one, and cautioned them against any further insurrection. Before departing for Europe via Damascus and Constantinople on 6 May Rothschild visited other Jewish settlements in the Jaffa area (Wadi el-Hanin, Ekron, Petah Tikva and Yahud) and lastly, Zikhron Ya'akov and Rosh Pinna.[4]

Among the various consequences of Rothschild's visit, the most far-reaching was his decision to purchase extensive stretches of land around Zikhron Ya'akov and Rosh Pinna. Although he ordered his representatives to pursue the matter while he was touring the colonies, the idea of increasing his land holdings was part of a plan envisaged when he was yet in Paris. In each of these two settlements, Rothschild hoped to establish a farming school that would train dozens of laborers, who would then be given land of their own.

During his visit to the northern colonies, Rothschild endeavored to strengthen ties with other inhabitants of the region, both Jewish and Arab. He welcomed the Arab peasants and dignitaries who called upon him, visited a neighboring Arab village, and met with Jewish personalities operating independently in the rural sector who were not affiliated with the Rothschild colonies.[5]

---

3   The timing of this visit had no relation whatsoever to the uprising in Rishon le-Zion. Planning for the trip began a year and a half earlier. See letter of Gordon to Sh. P. Rabinovitch, 24 November 1885, in Druyanow, *Documents*, I, col. 369.
4   Aaronsohn, *Baron*, p. 67, n. 12.
5   Ibid., pp. 67–69.

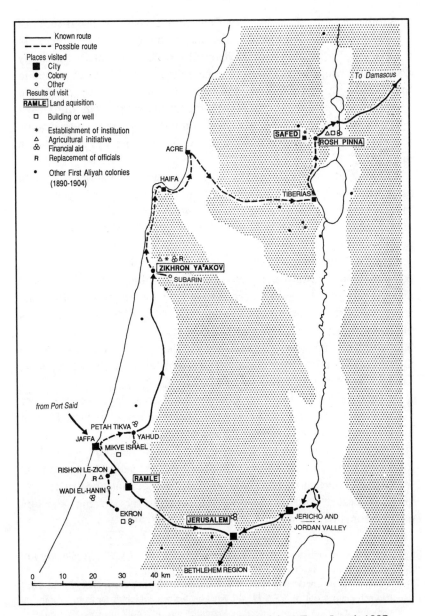

Map 3: Route and outcome of Rothschild's visit to Eretz Israel, 1887
Source: Data in this volume, pp. 87–88 (and references)

Another important outcome of Rothschild's visit was the shaping of a more systematic approach to the administration of the colonies. In the wake of the Rishon le-Zion revolt, Rothschild became increasingly wary of allowing the colonists to handle their own affairs, and opted in favor of the rigid, centralized system of organization to which he had been inclined from the outset. That same year, changes were introduced which were felt by the colonists and administrators alike: bureaucratic reorganization on the one hand, and less freedom for the colonists, on the other.

Not long after Rothschild's departure, three new regulations came into force: the colonists were prohibited from organizing, hosting outsiders in their homes and employing laborers without permission of the colony administrator. On 1 June 1887, the inhabitants of Rishon le-Zion were requested to sign a letter stating that they would abide by these rules as a prerequisite for continued support from Rothschild.[6] This measure was taken to neutralize subversive elements in the colony, which Rothschild and his advisors felt were nurtured through the formation of private associations, the presence of non-residents and the hiring of large numbers of Jewish laborers. Contrary to belief, these restrictions were not the brainchild of the colony administrators; they originated in Paris and their implementation was closely supervised by Rothschild's deputies, Erlanger and Scheid.[7]

At first, the majority of the colonists refused to sign, and an order was issued at the end of June to halt their income subsidies. Five of them gave in, but the remainder persisted in their refusal for three weeks, changing their minds only after Erlanger's visit to the colony on 18 July. Meanwhile, they made a living from odd jobs or selling produce from their farms. Several of the colonists were still defiant after Erlanger's visit, and at least three held out for three months by pawning or selling their personal belongings.[8]

---

6   The signed document (Hebrew manuscript) is in CZA A192/217. A photocopy of one of the drafts in French appears in Idelovich, p. 145.
7   Correspondence between Erlanger and Hirsch, 26 May, 9 June, and 17 June 1887 (French manuscript) in CZA J41/46. My conclusions, which differ from writings on the subject to date, are reinforced by Margalith, pp. 447–448, nn. 168–170, referring to another correspondence.
8   On the events following Rothschild's visit, see letter of Belkind to Lilienblum,

It should be borne in mind that behind the revolt in Rishon le-Zion lay an important economic factor: the colonists' opposition to reorganizing the farm economy and shifting the focus from grain crops to plantations.[9] In October 1887, after the ringleaders of the uprising were expelled from the colony and all the others signed the letter, an orderly transition to the new scheme was finally made possible.

The Druskieniki Conference which brought together all the Hovevei Zion societies in Russia, and the subsequent talks between Rothschild and Hovevei Zion chairman Leo Pinsker, also tied in with the events of 1887 which clinched Rothschild's relationship with the colonies. This conference, held on 28 June–1 July 1887, addressed two pressing issues: the failure of the movement to obtain official approval for its work in Russia, and the lack of progress in its settlement enterprise in Eretz Israel due to fiscal problems. Although most of the meetings were taken up with internal politics, three resolutions had a direct bearing on the activities of Baron de Rothschild: the decision to establish a central bureau in Jaffa, possibly headed by Samuel Hirsch; to continue support of Gedera, Yesud ha-Ma'ala and Petah Tikva but refrain for the time being from purchasing land or founding new colonies; and to reelect Erlanger as treasurer of Hovevei Zion and coordinator of its financial operations.[10] The supremacy of the Rothschild administration over Hovevei Zion was thus openly acknowledged. Over the next three months, members of the movement expressed their concern, both privately and in the Jewish press, that the revolt in Rishon le-Zion might dampen the baron's enthusiasm and adversely affect the colonization movement as a whole.[11]

Immediately after the Druskieniki Conference, Leo Pinsker met with Rothschild in Paris and secured his help in solving Petah Tikva's land

---

30 August 1887, in Druyanow, *Documents*, II, cols. 283–286 (Russian). The dates here are taken from Horowitz, *Diary*.

9 Aaronsohn, *Baron*, pp. 72–73.
10 Protocol of the conference in Druyanow, *Documents*, II, cols. 191–218; Lilienblum, pp. 86–89. Four of five letters written by participants in appreciation of Hovevei Zion's colonization work were addressed to Rothschild, Erlanger, Hirsch and Scheid. For more details, see Klausner, *Kattowitz*, pp. 130–140.
11 Ibid., summary of Hebrew correspondence, pp. 210–211; also see Ben-Yehuda, *Fickle*; Barzilai, *Memories*, no. 21, p. 5.

problems. Rothschild agreed to provide legal assistance, to collaborate with Hovevei Zion in buying back the land from society members who had never settled in Eretz Israel, and to distribute more land to colonists whose holdings were small. Although he had been unwilling to extend aid to Petah Tikva when he was in the country, his present decision was not out of line with the promises he had made to the colonists of Yesud ha-Ma'ala, who had sought his intervention in the matter of land registry and building permits for their colony.[12]

Rothschild's relationship with Gedera also revolved full circle. At first he would not even visit the colony or meet with its representatives. Erlanger and Hirsch were behind the expulsion of a Gedera pioneer who had been among the instigators of the revolt in Rishon le-Zion, and the incident led Hirsch to terminate his handling of the colony's land dispute. Yet this did not stop Rothschild from intervening on Gedera's behalf in 1887. When Scheid was sent on a mission to Constantinople that year, he convinced the Minister of the Interior to permit the registry of the lands of Gedera and to issue instructions to the local authorities in this regard. The colonists could thus go ahead with the excavation of a well for which funds had been lying in wait since 1886, and Rothschild contributed another 7,000 francs towards this purpose in February 1888. Hirsch resumed his negotiating efforts and succeeded in resolving the property feud the following month with the help of 2,500 francs from Baron de Rothschild.[13]

Thus it transpired that Rothschild was not deterred in his plans by the settlers' revolt, and he continued to work with determination to advance the colonization enterprise in Eretz Israel. In fact, the insurrection, coupled with his visit to the country, the resolutions of the Druskieniki Conference and his meeting with Pinsker, served to accelerate processes which were already in motion and lend a more calculated and permanent character to his decision-making and operational strategies. The events of

---

12   On Rothschild's agreement to aid Petah Tikva and Yesud ha-Ma'ala, see Pinsker, letter of 18 Tishrei, in Druyanow, *Documents*, II, pp. 322–323; Scheid, letter of 9 September 1888, ibid., pp. 595–596.
13   Laskov, pp. 270–276; letter of Pines to Pinsker, 21 May 1888, in Druyanow, *Documents*, II, pp. 540–541 (note 11); *Ha-melitz* 29 (1889), nos. 40–41.

1887 therefore exerted a cumulative influence which tipped the already tilted scales rather than heralding a revolutionary change.

Gedera and its settlers, 1892

Headway in the Rothschild Colonies

Two important strides were made at the end of 1887. First, Rothschild's bureaucracy was reorganized to incorporate officials of three ranks: the director-general, Elie Scheid, and a chief agricultural director, both of who operated from Paris; directors and agricultural advisors who supervised on a regional basis; and a network of local officials and agronomists who resided in individual colonies. By 1890, the lowest rank developed into a hierarchy in miniature, so that each colony had a chief agronomist, agronomists specializing in different branches, and assistant agronomists. Secondly, the central government in Istanbul issued a general kushan which gave Jews the right to colonize, purchase land, erect housing and dig wells after securing permission from the local authorities only.

Scheid's mission to Istanbul in September 1887 yielded three favorable decisions: construction on land belonging to Jews would now be under the jurisdiction of the *pasha* (regional governer) of Jerusalem and the *vali* (general governer) of Damascus, no longer requiring a permit from the central government in Constantinople; the pasha and the

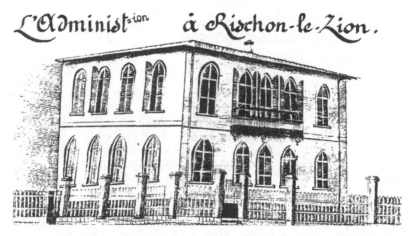

One of the administration buildings, Rishon le-Zion c. 1899

vali would assist rather than hinder colonization efforts; and authorization would be forthcoming for building in Gedera and the establishment of a winery in Rishon le-Zion.[14]

In the colonies, notable progress was achieved in three spheres: finalizing a clear-cut agricultural program, introducing professional training programs, and increasing the scope of non-agricultural building and investment. In April 1888, Rothschild collaborated with top aides Elie Scheid and Gérard Ermens, and other advisors such as Erlanger, Zadoc Kahn, and Professors Gayon and Mortier (the latter was in charge of Rothschild's estate in southern France, Château Lafite), with the aim of creating a new, comprehensive agricultural and industrial network for the colonies.[15] The choice of a marketing economy based on plantations was the product of realistic economic thinking rather than the cultural background or mentality of the planners, as so often assumed. Six years of farming experience in the region had shown that farms with field crops required at least 200–300 dunams to succeed. This was a serious drawback in light of the high cost and scarcity of land. In most colonies, there were no more than 100-150 dunams suitable for cultivation. As

---

14 Scheid, pp. 96, 195–196; letter of Scheid to Pinsker, 25 November 1887, in Druyanow, *Documents*, II, col. 385; Erlanger to Pinsker, 9 December 1887 and 3 January 1888, ibid., cols. 400, 437 (German).
15 Schama, p. 117; Scheid, p. 100.

one contemporary source notes, Zikhron Ya'akov had barely twenty-five dunams of arable land per family. A census conducted by Rothschild's officials in 1888 revealed that net earnings from dry farming in Zikhron Ya'akov, even under optimum conditions, did not approach the annual support provided by Rothschild, let alone set the colony on the path to financial independence.[16] By shifting to a more intensive type of farming, i.e., from field crops to plantations, it was possible to attain much higher yields on a smaller area of land. In this respect, Rothschild and his experts used the farms familiar to them in southern France and Algeria as a model.

The three principles behind the new scheme were the large-scale cultivation of orchards, the industrial processing of the bulk of the produce (even before 1888, it had been decided to open at least one winery), and experimentation to determine the most suitable crops. A recommendation in favor of monoculture farming which would involve vineyards alone was notably absent. As we shall see, grapes were indeed central to the Rothschild plan, but at this stage, and well into the 1890s, a variety of industrial crops were grown, including mulberry trees for the silk industry, citrus fruits for preserves and aromatic plants for perfume. Other experimental crops were caster-oil plants, tea, coffee and cotton.[17]

Five of these were tropical or sub-tropical crops which Rothschild recommended because he perceived Eretz Israel as a "hot country."[18] However, it was the perennial Mediterranean crops that proved most successful and began to be planted on a commercial scale. All the Rothschild colonies set aside land for "experimental fields" (*champs d'expérience*). The nursery in Rishon le-Zion experimented in 1888 with non-fruitbearing trees such as eucalyptus, cypress, she-oak, ficus, bamboo, jacaranda, and greviella. Other trees grown in the colonies

---

16 Hissin, *Diary*, p. 306; ibid., pp. 87–88. On the agricultural census in Zikhron Ya'akov from 1888, see Ever-Hadani, *Vinegrowers*, p. 46.
17 See Pukhachewsky, Founders, nos. 28–40; also see chapter on agriculture below.
18 According to the memoirs of one of the assistant agronomists, Rothschild devoted a special section in Yesud ha-Ma'ala to "sub-tropical" experiments beginning in 1887 (see ibid., 26). According to another source, Rothschild was searching for "an agronomist with experience in hot countries who would agree to go to Palestine on a research and study mission" (Ever-Hadani, *Vinegrowers*, p. 44).

during this period, aside from mulberry and citrus, were olive, almond and apricot.[19]

Rothschild's decision to establish training programs for skilled laborers was motivated by both economic and cultural-ideological considerations. From the earliest days of the colonization enterprise, hiring Arab peasants to work in the fields was proposed as a solution for the colonists' lack of farming experience and familiarity with local conditions. Rothschild, on those occasions when he voiced an opinion, consistently favored Jewish labor. His views were put into practice in 1886 when a clause in the contract for the sale of the Ayūn Qāra lands to private settlers stipulated the employment of Jewish workers only. Ideology aside, it seems that hiring Jews also had a practical side: skilled workers were needed in growing numbers as the colonies underwent a transition from grain to plantations.[20]

Rothschild invested in three types of training: programs for the children of colonists at the Mikve Israel agricultural school, advanced overseas training for outstanding students, and farming schools in the colonies themselves. The colonists' children had been sent to Mikve Israel in small numbers since the beginning of the colonization movement. However, this was not done on an organized basis or funded by Rothschild until his visit to the country in 1887. He arranged for the children of Rishon le-Zion to attend the school as of 1887/88.[21]

In 1887, prior to Rothschild's decision to send promising students abroad, his officials appointed some of the more capable young people of Zihkron Ya'akov and Rosh Pinna to positions of responsibility. Towards the end of the 1880s, they were enrolled at agricultural schools in France or Algeria (Versailles and Ruaiba), where they attended professional courses for periods of two and three years. At the same time, some of the outstanding female students were sent to the teachers' seminary of

---

19   Pukhachewsky, Founders, no. 33, pp. 14–15; Scheid, p. 84; Freiman, I, p. 25; II, p. 17.
20   Aaronsohn, *Baron*, pp. 77–78.
21   Letter of AIU to Hirsch dated 24 June 1887, CZA J41/23/3. Hirsch's letters to the AIU between 1882 and 1890, preserved in the AIU archives in Paris, contain dozens of references to students from the colonies. For example, his report for 1884 (AIU Archive, France b/2679/3) and the student list for 1889/90 (ibid., g974).

the Alliance Israélite Universelle in Paris, and were hired to teach at the colony schools upon their return.

During, Rothschild's sojourn in Eretz Israel, he declared his intention to found farming schools in Zikhron Ya'akov, Rosh Pinna and Rishon le-Zion.[22] However, an *arbeiterschule*, as this type of school was known in Yiddish, opened only in Zikhron Ya'akov and began to operate in the autumn of 1887, as soon as the building was complete. There were no entrance requirements save a promise to work diligently. Students received a monthly wage of thirty francs, accommodation, clothing, a pair of work shoes, and assurances that Rothschild would set them up as farmers at the end of three years. The only branch of agriculture taught was viticulture; no less time was devoted to preparatory work such as construction and clearing away stones. Not surprisingly, the students played a role in Zikhron Ya'akov even before they completed their studies: they constituted a reliable source of cheap labor and were put to work on communal projects.[23] In addition, the availability of such a work force presumably lowered costs and raised professional standards in Zikhron Ya'akov.

During this stage, between 1887 and 1890, greater attention was paid to building and investments that were not connected with agriculture. Rothschild began to devote himself to public services such as education and health, particularly towards the end of the decade. However, we shall return to this subject below.

Land Purchases and the Beginnings of Be'er Tuviya, Bat Shlomo and Meir Shefeya

Until 1887, Rothschild's land purchases were carried out on a limited scale, mainly in the vicinity of the existing colonies, and he refused to cooperate with the various Hovevei Zion societies who asked him to acquire tracts of land for their members and assist in their settlement. Towards the end of 1887, he acquired property in Shawiye, which was

---

22 Aaronsohn, *Baron*, pp. 78–79.
23 For an authentic description of the school and those who attended it, see student letters: Kantor, Basic, Bronstein; more details in Samsonov, pp. 189ff.

to become the colony of Shefeya, east of Zihkron Ya'akov, and in 1889, more land on the outskirts of Rosh Pinna, Yesud ha-Ma'ala and Rishon le-Zion.[24] Furthermore, for the first time, attempts were made to purchase land and establish colonies in new geographical sites, far removed from the current core of settlement.

This brings us to a plan drawn up in late 1887 for settling in Transjordan a group of sixty financially independent Jews who had served in foreign armies, primarily that of Russia. For two years, Rothschild's officials and the leaders of Hovevei Zion negotiated for the purchase of land in the region, but without success. Rothschild's idea seems to have been to establish a colony which would not be dependent upon him financially, but managed by his administrators. He hoped to take advantage of the inexpensive land in Transjordan, which allowed for colonization with relatively little investment. He considered remoteness from government centers to be an advantage and the problem of security could be solved by utilizing the military background of the colonists and establishing a chain of settlements along a broad stretch of land. Among the candidates for settlement were graduates of the farming school in Zikhron Ya'akov and members of Hovevei Zion societies which had been in contact with Rothschild (including the Bessarabia society, which rejected the Transjordan site and later settled in Be'er Tuviya).[25]

As it transpired, only one colony was established in Transjordan, and not by Rothschild. A group of Jews from the "Old Yishuv" of Safed banded together in 1886–1887 and attempted to set up the colony of Bnei Yehuda on 14,000 dunams of land which had been purchased from the Circassian village of Rumthaniyya in the central Golan. Due to financial hardship and the long wait for a kushan, the men worked in shifts of ten and their families resided in Safed. The colony was abandoned after two agricultural seasons. At the end of 1888, the pioneers reorganized and tried to colonize in a new location: Bir esh-Shkūm in the southern Golan. Again, they found themselves in serious difficulty, and most of the land

---

24 On Ossowetzky's purchase of additional land from the village of Ja'une, see Epstein, Question, p. 195. The area of Rishon le-Zion was increased by 1,540 dunams when Epstein, a wealthy member of Hovevei Zion in Odessa, succeeded in purchasing land from an Arab effendi in October 1889 (see Map 6).

25 Aaronsohn, *Baron*, p. 80, nn. 50–52.

continued to be cultivated by Arab tenants. Over the next two years, the colonists remained on the site only during planting and harvesting. In the summer of 1891, however, several families did settle down and begin to construct permanent housing.[26]

Aside from a new receptivity to colonization in other geographical locations, another change in Rothschild's settlement policy became evident in 1887. Until this time, his endeavors outside the colonies addressed members of the middle-class, who were encouraged to settle in the rural sector regardless of age or farm experience; the only qualification was financial, as in Ayūn Qāra (near Rishon le-Zion) and the wine-growing colonies planned on the outskirts of Zikhron Ya'akov in 1886. Hereafter, Rothschild began to give thought to the plight of destitute laborers and landless second-generation colonists, which resulted in the establishment of Bat Shlomo and Meir Shefeya. He was also prepared to tender assistance to select groups of Hovevei Zion pioneers, as in the unsuccessful Transjordan scheme and the founding of Be'er Tuviya. Rothschild's guidelines were identical in all three cases.[27] His idea was to establish colonies that would develop under administrative supervision and achieve self-sufficiency within a year, without his having to assume the financial burden of their upkeep. Reality proved otherwise.

Bat Shlomo and Meir Shefeya, the daughter colonies of Zikhron Ya'akov, were founded to solve a problem which had a far greater impact on the history of the First Aliya than once believed. As the population in the older colonies swelled, so did the pressure on resources, particularly land. In the 1880s, the children of the founders reached adulthood and began families of their own. The population was also augmented by large numbers of landless laborers.[28] To accommodate some of this demand, new colonies were founded in the second half of 1890, not all of them under Rothschild's auspices. For example, the large family estates belonging to Reuben Lehrer in Wadi el-Hanin (Nahalat Reuven) and Mordechai Lubovsky in Shoshanat ha-Yarden

---

26 For these attempts, see above, p. 81, and Ilan, pp. 64–74, and references there.
27 Scheid, *Ha-melitz* 29 no. 79 (1689), ibid., no. 115; *Ha-zvi*, 6 (1889), no. 3.
28 Aaronsohn, Establishment, pp. 50–51. No distinct proletarian class developed during the First Aliya period; both laborers and colonists' sons shared the ambition of becoming farmers.

Bat Shlomo, c. 1898

were parcelled out and sold to land-hungry laborers beginning in 1887, becoming the colonies of Nes Ziona and Mishmar ha-Yarden at the end of 1890.[29]

The colony of Bat Shlomo was the baron's first full-scale colonization enterprise since Ekron. It was located on 2,500 dunams of land in Umm el-Jamal, which had been acquired by Rothschild in November 1885 along with 17,000 dunams in Nazla, Umm el-Tut and Shawiye in a bid to increase his land holdings in the Zikhron Ya'akov region.[30] The new colony, an hour's journey east of Zikhron Ya'akov, was a solution to the shortage of arable land in the older colony, a problem made more acute by natural increase, the influx of Jewish laborers and the aspirations of the farming school's students (see Map 2).

Nearly two years after the property was purchased, three young farmers from Zikhron Ya'akov pitched their tents on the land and set to work to establish a claim (Arab tenants from the village of Umm el-Tut continued to farm the land through 1886). When the decision to found Bat Shlomo was reached in 1888, another five farmers from Zikhron Ya'akov joined them to ready the fields and build housing. At a public ceremony in June 1888, Elie Scheid was given the honor of laying the cornerstone. Fifteen graduates of the Zikhron Ya'akov farming school settled in Bat Shlomo

29 Aaronsohn, *Building*, pp. 244–245, 255–256.
30 The sources differ on the size of these tracts. Establishing accurate dimensions is difficult in light of the numerous estimates and the unreliability of the land registry system. The lands of Bat Shlomo measured 4,000–5,800 dunams, but only 2,534 were entered in the official register. See Hissin, *Journey*, p. 330; Meerovitch, *Description*, p. 192.

in September–October 1889, and seven stone houses and a stable had been completed by the end of 1890.[31]

The procedures followed in the establishment of Bat Shlomo were geared to making the colony economically viable from the very first year. Candidates were screened in advance, communal funds were spent cautiously, a one-time grant was provided for establishment expenses and dry farming was introduced as the principal branch of agriculture. Only the children of colonists and unmarried laborers with agricultural experience were accepted, and it was decided that all communal services, with the exception of a synagogue, would be provided at Zikhron Ya'akov. Each colonist received a house, a plot of 220 dunams, a long-term loan, and all the tools, housewares and livestock needed to operate a farm without further support from Rothschild.[32] The grain harvest was supposed to provide sufficient income for the achievement of economic stability within a year.

This new farming pattern had an immediate impact on the landscape. Public building or plans for such construction was minimal, housing units were small and designed for communal-living, the entire colony was small-scale and compact, and farmland was carved out in large, uniform blocks.

The colony of Be'er Tuviya, which continued to be known by its Arabic name, Castina, was founded by the Hovevei Zion group from Bessarabia for whom Rothschild had agreed to buy land at the end of 1887. In certain respects, Be'er Tuviya was similar to Ekron. Both were "model colonies" populated by pioneers who immigrated to Eretz Israel on their own initiative, paying their own way. On the other hand, the colonists of Ekron had a background in farming, whereas the Be'er Tuviya colonists did not, and the Bessarabians — unlike the Ekron pioneers — shared in the cost of the land.[33]

The lengthy organizational process was again reminiscent of Ekron.

---

31 Rokeah, Evil Writs, pp. 35–36; Samsonov, pp. 180–189, 212; Rokeah, Colonies 1888, p. 249.
32 Hissin, *Journey*, pp. 329–332; Herschberg, *Oriental Lands*, pp. 137–138.
33 Erlanger to Pines, 22 December 1887 and 3 May 1888 (German), in Druyanow, *Documents*, II, pp. 428–429, 521; Erlanger to Hirsch, 21 January 1889 (French manuscript), CZA J41/46. Castina has been the subject of much research, including a monograph: Giladi, Be'er Tuviya and references there. However, some data has

The Be'er Tuviya settlers — 18 families numbering 150 persons — were forced to wait in Jaffa for several months after their arrival on 13 March 1888, because the Rothschild administration had not yet purchased land. Meanwhile a monthly stipend of twelve francs was distributed to them by Emil Ettinger, who was appointed colony administrator.[34] Joshua Ossowetzky, who represented Rothschild in dealings with the authorities and had been in charge of land purchases in the south of the country since his transfer to Petah Tikva, eventually acquired 6,500 dunams of land from two residents of Castina, an Arab village about twelve kilometers south of Gedera. After much negotiation and payment of bribes, a kushan (for 5,623 of the 6,500 dunams) and a permit to build housing were obtained from the local authorities (the *pasha* of Jerusalem and *kaymakam* of Gaza).[35] As this license was contrary to the orders of the central government, which allowed only cow sheds and stables, it was valid for no more than fifteen days. To meet this deadline, prefabricated huts were built in Rishon le-Zion and then dismantled and reassembled in Be'er Tuviya on 13 September 1888, the colony's official date of establishment. This was done by carpenters and laborers working around the clock, who completed the construction of homes even before the arrival of the first colonists.[36]

---

been distorted or entirely overlooked. The short history of Be'er Tuviya provided here is based on previously unknown primary sources.

34   Rokeah, Colonies 1888, pp. 29–30, 244. Also see Rokeah, Colony, pp. 85–87. Date in Rokeah, Colonies 1888, p. 261. This author provides two population estimates: fifteen families and eighteen families (Rokeah, Colonies 1889, p. 146). The most common figure is twenty-five persons; but one source goes as high as one hundred (Izraelit, p.1). My data relies on Erlanger's letter to Hirsch, 21 January 1889, CZA J41/46 and the appended list. The number of founding families may have reached twenty if we include the families of two emissaries who returned to Paris in early 1890.

35   Goldman, Be'er Tuviya, pp. 15–23. The transaction took place in the summer of 1888, but the precise date is unknown. The earliest date I was able to find was June. See Rokeah, Colonies 1888, p. 244. For further details, see Izraelit, pp. 2–3.

36   Ibid., p. 4. This source cites twenty-five wooden cabins. Figures cited by other sources are between twenty and twenty-three, and thirteen. More on this subject in Pukhachewsky, Founders, no. 33, pp. 14–15; Goldman, Be'er Tuviya.

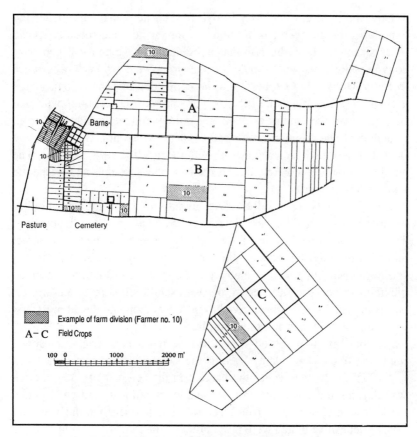

Map 4: Lands of Castina (Be'er Tuviya), 1896
Source: Slor, Outline plan of Be'er Tuviya, 1896
(JNF map 4614, Hebrew University map collection)

Now the pioneers of Be'er Tuviya faced a new challenge. After the experience of the revolt in Rishon le-Zion, which had recently spread to Zikhron Ya'akov, the regional administrator, Alphonse Bloch, was convinced that measures should be taken to prevent any such occurrence in Be'er Tuviya. In October 1888, he demanded that the colonists sign a contract which relegated them to the status of day laborers who had no rights over the land or assets of the colony and were prohibited from organizing. The colonists, who had contributed towards the cost of the land and assumed they would be running private farms, refused. The administration immediately cut off their income subsidies and leased the land to Arab tenants.[37]

On 27 January 1889, after seven months in Jaffa, thirteen families numbering one hundred persons packed their bags and left the country. The remaining five families, a total of fifty persons, signed the contract and became hired laborers of the baron. First they were sent to Rishon le-Zion, where they were joined by a group of 20–30 laborers deemed qualified to become farmers by the Rothschild administration, and towards the end of year, they moved to the new colony — the laborers first and then the colonists and their families.[38]

As soon as they settled down, the winter wheat crop was sown, mulberry trees were planted along the colony's only road and work began on a new well. After the harvest in the summer of 1889, a ditch was dug around the colony to demarcate its borders, and an irrigated orchard with a variety of fruit trees was planted near the old well and pool to determine which were most suited to the local soil conditions and climate (see Maps 4 and 5). Twelve of the colonists worked as tenant farmers under the supervision of the resident agronomist, earning a wage of 1.5 francs per day.[39]

The settlers of Be'er Tuviya faced numerous hardships during their first

---

37 The Bessarabian pioneers envisaged a mixed farm economy which included grain, vegetables, poultry, honey, vineyards and fruit trees. See Cohen, Be'er Tuviya, p. 17. On the contract, see Rokeah, Colonies 1888, pp. 49–50; on the colonists' reaction, see ibid., pp. 50–53, 59–62; and Rokeach, Colony, pp. 86–87.
38 Rosen, p. 334; "Reckoning of the Yishuv," *Ha-maggid* 33 (1889), no. 6, pp. 41–42. The sources offer various data on the population of laborers. I was unable to determine the precise total or ascertain whether there was any fluctuation.
39 Cohen, Be'er Tuviya; Pukhachewsky, Founders, nos. 32–34; *Ha-zvi* 5 (1889),

year. Their own water sources were so unreliable they had to buy water from their Arab neighbors in Beit Daras. They were located far from Jewish population centers, which isolated them socially and cut them off totally when the winter rains came. Work in the fields was backbreaking, and many died from malaria. Unresolved disputes over boundary lines led to harassment and attacks from the surrounding villagers. No substantial assistance came from the administration even in two spheres that were supposedly under its jurisdiction: the inexperience of both colonists and laborers in dry farming, and poor farm management, which led to a shortage of tools and draft animals when they were most needed.[40]

Yet this is not what brought about the collapse of Be'er Tuviya. After all, many other colonies had endured hardships just as severe. The true reason was the unhealthy relationship which existed in the colony between the administrators, farmers and laborers. The Rothschild administration was responsible for creating two separate groups — farmers and laborers — each of which was small, weak and working at cross purposes. Relations with the officials were tense, and the colonists also fought between themselves. The breakdown began even before the colonists settled on the land, with the departure of so many families creating an atmosphere of transience and uncertainty which was further compounded by the frequent changes in administrative personnel.[41]

Individual laborers began leaving the colony during the first year; by the next year, nearly none were left. Some of the families also moved out: they were bitter over their status as hired workers and had lost all hope of ever becoming independent landowners. Within two years, Be'er Tuviya had deteriorated from a colony to an ordinary farm. A few workers remained, but most of the land was leased to Arab tenants.[42] In the summer of 1896, an attempt was made to revive the colony.

---

        no. 26, p. 100; letter of Castina farmers to Greenberg in Druyanow, *Documents*, III, pp. 107–110.

40   Ibid.; Izraelit, pp. 3–9; Rokeah, Colonies 1888, p. 49; Rokeah, Lament, pp. 144–145.

41   On the death of one of the laborers and the friction between the administrator and the agronomist, see ibid., ibid. In the span of one year (1889), these two officials were replaced four times, and the non-resident supervisor, twice.

42   Druyanow, *Documents*, III, p. 110; Izraelit, p. 5. On the changes in land ownership, and cultivation, Barzilai, *Beit Halevi*, p. 38.

Among the seventeen Hovevei Zion pioneers who returned to the site and reinhabited the old buildings were three families from the group of Bessarabians who had originally settled there.[43]

In September 1889, about a year after the establishment of Be'er Tuviya, Zikhron Ya'akov gained another daughter colony: Meir Shefeya. The land had been purchased in the summer of 1886, but cultivation began only two years later, as in Bat Shlomo. However, in contrast to Bat Shlomo, a Jewish tenant farmer was hired to tend the wheat fields, while the agricultural school students cleared the land under the supervision of J. Dugourd.[44] At the end of 1889, ten bachelors from Zikhron Ya'akov took up residence in an old stone house in the Arab village of Shawiye. When the planting season came around, they planted grapevines and a variety of fruit trees, including almond and apricot. The first permanent housing was constructed in a new location west of Shawiye, and the colonists settled there in the summer of 1890.

Screening procedures and planning in Shefeya basically followed the same social and economic principles as in Bat Shlomo, although reforms were introduced in two spheres: it was decided to provide communal services, however minimal, to alleviate the problem of total dependency on the mother colony, and the main agricultural branch was changed from dry farming to plantations.[45]

Geographically, Shefeya enjoyed an advantage over Bat Shlomo. It was much larger, encompassing 8,519 dunams, only half an hour's walk to Zikhron Ya'akov. As a result, the younger colony gained ascendancy during the 1890s, overshadowing its elder sister. In neither daughter-colony, however, did the pioneers achieve the financial independence they sought; both remained beholden to Rothschild and his administrators for many years to come. Over the next decade,

---

43 "List of Castina colonists," Odessa Committee report for 1896–1898, in Giladi, Be'er Tuviya.
44 The founding dates and order of establishment of the various colonies are determined here and elsewhere in this volume by the date on which the pioneers, generally the men, camped on the site and commenced agricultural activities. On the work in Shefeya, see Samsonov, pp. 130ff. According to one source, negotiations with the owner of the estate commenced in early 1885. See Hissin, *Journey*, p. 333.
45 Ibid., pp. 330–335; Samsonov, p. 190.

The colony of Shefeya, 1898

the farm economy became more varied, and the colonists supplemented their income by doing day labor for the baron in the nurseries and orchards.

With all its drawbacks, the farming model employed in the establishment of Bat Shlomo, Be'er Tuviya and Meir Shefeya in the 1880s was adhered to, with minor adjustments, in most of the colonies which emerged later: Metulla (the northernmost Jewish settlement in Upper Galilee) and the resurgent colony of Be'er Tuviya in the 1890s, as well as the dry farming colonies of Lower Galilee and in the Zihkron Ya'akov region at the turn of the century.[46]

---

46 Scheid, pp. 95–96; Aaronsohn, Building, pp. 266–272 (including references).

The Circle Widens: Petah Tikva and Yesud ha-Ma'ala as Colonies of the Baron

When Rothschild visited the Holy Land in the spring of 1887, much of his time and energy were devoted to projects outside the colonies, notably his support of public institutions in the Jewish urban sector. Among his activities were the establishment of schools and the purchase of land for a hospital in Safed (the plans for the hospital never materialized), the purchase of land for the Ezrat Nashim hospital in Jerusalem and a synagogue in Ramle, the renovation of the ritual bath and cemetery in Gaza, and the upkeep of a synagogue in Nablus.[47] Other assistance to the urban communities was provided through the creation of job opportunities in the Rothschild colonies, the distribution of food items, and the offer of one-time loans and individual grants in the form of money or production supplies.

However, Rothschild's generosity was most evident in the Jewish rural sector. Aside from his valuable aid to the Hovevei Zion colonies in both the early and later stages of their development, there was hardly a Jewish cause in the rural sector to which Rothschild did not donate. In one settlement, he paid the salary of the ritual slaughterer and the teacher, in another he financed the drilling of a well, and in yet another, he extended loans to private settlers.[48]

The inclusion of the Hovevei Zion colonies of Petah Tikva and Yesud ha-Ma'ala in his financial patronage scheme constituted Rothschild's major undertaking in the agricultural sector outside the bounds of his own colonies. Although the pioneers of the three Hovevei Zion colonies remained masters of their own fate during the second half of the 1880s, the future looked bleak. Development work was at a standstill, wheat harvests were poor, and large stretches of land lay barren or were leased to Arab tenants. Living standards were very low, even in Petah Tikva which was better off than both Gedera and Yesud ha-Ma'ala. The most pressing problem was land registry and obtaining building permits. Without these,

---

47   AIU Archives, Paris, letter dated 6 June 1888, no. f684/7; Luncz, Rothschild, p. 203; Luncz, *Guide*, pp. 83, 212, 248. For more particulars, see Aaronsohn, *Baron*, Table 28.
48   Ibid., p. 89.

no housing or wells could be constructed, property disputes erupted between the neighbors, the land could not be divided into plots, and certain portions remained unfarmed. The Odessa Committee tried to work out a solution through its representatives in Eretz Israel, but without success.[49]

The colonists of Yesud ha-Ma'ala suffered most of all. Their housing consisted of huts made of a mixture of mud and straw, or tents woven from swamp-reeds in the manner of the Bedouin. Confronted with their own powerlessness, Hovevei Zion appealed in March 1866 to an official of the Rothschild administration, L. Wormser, asking him to intervene on the colony's behalf, and indeed, some aid from Rothschild did materialize in the mid-eighties.

When Rothschild visited Rosh Pinna in May 1887, he also met representatives from Yesud ha-Ma'ala. In response to their requests for assistance, he sent in officials that same summer to establish a nursery and a station for agricultural experiments. In Paris, a plan was being worked out to buy back the land of Hovevei Zion members who had purchased large tracts in Yesud ha-Ma'ala but never settled there. This land would then be divided between the colonists whose farms were very small. Such a plan was alluded to in the summer of 1888, when Scheid and Ermens tried to explain to the pioneers of Yesud ha-Ma'ala why Rothschild was not prepared to take over the colony. Towards the end of the year, his basically favorable attitude became more articulate: he asked Hovevei Zion to organize the property holdings of all absentee landowners so that he could purchase them as a single bloc and use the land to build greenhouses and start a flower industry.[50]

In early 1889, Rothschild took another step in his dealings with Yesud ha-Ma'ala. He permitted Ossowetzky to reside in the colony as the local Hovevei Zion official, agreed in principle to settle the colony's debts, and contributed an additional sum as emergency aid. He also instructed Ossowetzky to purchase another 2,000–3,000 dunams of land in the vicinity. Although this transaction was completed only in the 1890s, Hovevei Zion was able to organize the property

---

49 Klausner, *Kattowitz*, I, pp. 140–168, 297–313, 360–368.
50 *Ha-melitz* 28 (1888), no. 13; on Rothschild's proposal, see letters of Scheid to Pinsker, 9 September and 25 October 1888, in Druyanow, *Documents*, II, pp. 595–596, 610.

Yesud ha-Ma'ala, 1898

of the absentee landowners by the end of the summer of 1889, which paved the way for Rothschild's next decision.[51]

In September 1889, he announced his willingness to take the colony under his wing: he would build housing, establish communal services and pay the farmers' wages, again on condition that all the land be turned over to him. After a brief spell of opposition, the colonists agreed and the entire estate came into Rothschild's possession following the exchange of 1,200 dunams for part of his land in Castina.[52] A resident administrator and an agronomist were appointed, a road was paved from Yesud ha-Ma'ala to Rosh Pinna, and upon receiving a permit in the first half of 1890, work began on permanent housing.[53]

The transfer of Petah Tikva to the baron was a more complicated affair, although in general lines, the process was similar. As in Yesud ha-Ma'ala, Rothschild refused at first to undertake financial responsibility, declaring that assistance should come from Hovevei Zion. Nevertheless, he did

---

51 Hissin, *Journey*, p. 409; Scheid, p.164. Some sources say the nursery was established only in the spring of 1889. Perhaps the facility was enlarged at this time. See *Ha-melitz* 29 (1889), nos. 96, 151, 236, 15 May, 9 June and 26 June respectively.
52 Letter to Lilienblum, ibid., no. 220, 2 June 1889; Pines to Greenberg, 1 October 1889 in Druyanow, *Documents*, III, p. 1; Hacohen, Land of Israel.
53 *Ha-maggid* 34 (1890), no. 2; Hissin, *Journey*, pp. 409–411.

contribute from time to time towards various community projects. Only after his visit to the colony at the end of May 1887 did he take upon himself all communal expenses, which included paying the salaries of the rabbi, teachers, midwife and pharmacist, maintaining the pharmacy, repaying government debts, and putting up the capital for livestock and a pump. He even extended private aid to farmers who wished to plant vineyards.[54] However, this did not yet constitute genuine patronage.

Petah Tikva came closer to sponsorship at the end of 1887, when Rothschild agreed to work together with Hovevei Zion. All the property in the colony belonging to absentee landowners residing overseas was organized by Hovevei Zion, while the baron's officials worked on securing the lands of those residing in the country. By early 1888, Rothschild assumed ownership of 3,000 dunams (on which he originally planned to settle the pioneers from Bessarabia), and Ossowetzky, who represented the baron's interests in Petah Tikva, instructed some of it to be planted with grapes and the remainder to be distributed among colonists whose farms were small. Gérard Ermens, who visited the colony at this time, recommended the introduction of citrus groves and experimental crops of coffee and cotton. Rothschild also approved a plan for the purchase of another 3,000 dunams near the village of Yahud for the purpose of private settlement.[55]

By 1889, the stage had been set for a new relationship between Rothschild and Petah Tikva. After his promise to construct housing and stables for individual farmers, he offered to take full responsibility for a certain sector of the colony. In September 1889, the inhabitants were divided into three groups, and Rothschild agreed to sponsor those who had been working in agriculture since the early days of the colony and owned farms of at least 80–160 dunams — a total of twenty-eight families.[56] The other forty-five families belonged to one of two categories: independent

---

54 Pinsker's letters in Lilienblum, p. 113; and in Druyanow, *Documents*, II, pp. 481–482. On assistance from 1887 (chiefly land registration), see Erlanger to Hirsch, February 1882 (French manuscript), CZA J41/46; Hirsch to AIU, 27 February and 27 March 1887 (French manuscript), AIU Archives, France, e2674/7, e2816/3, e2953/3 respectively.
55 Ossowetzky to Levontin, 11 November 1887, CZA A34/18; "Short History...," document in Horowitz, Yesud ha-Ma'ala, p. 249.
56 Pines to Greenberg, 3 October 1889, Druyanow, *Documents*, III, p. 3.

farmers or veteran farmers with less than eighty dunams, and newcomers. Although they retained their financial autonomy, they, too, enjoyed the public services and coverage of general expenses undertaken by Baron de Rothschild (Table 1).

Table 1
The Rothschild colonies in the 1880s:
A chronology of establishment and patronage

Involvement of Rothschild and his officials

stages	independent settlement[1]	financial aid: for individual	financial aid: for groups	patronage	establishment decision	land purchase	initial settlement[1]	permanent settlement
Rishon le-Zion	July 82	—	Nov. 82	July 83				
Zikhron Ya'akov	Dec. 82	July 83	—	Oct. 83				
Rosh Pinna	Sep. 82[2]	July 83	—	Nov. 83				
Yesud ha-Ma'ala	Mar. 84	May–June 86	June–Aug. 87	Sep. 89				
Petah Tikva	Oct. 82[2]	Feb. 84	Mar. 87	Oct. 89				
Mazkeret Batya					Oct. 82	Oct. 83	Nov. 83	Sep. 84
Bat Shlomo					85–87	Sep. 85	May–July 87	Oct. 89
Meir Shefeya					85–87	Aug. 87	Sep. 89	May–June 90
Be'er Tuviya					May–July 87	June–Aug. 88	Sep. 88	Feb.–Mar. 89

1 Settling on the land to begin farming (usually by the men only).
2 Resettlement after a period of abandonment (the first settlement by Jews was in 1878).

The progression from independence to patronage of the two Hovevei Zion colonies was similar in five respects. First, there was a long period during which Rothschild avoided becoming involved in the colonies' internal affairs. This was followed by a period of groping and sporadic assistance which intensified in stages, followed by a period of bureaucratic intervention in the sphere of land ownership which served as a catalyst for the next step, involving the actual transfer of the lands to Rothschild. Finally, plans were drawn up to promote the development of the colony through the plantation of annual and perennial crops.

Stage Three: A Completed Process

The events of 1887 set in motion the final stage of Rothschild's relationship with the Jewish colonies in Eretz Israel, which assumed a new and broader radius. From a spatial standpoint, the plans pursued during this period took Rothschild and his officials to regions never considered before, such as Transjordan, and nourished schemes in urban and rural areas which were not necessarily contiguous with the four colonies in which Rothschild had invested the bulk of his energies heretofore. A few of his efforts to improve the welfare of the Old and New Jewish communities in the cities were personal endeavors rather than initiatives of the House of Rothschild. Yet even now, most of his efforts were concentrated in the rural sector. In addition to promoting the development of the existing colonies, he assumed responsibility for two of the three Hovevei Zion colonies, increased his land holdings and founded three new colonies. Two were offshoots of older ones and located nearby; the third was in a new region entirely. Thus we see that by 1890 Rothschild held a virtual monopoly over Jewish colonization in Eretz Israel. Nine of the eleven agricultural settlements (or thirteen, counting Mikve Israel and Nahalat Reuven) operating in the country at the time were owned by him and managed by his administrative network.

During this stage, the range of activities engaged in by Rothschild's officials became increasingly diverse. There was an administrator in charge of every aspect of colony life, and even outside the so-called

Rothschild colonies, every Jewish farmer in the countryside was a consumer of the agricultural and social services provided by Baron de Rothschild. As for the length of time Rothschild was prepared to remain involved in the colonization enterprise, here, too, he went far beyond his original intentions. He consciously agreed to continue his support until the farmers' plantations bore fruit, which meant at least four years for vineyards and ten to fifteen years for almond and olive groves. The loans he granted to private farmers were also repayable over a long period of time.

It was now firmly established that plantations were preferable over dry farming, and that various industrial crops would be raised, with an emphasis on wine grapes. Rothschild's macro-economic program took another step forward with his decision to establish processing plants in the colonies. A winery was built in Rishon le-Zion in 1889, and plans were drawn up for other factories. Despite the priority given to industrial crops, alternate branches were not ruled out. The Rothschild administration assisted several farmers who grew wheat in the older colonies, and even planned dry farming as the main branch in the three new colonies founded at the end of the decade.

The transition to plantations was one of the decisions reached in the course of introducing a centralized, coercive organizational system in the colonies — a system in which the colonists were left out of the decision-making process. In signing their land over to Rothschild, the colonists enabled the baron's officials to implement far-reaching agrarian reforms in which the settlers had no legal say and ultimately lost their ability to influence the development of their farms. Collectively, they engaged in planting and other farm chores as day laborers of the Baron, and their land was redivided and returned to them only in the 1890s (whereas the legal transfer of ownership was not completed until World War II!).

It should be emphasized, however, that the process was not an abrupt one. The seeds had been planted much earlier, in the form of aid to urban Jewish communities, twelve-year loans to farmers outside the colonies, plans to establish daughter colonies, distribution of land for vineyards, explicit statements about a winery, and traces of administrative inflexibility. All the signs of Rothschild's impending role, including the imbalance between him and Hovevei Zion, were discernable before 1887. It was after this period that the seeds germinated at a rapid pace and assumed proportions which could no longer be dismissed. Hovevei Zion bowed to Rothschild's dominance in the sphere of Jewish colonization, and made no attempt to disguise its reliance upon his administrative network in the late eighties. When two out of three Hovevei Zion colonies came under his jurisdiction on the eve of 1890, Rothschild's involvement in Jewish colonization entered its third and final phase.

PART TWO

THE ROTHSCHILD ADMINISTRATION: HIERARCHY, ACTION AND IMPACT

Introduction: Responsibilities of the Administration

Baron de Rothschild's status in the colonies was technically that of an absentee landlord. All property belonged to him, but like King Leopold of Belgium, owner of a large part of the Congo, the French millionaire who purchased the island of Anti-Costi off the Canadian coast and many others he was not physically present on his land and required others to operate it on his behalf.[1] Within Eretz Israel, Rothschild's position was similar to the city-dwelling Arab effendis who employed agents (*wakil* and *bayarji*) to tend their fields and citrus groves, and on a smaller scale, Jewish landowners such as the Shmulechansky brothers of Russia whose estates in Gedera and Rishon le-Zion were managed by Isaac Frank, or Emil Lachman of Berlin whose farm in Petah Tikva was run by Arieh Leib Frumkin.[2]

The closest approximation of the baron's organizational network in the colonies was the apparatus devised by the Central Committee in Galatz, Rumania, to oversee the development of the colony of Zammarin, later Zikhron Ya'akov, at the end of 1882. The Committee empowered Emile Franck, a wealthy businessman and leading member of the Alliance Israélite Universelle in Beirut, to conduct its affairs in Zammarin. Franck continued to reside in Lebanon, but sent one of his associates, Louis Brasseur, to direct the colony in his name. Brasseur settled in Haifa, where the families of the colonists were staying temporarily, and a farming instructor, Solomon Brill, was sent from Rumania to supervise the work of the pioneers on site. This arrangement remained in force until Rothschild assumed financial responsibility for the colony at the end of 1883.[3]

For Rothschild, too, the only way to maintain control over his assets was to appoint agents to run the colonies for him. However, given the fact that his designs extended far beyond the technical management

---

1 There were various categories and degrees of absentee ownership. On the establishment of settlements in Eretz Israel in the early twentieth century as a form of absentee ownership, see Katz, Ahuzot, pp. 150–157.
2 Aaronsohn, *Baron*, p. 97, n. 2.
3 Aaronsohn, Establishment, pp. 16–17; Hissin, *Journey*, pp. 301–304; for more details, see below.

Baron Edmond de Rothschild

of farms, the employment of clerks and administrators was not enough. To achieve the economic and social aims that were an integral part of his plan, Rothschild called in professionals in the sphere of agriculture and communal services. As his relationship with the colonies and interest in Jewish settlement throughout the country intensified in the 1880s, the size and diversity of the workforce increased, and the emphasis began to move away from agriculture. By the time the Rothschild administration assumed its final form, there were dozens of officials specializing in at least ten different fields:

a) Legal affairs — contacts with the central and regional authorities to register land and obtain building permits in the colonies and other rural settlements; liaison with outside elements such as the Arabs and local government.

b) Manpower management — hiring salaried workers and manipulating a huge staff of permanent and temporary employees, including tenders, interviews, signing contracts and insuring that their terms were carried out; coordinating the work of the colonists and other farmers sponsored by Rothschild.

c) Finance — distributing income subsidies to the colonists, and granting loans to independent settlers and private organizations.

d) Land purchase — surveying properties for sale and acquiring land for expansion and establishment of new colonies; arranging for the repurchase of land from Jewish absentee owners.

e) Physical development — supervising land improvement, development of infrastructure (roads, water supply), construction of housing, farm buildings and public buildings.

f) Farm production — supervising agricultural activities, providing instruction to farmers, distributing equipment and animals, direct management of the Rothschild enterprises.

g) Agro-industry — experimenting with industrial crops and processing (wineries, etc.).

h) Commerce — developing local and overseas markets for the purchase of supplies and marketing of goods produced in the colonies.

i) Public services — establishing and operating communal institutions in the spheres of health, sanitation, religion and education for the benefit of the colonists and, to some degree, outsiders.

j) Planning — drawing up detailed plans for all the above (such as building plans and programs for economic development); budgeting and allocation of land use for approved plans.

Most of these employees were not administrators in the narrow sense, but providers of a wide variety of agricultural and public services. Among the Rothschild officials were teachers, religious functionaries, doctors, nurses, paramedics, farming instructors, builders, engineers, and others. The following discussion has been limited to genuine "employees": those executives, agronomists and community workers whose names appeared on the payroll as recipients of a monthly wage.[4]

---

4   In his memoirs, Scheid distinguishes between three job categories: "Ar" for *administrateurs*, "Jr" for *jardiniers*, "Dr" for *docteurs*. See Scheid, "Mémoires sur les colonies Juives et ses voyages en Palestine et en Syrie," I, p. 3, CZA J15/7245; also see Scheid, p. 21, n. 2.

CHAPTER FOUR

ADMINISTRATORS AND CLERKS

Development of the Administrative Sector

As Rothschild's undertakings in the Jewish colonies became broader and more diverse, and he assumed the financial burden for a larger number of colonies, the need for administrators to coordinate his activities grew without stop. In the early period, during 1882 and 1883, this work was entrusted to four officials: Dugourd, Ossowetzky, Benschimol and Scheid. The first and last, Dugourd and Scheid, fulfilled an administrative role in addition to their professional duties.

Justin Dugourd was sent to Rishon le-Zion in November 1882 after the receipt of Rothschild's first loan. As no other officials had yet been hired, Dugourd, a trained agronomist, was also responsible for keeping an eye on public spending and supervising the public works that Rothschild had agreed to finance. Only after his transfer to the northern colonies in November 1883 did he give up these duties and devote himself entirely to his profession, which he pursued until leaving the country in 1891.[1]

Samuel Hirsch, the headmaster of the Mikve Israel agricultural school, assisted Dugourd in his managerial efforts in the colonies after receiving special permission from the Alliance Israélite Universelle at the end of October 1882 (see pp. 55ff). His work in Rishon le-Zion, which was wholly voluntary, continued throughout the 1880s alongside his educational duties.[2] Rothschild wired money through the AIU headquarters

---

1   On Dugourd's background and his work as an agronomist, see pp. 59–62. The official appointed after Dugourd was Jacob Papo, a mechanic, who arrived at the end of 1882.
2   The AIU in Paris voiced its consent in a letter to Hirsch, 20 October 1882, in Idelovitch, p. 115. More on Hirsch in the section on voluntary supervisors, p. 154ff.

in Paris and Hirsch relayed it to the Rishon le-Zion settlers' committee and Dugourd for distribution among the needy and funding of public works. Rothschild and his deputies (chiefly Michael Erlanger) regularly corresponded with Hirsch and Dugourd, creating an open channel for communication in both directions.

Hirsch functioned in a similar capacity, as an intermediary in the transfer of funds and an overseer of development work, when the Radom pioneers founded the colony of Ekron. The person in direct contact with the pioneers was Abraham Moyal, a prominent Jaffa Jew, who assisted them from their earliest days in the country and voluntarily managed the colony for the first six months (November 1883–March 1884) until a salaried director was appointed.[3]

Thus we see that during the preliminary stage of Rothschild's involvement in the colonies, no special organizational body existed and Rothschild relied on certain persons who happened to be there — an agronomist (Dugourd) and two volunteers (Hirsch and Moyal). Only after taking Rishon le-Zion under his wing in July 1883 and considering patronage of other colonies did Rothschild give thought to "envoyer quelqu'un pour s'occuper specialement de la directione et de la surveillance des colonies qu'il prendra sous son patronage (c'est toujours indirect que je le sais)."[4] Towards the end of the year, Rothschild went ahead with this idea and hired two teachers from Mikve Israel, Jacob Benschimol and Joshua Ossowetzky. Benschimol's engagement as director of Rishon le-Zion in December 1883 constituted the first permanent appointment in the Rothschild administration since the commencement of the colonization enterprise. Moroccan-born Benschimol was a graduate of the teachers' seminary of the AIU in Paris who had been working at Mikve Israel since 1879 as a French teacher, bookkeeper and substitute headmaster. When Hirsch nominated him as a candidate for colony director, Benschimol took an unpaid leave of absence and travelled to Paris to meet Rothschild.[5]

In November, it was decided to transfer Dugourd to the northern

---

3   Erlanger's letters to Hirsch, 30 November 1882 and 28 December 1882, in Yavne'eli, II, pp. 242, 244. More on Moyal above, p. 154.
4   Erlanger's letter to Hirsch, 27 July 1883, CZA J41/43.
5   Erlanger's letters to Hirsch, 10 and 17 August 1882, in Yavne'eli, II, p. 236. On Benschimol see Tidhar, VI, p. 2579; Idelovitch, pp. 438–439.

colonies. To fill the vacancy until Benschimol's official appointment and return, Joshua Ossowetzky, another teacher from Mikve Israel, was appointed temporary director of Rishon le-Zion and Ekron.[6] Ossowetzky, an erudite Jew from Brody, had been selected by Charles Netter to escort twenty-eight Jewish children to Mikve Israel following the pogroms in Russia in January 1882. At Rothschild's bidding, he, too, arranged for an unpaid leave of absence from the AIU and embarked upon a lengthy career in the service of the baron which began with a one-month stint as a stand-in for Benschimol.

Elie Scheid was another official appointed by Rothschild during his first stage of involvement in Jewish colonization. Scheid was born in Haguenau, Alsace, to a lower middle-class family. Despite his humble background and minimal schooling, he became a successful accountant, businessman and city councilman, and wrote a history of the Jews of Alsace. At the beginning of 1883, he was elected secretary of the Comité de Bienfaisance Israélite de Paris presided over by Baron de Rothschild. Towards the end of that year, Rothschild sent him on a six-week mission to Eretz Israel to arrange his financial take-over of the northern colonies.[7] Contrary to plan, Scheid remained for four months, from October 1883 to February 1884 and assumed the directorship of Zikhron Ya'akov and Rosh Pinna. From his seat in Haifa, he closely supervised building and infrastructure work throughout the months of December and January, and as Hirsch had done in the Judean colonies, he received money from Rothschild and relayed it to Dugourd, the resident agronomist. The permanent director, Judah Wormser, arrived at the end of January; after two weeks of working alongside one another, Scheid returned to Paris.[8]

6   Hirsch's proposal in a letter to Erlanger, 21 September 1882, in Yavnielli, II, p. 239. On the employment of Ossowetzky, see telegram from Hirsch on 5 November 1882, cited in Erlanger's letter of 9 November 1882, and details in Erlanger's letter of 21 December 1882, ibid., pp. 241, 243. Also see Smilansky, *Family*, II, pp. 120–125; Harosen, pp. 413–416; Idelovitch, pp. 441–442; Tidhar, III, p. 1318; Eliav, *First Aliyah*, II, p. 405.
7   On Scheid, see CZA A192/180/64; biography by S. Schwartzfuchs in introduction to Scheid, pp. 7–17; Tidhar, I, pp. 206–207; Aaronsohn, Officials, p. 163 (no. 13).
8   Scheid, pp. 58–60, 63, 68–70, 129; letter dated 8 February 1884 in Idelovitch, pp. 76–78; and operational expenses from end of 1883 to beginning of 1884 in Zikhron Ya'akov and Rosh Pinna account books, CZA (French manuscript) J15/5956, J15/6355.

Over the next seven years, Scheid served as superintendent of the Rothschild colonies in Eretz Israel. This position was voluntary and pursued in addition to his full-time salaried job as secretary of the Comité de Bienfaisance Israélite. His days, said Scheid, were devoted to charity, and his nights to colonization in the Holy Land.[9] From Paris he conducted a steady stream of correspondence with officials in the colonies, which he visited once or twice a year, and also traveled to the Levant and Turkey whenever necessary to deal with the central government.

Ossowetzky and Benschimol remained in Rothschild's employ until the late 1890s. After Benschimol's return from Paris in December 1883, Ossowetzky made the trip, too, and returned as assistant director of Rishon le-Zion. He served in this capacity between March 1884 and October 1885, and was then promoted to director. At the same time, he was asked to assume this position in Ekron, which still lacked a chief administrator.[10] When the colonists of Rishon le-Zion rebelled against his authority in February 1887, Ossowetzy was sent to Petah Tikva where he represented the baron for nearly a year and a half, from May 1887 to October 1888. He finally settled down in Rosh Pinna as a replacement for Benschimol. He supervised this colony over the next ten years, until 1897, in addition to handling all Rothschild's affairs in the Galilee.

Benschimol also relocated frequently until finding a permanent niche. A relapse of malaria forced him to leave Rishon le-Zion in October 1884. After many months of recuperation in Morocco, France and Switzerland (the bills were paid by Rothschild), he returned briefly to Rishon le-Zion in or around December 1885. In April 1886, he was apparently transferred to Rosh Pinna, and in October 1888, to Zikhron

---

9 S. Schwartzfuchs in introduction to Scheid, pp. 11, 15. Scheid's letters to Hirsch reveal that he replaced a non-Jewish secretary who had been in charge of correspondence with the colonies until early 1884 (letters of 8 February and 14 April 1884, CZA J41/28/32).

10 Rothschild confirmed Ossowetzky's appointment as director of Ekron and Rishon le-Zion in a letter dated 19 October 1885, CZA J41/72 (French manuscript; photocopy in J15/36). Ossowetzky left Ekron (now officially Mazkeret Batya) at some point between May 1887 and October 1888.

Ya'akov, where he remained director for twelve years, until August 1899.[11]

Administrator and settlers in the main street of Zikhron Ya'akov (1886?)

Judah Leon (Leib) Wormser, a Parisian teacher born in Alsace, was the first of Rothschild's officials to be personally selected by him. He arrived in Zikhron Ya'akov at the end of January 1884 as a replacement for Elie Scheid, and managed the colony until the settlers rebelled in October 1888. He then resigned and returned to France.[12]

Another teacher at Mikve Israel proposed by Hirsch in August 1883 as a possible administrator for the northern colonies was Isaac Oschri, a well-educated Jew fluent in several languages who had fled the pogroms in Russia. Like Ossowetzky, he was sent to Mikve Israel in January 1882 by Charles Netter. From May to August 1884, Oschri was employed as Wormser's assistant in Zikhron Ya'akov and was then transferred to Rosh Pinna as colony director. This appointment was less than successful and was scheduled to end in October. However, his replacement, Benschimol, fell ill, and Oschri stayed at his post until the colonists revolted in the

11 It is not clear when Benschimol commenced his work in Rosh Pinna. The sources cite various dates between January and June 1886. Also unknown are the precise date of his return from overseas and his duties in Zikhron Ya'akov.
12 Aaronsohn, Officials, p. 163 (no. 8).

spring of 1885 and the Paris administration had no choice but to remove him. The management of the colony was taken over by Emil Ettinger until Benschimol's recovery at the beginning of 1886, and Oschri became a teacher of French in Zikhron Ya'akov, never to resume his career as a Rothschild official.[13]

Emil Ettinger of Alsace, described as a former French soldier, fared even more poorly as a colony director than Oschri, despite having been hand-picked by Rothschild. Although the data is vague, he apparently began working in Rishon le-Zion early in 1885, prior to the arrival of the new director, M. Lyon, and was transferred to Rosh Pinna to replace Oschri towards the middle of that year.[14] Over the span of five years, he moved from one colony to the next, serving as director or assistant director for short intervals in Rishon le-Zion, Rosh Pinna, Ekron, Zikhron Ya'akov, Be'er Tuviya and Petah Tikva. A permanent position was found for him only in the early nineties, when he became assistant director in Rishon le-Zion.

Moroccan-born David Hayim joined the staff of Mikve Israel in 1882 as a teacher and manager of its vineyards; in 1886, he took charge of accounting and substituted for the headmaster. At Hirsch's recommendation, he was appointed temporary director of Petah Tikva at the beginning of March 1887. According to plan, he was to stay on for three months, but was sent to Rishon le-Zion in mid-May after Ossowetzky's removal. By December, he left this colony, too, and dropped out of Rothschild's service entirely.[15]

Thus we see that during the years 1884-1887, the second stage of Rothschild's involvement, the Benschimol–Ossowetzky team was joined by several new people. In contrast to the reliance on local manpower which characterized the first stage, three of the officials of the second stage — Wormser, Ettinger and Lyon — were personally selected by Rothschild in Paris, and only Hayim and Oschri were members of the teaching staff at Mikve Israel.

13 On Oschri, ibid., p. 162 (no. 4).
14 Idelovitch, pp. 444–445.
15 Ibid., pp. 442–443; on his transfer to Petah Tikva, see AIU Archives, France, letters e2617/2 (19 January 1887), e2674/7 (27 February 1887). David Hayim's letter from Petah Tikva (French) dated 12 April 1887, is published in Druyanow, *Documents*, II, pp. 149–151.

As Rothschild's relationship with the colonies solidified in 1887–1890, eight more officials were hired, three of them in executive positions: Bloch, Boris Ossowetzky and Aboulafia. Alphonse Adolf Bloch, of Alsace, was an elderly, unmarried businessman who spoke French, Arabic, Turkish and German and represented various French organizations in Constantinopole. In December 1887, Rothschild engaged him as director of Rishon le-Zion and Ekron, where he remained for almost seven years. As chief overseer of the Judean colonies, Bloch supervised Rothschild's projects in Petah Tikva and the Jaffa region, and assisted in the efforts to found a colony in Castina in 1888–1890. Early in 1894 he tendered in his resignation and returned to France.[16]

Boris Ossowetzky, younger brother of Joshua, was a broadly-educated Jew who resided in his native city of Kiev until moving to Rishon le-Zion in the summer of 1886. He worked under Bloch as assistant director of Ekron from the end of 1888 and at the end of 1889 returned to Rishon le-Zion as financial director and auditor of the colony's new winery.[17] This seems to have been his speciality, given the fact that from the beginning of 1891 to the end of 1892, he was taken on in the same capacity at the winery in Zikhron Ya'akov. Over the next decade, Boris served as a wine-expert and manager of the winery in Rishon le-Zion.

Meir Aboulafia of Damascus was sent to Petah Tikva in October 1888 to represent Rothschild's interests after the dismissal of Joshua Ossowetsky. In 1892, he was transferred to Yesud ha-Ma'ala and in 1896, to Metulla.[18]

The other five officials employed towards the end of the 1880s were professional farming instructors who, like Dugourd during the first stage, were invested with additional administrative duties. The importance of administrative developments during the first decade of Baron de Rothschild's involvement in the colonies can be measured quantitatively, as well as qualitatively. The three most important officials of the 1890s — Bloch, Boris Ossowetzky and Benschimol — as well as Scheid, who became chief superintendent of the Rothschild colonies,

---

16 On Bloch, see Idelovitch, pp. 443–444; Eliav, *First Aliyah*, II, p. 409; and Aaronsohn, Officials, pp. 162–163 (no. 6).
17 On Boris Ossowetzky, see ibid., p. 162 (no. 2).
18 No more is known about him.

Members of the Baron's administration (E. Scheid in the center), Zikhron Ya'akov, c. 1897

all entered the baron's service during the 1880s. To these one should perhaps add Wormser, Rothschild's personal secretary.[19]

Characterizing the Officials

Previous studies of the Rothschild colonies have emphasized the large number of French Christians among the administrative personnel and especially those in top executive positions. It has been assumed that French culture was highly significant in the development of the colonies, and that much of the tension between the administrators and the farmers was the result of the "foreignness" of those in positions of authority.[20]

While the Frenchmen were the larger group, they accounted for seven out of eighteen, or less than forty percent of all the baron's administrators during the first decade. Aside from the French officials, four of whom

---

19 More details with some observations in Aaronsohn, *Baron*, pp. 110–111.
20 Kressel, *Father*, p. 37; Gvati, I, pp. 72–76.

were natives of Alsace, Rothschild's staff included six East Europeans (five from Czarist Russia) and five Mediterraneans (including one born in Eretz Israel). On the other hand, the Mediterraneans were all students or teachers affiliated with the Alliance Israélite Universelle and steeped in French culture. Grouping them together with the Frenchmen would bring the ratio to thirteen "French" officials, and let us not forget that the cultural background of other Rothschild agents such as Hirsch, Moyal and Franck was French, too. As a result, French culture was an influential factor not only on the higher echelons in Paris (Rothschild and his advisors, and Scheid as superintendent) but on a local level, inside the colonies.

Be that as it may, a French background was neither a major qualification for colony directors nor crucial, for the first two years, at least, in the decision to employ a particular candidate. Of the four or five administrators hired in 1884, two (Oschri and Ossowetzky) were Russians with a limited knowledge of French. As for being Christians, only two of the French officials — agronomists Dugourd and Deshays — fell into this category (i.e., ten percent of all the Rothschild officials), and their administrative duties were pursued for no more than a year or two.

Operational and Spatial Hierarchy

A further understanding of the Rothschild administration can be gained through a study of its operational and spatial hierarchy, by which we mean the ranking of officials and colonies on a scale of importance that was already evident in the 1880s.

Occupying the top rung of the spatial hierarchy was Paris, as the chief executive center. Next came Mikve Israel and Beirut as the national centers, responsible for all administrative activities pursued inside and outside the country. These two echelons were alike in that neither had physical contact with the colonies. On the third rung were the regional colonies of Rishon le-Zion, Zikhron Ya'akov and Rosh Pinna, and on the fourth were the other colonies of the baron: Ekron, Petah Tikva, Be'er Tuviya, Bat Shlomo, Shefeya, Yesud ha-Ma'ala (and later — Metulla and Ein Zeitim).

Table 2
**Spatial and functional hierarchy:
The colonies and Rothschild officials**

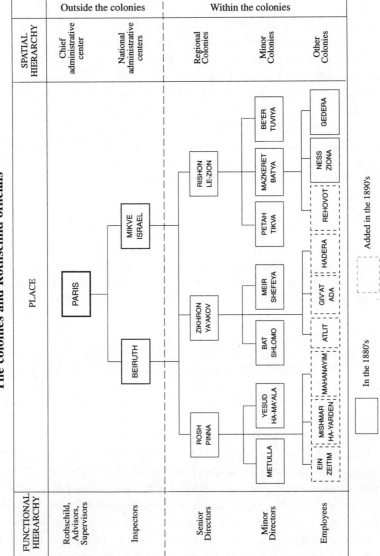

Simultaneously, an operational hierarchy emerged in which Rothschild reigned as "commander-in-chief," followed by Scheid as superintendent, with Michael Erlanger and Rabbi Zadoc Kahn as his closest advisors. On the second rung were the colony inspectors, a position occupied by Hirsch and after 1887 by Hirsch and Emile Franck. Third in line were the regional directors, which included Benschimol, Wormser and Oschri in the early 1880s and Benschimol, Ossowetzky and Bloch at the end of the decade. Lyon and Hayim also served in this capacity for several months in mid-decade. Finally, there were the resident directors and administrators; in the 1880s, these were Dugourd, Ettinger, A. Brill, B. Ossowetzky, Aboulafia, Deshays, and others (Elhadaf, Horowitz, Pukhachewsky and Lustgarten).

Officials of the two lower ranks were paid a monthly wage. For the regional directors, this amounted to 250 francs a month or 3,000 francs a year during the 1880s. The resident directors probably received somewhat more than half as much.[21] Usually, but not always, there was one resident director in each colony reporting back to the regional director who lived in Rishon le-Zion, Zikhron Ya'akov or Rosh Pinna. This was so in Ekron, Petah Tikva and Yesud ha-Ma'ala when they became Rothschild colonies.

The hierarchy presented here obviously represents the state of affairs only in the third and final stage of Rothschild's liaison with the colonies, during the late 1880s, when the administrative mechanism was more fully developed. It continued to operate in this manner throughout the 1890s, when Metulla and Ein Zeitim came under the patronage scheme (see Table 2). Why did it take this particular form?

The answer lies in Rothschild's belief in centralism as a fundamental principle in the administration of the colonization enterprise. This was the common organizational method in France and its colonies in North Africa, and satisfied the needs of Rothschild himself, given his lack of confidence in the colonists' farming ability and his paternalistic concern for their welfare.[22] Centralism allowed him to delegate authority and operate a ramified network of officials while maintaining a firm grip

---

21 Data and analogies in Aaronsohn, *Baron*, p. 114, n. 30.
22 See, for example, Schama, pp. 67–71; Giladi, Rothschild, pp. 183–184. For a more extensive discussion see Aaronsohn, *Baron*, pp. 115–117.

on the reins in every sphere and at all levels of the hierarchy. Towards this end, he carefully monitored progress in the colonies through regular reports from his officials.

Indirect reports were received at least once a week from his chief advisors in France, i.e., Scheid, Erlanger and Kahn, and from his superintendents in Eretz Israel, Hirsch and Franck, who wrote to him whenever necessary on the basis of dispatches from the administrators in the colonies. At the same time, the regional directors, and in the 1880s especially, some of the lower officials, reported to Rothschild directly.[23] He also kept abreast of developments in the colonies by meeting personally with any officials or colonists visiting Paris, and by visiting Eretz Israel five times between 1887 and 1925.

Did the system work? With its help was Rothschild able to take charge of the colonies not only on a strategic level, but tactically, on a day-to-day basis? In principle, the answer is yes. The sources demonstrate that officials all down the line conformed strictly with the demands of the hierarchy and accepted the authority of their superiors.[24] While Rothschild occasionally acted without prior coordination with the responsible officials and upset the established order, he stood firmly behind his administrators in times of conflict and even defended them against the colonists as long as they carefully followed standard procedures and worked through the proper channels.[25]

---

23 On the transfer of new bills (along with the receipts) directly to Rothschild, at least until the end of 1886, see Erlanger's letter to Hirsch, 13 October 1886, CZA J41/45. On Rothschild's request for ongoing reports from Ossowetzky and Benschimol, see his letters to Hirsch, 17 August 1884 and 19 October 1885 (French manuscript), CZA J41/72; on Wormser's reports to Rothschild, see Erlanger's letter, 13 July 1885 (German) in Druyanow, *Documents*, III, p. 771. Direct correspondence between Rothschild and the regional directors continued into the 1890s. See, for example, his letters to Benschimol, CZA K12/42/2.
24 "Ossowetzky as director is subordinate to Mr. Hirsch and operates in his name" (Erlanger to Pinsker, 8 April 1887, in Druyanow, *Documents*, II, p. 148); "I [Erlanger] am Hirsch's sole correspondent on the subject of the colonies" (Erlanger to Pinsker, 14 July 1888, ibid., II, p. 542). Erlanger repeats in many of his letters that aside from minor matters, all his orders came directly from Rothschild.
25 Erlanger to Hirsch, 26 May and 17 June 1887, CZA J41/46 (French manuscript); Erlanger to Pinsker, 8 April 1887 (German) in Druyanow, *Documents*, II, p. 149.

CHAPTER FIVE

AGRONOMISTS AND TECHNICIANS

The non-administrative personnel employed by Rothschild in the colonies were either agronomic experts or providers of community services. The section below will focus on the agricultural employees who received a monthly wage, which excludes dozens of skilled workers and professionals who were engaged on a part-time basis (see pp. 162–165 below). While most of these others worked in farm infrastructure, the employees in question were mainly agronomists (*jardiniers*).

Categorizing the Agronomists

As we have seen, the first official hired by Rothschild was the agronomist Dugourd. By the 1880s, there were five other "agronomist-clerks," representing one-third of all the Rothschild administrators in the colonies. In addition, there were at least thirty-three agronomists who did professional work only, which brings the total figure to thirty-nine. We have divided them into five groups: chief agronomists, Russian trainees, young natives, farm school students and Arab agronomists.

There were five chief agronomists during the 1880s, all of them French Christians: Dugourd, Cavelan, Deshays, Ermens and Forey.[1] Justin Dugourd received his training at the agricultural school in Versailles and worked in agronomy in Paris, Algeria and Egypt, where he learned Arabic. His first assignment in the colonies was a year as chief

---

1 Schama, p. 63; Giladi, *Rothschild*, p. 187; Idelovitch, p. 438. For further details and source material on agronomists, see Aaronsohn *Baron*, pp. 120–121; Aaronsohn, Officials.

agronomist of Rishon le-Zion, after which he spent six years in Zikhron Ya'akov. In 1891, he was forced to return to Paris due to ill health.

To replace Dugourd in Rishon le-Zion, Rothschild employed F. G. Cavelan, another graduate of the Versailles school whose specialty was flowers. Cavelan took up his post in November 1883, and although he contracted malaria two months later, he remained in Rishon le-Zion for more than twelve years, until 1896.

Jules Deshays, also of the Versailles school, had gone to Spain to specialize in viticulture. He was hired as Rosh Pinna's first resident agronomist and worked there for eight years, from April 1886 to April 1894.

Gérard Ermens came to the colonies after years of experience in Paris, Senegal, Cairo and Kashmir. Ermens was an expert in transplanting flowers and grapevines from one region to another (Algeria to Senegal and France to India), which was no doubt a factor in his appointment. Following his visit to the country in 1887, Rothschild sought an agronomist to supervise agricultural activities on a national scale. At the recommendation of the headmaster of Versailles, Ermens was chosen for the position at the end of that year, and worked as an agricultural supervisor for an entire decade.

The fifth French Christian agronomist, P. Forey, was hired in the summer of 1889. Forey, an experienced winegrower, spent nearly two years supervising the planting of vineyards. Due to ill health, he returned to France in 1892.

At the end of 1885, the second group of agronomists arrived: the Russian trainees. Six young members of Hovevei Zion were sent over by Rothschild to be trained as agronomists and future farming instructors.[2] In Rishon le-Zion, to where they went directly, they were put to work in the fields. The emphasis was on raising flowers and vegetables, along with many hours spent in preparing land for planting, construction, paving roads and other physical labor. During that year, one of the trainees died of malaria and a second became seriously ill. The remaining four were sent to Rosh Pinna for another year of more specialized training. As assistants to the resident agronomist, they worked in the orchards,

---

2 Zimmel to Sheffer 27 May 1885 in Druyanow, *Documents*, III, pp. 750–751 (Russian). For further details, see Aaronsohn, *Baron*, pp. 164–167.

practiced trimming and pruning, learned modern techniques of irrigation, fertilization and greenhouse cultivation, and received theoretical instruction in viticulture and the development of agricultural industries (wine, alcohol and perfume). Rothschild paid for their accommodation and clothing and provided a small monthly wage of thirty francs throughout their apprenticeship. When the two-year training period was over, he hired them as part of his regular staff.[3]

The third and largest group of agronomists, young experts born in the country, were taken on by the Rothschild administration beginning in 1886. Of the twenty-three native-born Jewish agronomists, four had been brought up in the city and nineteen in the colonies. Those from the city (chiefly Jerusalemites) belonged to the first graduating class of Mikve Israel. A few of those raised in the colonies had also studied at Mikve Israel, but the majority received their training at home, under the tutelage of Rothschild's chief agronomists. A large number had been sent overseas for advanced courses — the urban students by the AIU and the second-generation colonists by Rothschild. Usually they attended agricultural schools in the French cities of Versailles or Montpellier, though some pursued further specialization in Spain, Italy or India. Upon their return, they worked as assistant agronomists in the colonies and among those who stayed on during and after the 1890s, several attained positions of influence in the Rothschild hierarchy.[4]

Students of the agricultural school in Zikhron Ya'akov made up the fourth group of agronomists in the Rothschild colonies. When Rothschild visited Zikhron Ya'akov in 1887, he announced his intention to establish an agricultural training program for sixty young immigrants who would work as farm laborers for three years and then receive plots of land on the outskirts of the colony to establish their own farms. When enrollment for the program began that year, virtually anyone who applied was

---

3   Epstein to Pinsker, 3 Kislev 5646, Druyanow, *Documents*, II, cols. 43–44; Gurevitch (Horowitz) to Sheffer, 18 Adar Aleph 5646, ibid., I, cols. 721–722 (Russian) and translation in Samsonov, pp. 124–125; Pukhachewsky to his parents, 9 Adar Bet 5646, *Ha-melitz* 31 May 1886 (reprinted in Samsonov, p. 123); Yigli, Warhaftig, Epstein and Gurevitch to Pinsker, 14 Adar Aleph 5646, translated into Hebrew in Samsonov, p. 124; Pukhachewsky, Founders, no. 24, pp. 11–12.

4   More on the twenty-three native-born agronomists in Aaronsohn, *Baron*, pp. 122–126.

A young colonist as a pupil in
Mikveh Israel, c. 1898

accepted.⁵ There was no theoretical training: the students tended the vineyards and orchards, and worked on infrastructure (mainly clearing away stones and construction). In exchange, they received a monthly wage of thirty francs, accommodation, clothing and footwear, religious and health services, and the promise of being set up as farmers after three years. In practice, their training lasted two years, and often no more than one. Within this period, at least thirty-four of the students began tending their own farms, either in Zikhron Ya'akov or in one of its daughter colonies. Those who completed the course were employed by Rothschild

5 Bronstein, pp. 1–2; R. (Rokeah), "Dam Halalim," *Ha-havazzelet* 19 (1889), no. 15, pp. 37–39; Samsonov, pp. 146–147, 168.

in the northern colonies, generally as assistant agronomists, and two graduates went on to become senior administrators in Rosh Pinna and Zikhron Ya'akov in the 1890s.[6]

The Arab agronomists were not very numerous. In fact, the sources make explicit reference to only two, who worked in Zikhron Ya'akov in 1889 as "field gardeners." They were responsible for the grain crops and offered guidance in dry farming techniques. In this respect, they differed little from the Arab instructor at Mikve Israel agricultural school and the Arabs brought in to assist the early pioneers of Rosh Pinna and Ekron. Chronologically, they were the last group of agronomists to enter the baron's service.[7]

The pattern that emerges is a gradual shift towards specialization in the agricultural sector. During the first half of the 1880s, it was common for a single agronomist to take charge of all aspects of farming in the colony where he was stationed, including paperwork, construction and the development of all agricultural branches. Towards the end of the decade, this was so only in the smaller colonies. Agronomists taken on in the regional colonies were experts in specific areas and were to devote full attention to their specialities, thus creating a need for a larger work force. By the late 1880s, seven non-Jews (five French Christians and two Arabs) and a minimum of thirty-two Jews earned their livelihood as agricultural officials in the Rothschild administration.

Modification and Change

The French agronomists were all highly accomplished in their field. Two of them had worked in France before coming to the colonies, and three had additional experience in the Mediterranean area (Spain, Algeria and Egypt). Over time, the most noticeable change was that the early agronomists, those employed in 1882–1883, were experts in

---

6   Ibid., pp. 147, 189–193; Kantor, Basic, pp. 1187–1188. For further details and references, see Aaronsohn, *Baron*, pp. 126–128.
7   The Arab agronomists are mentioned in the Zikhron Ya'akov account book, CZA (French manuscript), J15/5960 (no pagination). On the cessation of their work in the mid-1890s, see Rothschild's letter to Benschimol, 15 March 1895 (French manuscript), CZA K12/42/2.

gardening, whereas those who came later, between 1886 and 1889, specialized in viticulture. On the whole, they were a stable group. Their work in the colonies continued into the 1890s, when most of them resigned for health reasons, and all except one remained in the baron's employ for eight to twelve years.

In 1886, five Jewish trainees were taken on as assistant agronomists in three colonies. The four who were still in service between 1887 and 1890 comprised a mobile work force and were transferred from colony to colony as necessary. They continued to hold positions of responsibility in the 1890s, and towards the end of that decade three of them settled permanently in the colonies to which they were assigned.

The native-born agronomists had been trained before their employment in the colonies, either at Mikve Israel followed by advanced study in France, or on the farms where they were born. Most of them were between sixteen and twenty-one years old when taken on, and continued working for Rothschild throughout the 1890s. Some remained at their posts when the Jewish Colonization Association took over the colonies in the early twentieth century.

Numerically, the Jewish agronomists clearly enjoyed the upper hand throughout the decade. During the first and second stages, Rothschild employed between seven and thirteen Jews compared with three Christians, and during the third stage, at least thirty Jews compared to seven Christians and Arabs.[8] However, a glimpse at the operational and spatial hierarchy reveals that it was the Christians rather than the Jews who occupied the most important positions. In 1890, for instance, the top-ranking agronomist was Ermens, a Frenchman operating out of Paris. The chief agronomists, also French, lived with their assistants in the regional colonies of Rishon le-Zion, Rosh Pinna and Zikhron Ya'akov. At the lowest level were the local, Jewish agronomists who were dispersed among the other colonies.

The wages of the agronomists increased dramatically as we go up the hierarchical scale. Whereas trainees received thirty francs a month, and the assistant and local agronomists between sixty and one hundred

---

8 These figures are provided to highlight certain trends and may not be absolute. As for other sectors of the Rothschild administration, there may be officials we have not accounted for.

francs, the chief agronomists earned four hundred and more, which was higher than the salary of a regional colony director of the same standing.[9]

The agronomic hierarchy differed from the admistrative hierarchy in having no national center equivalent to Beirut and Mikve Israel. On the other hand, in the regional colonies there were three additional subordinates to the chief agronomist: branch supervisors (head of the vineyards, orchards or wheat fields), assistants and aides, and trainees who served as "supervisors" or "head supervisors" as part of their training.[10]

At the bottom of the scale were the Jewish agronomists, some of whom worked themselves up to mid-level as time went on. The only ones who were initially hired at this level were five Mikve Israel graduates. All senior positions were manned by non-Jews who were formally trained in France and had years of experience in Mediterranean, sub-tropical or tropical countries (Algeria, Spain, Egypt, Senegal and Kashmir).

In sum, the principal trends during the 1880s were the employment at the helm of a small but stable team of French Christians with formal training and experience in hot climates; the later employment of Jewish agronomists, mostly untrained, who were promoted to associate positions after attending one of the training programs developed during the second half of the decade; a notable increase in the number of second-generation colonists, especially towards the end of the decade when they virtually monopolized the agricultural sector; a steady rise in the percentage of Jews although the Frenchmen retained the uppermost positions; and a shift towards local manpower through the employment of native-born agronomists and Arabs, possibly in response to charges that the French agronomists were "ordinary gardeners from Egypt and Algeria, frivolous types interested only in their salaries and not in their work."[11] Some years later, Scheid explained that "enemies of the Jews" had accused the colonization enterprise of depending on Christian winegrowers and

---

9 Pukhachewsky, Founders, no. 40, p. 11; Hirsch's letter of 26 December 1883, AIU Archives b322/5; Margalith and Goldstein, p. 480, nn. 346–350.

10 For a description of four intermediate positions on the agronomic scale at the end of the 1880s, see Smilansky, Memoirs, II, p. 24. In the 1890s, they were called maitres, contre-maitres, jardiniers and chefs de culture. See letters of Starkmeth, CZA J15/63.

11 Idelovitch to Levi, 15 December 1889, in Druyanow, First Days, I, p. 53.

Arab labor as the Jews just stood by and watched, incapable of manual labor. By 1897, Scheid could state with pride that "we now have Jewish agronomists, nearly all of them the sons of farmers or Jewish inhabitants of Eretz Israel."[12]

Technical Staff

Although most of the craftsmen and professionals hired by the Rothschild administration worked on a part-time, temporary basis and were therefore excluded from the category of officials as defined above, at least four were already permanent staff members in the 1880s and recipients of a monthly wage.

First water tower, built in Zikhron Ya'akov 1891

---

12   Lecture delivered by Elie Scheid in Paris, *Ha-zvi* 13 (1897), no. 19. On the gradual cutback in the employment of Arabs, see Rothschild's letter to Benschimol, 15 March 1895 (French manuscript), CZA K12/42/2.

Chapter Five

The first was Jacob Papo, a native of Jerusalem who had attended the local school of the Alliance Israélite Universelle and graduated from Mikve Israel. In September 1882, he was sent by Rothschild to study under a hydraulic engineer in France and upon his return in early 1883, he became the second official, after Dugourd, to join the Rothschild administration. His career as a "mechanic" in the Judean colonies was to span over twenty years.[13] Papo's employment was apparently a direct result of the talks between Rothschild and Charles Netter, during which they discussed the importance of establishing farm colonies and developing water sources in the Holy Land.[14]

The Rishon le-Zion winery provided a source of employment for a wide array of agricultural and administrative personnel. Among the technical officials working in the colony when the winery opened its doors in the summer of 1890 were Papo and another Jewish mechanic, Nahum Miller, as well as a French Christian wine expert, Dupuy (Dupuis in some sources), who came from an old family of winegrowers from Bordeaux and was considered highly knowledgeable and experienced in his field. After managing the winery for a year and a half, Dupuy returned to France. The official reason for his departure was malaria, but he may have been frustrated by a professional problem — rapid fermentation brought on by the heat — that was solved by his successor, Peychaud.[15] Nahum Miller of Kovno was appointed chief mechanic at the Rishon le-Zion winery in early 1890. Two years later, he moved to the winery in Zikhron Ya'akov and worked there both as chief mechanic and workshop director until 1906.[16]

The sources allude to three other technical staff members employed at the Rishon le-Zion winery before it produced its first vintage. Elhanan Bolkin (Greenberg), a Jewish textile manufacturer from Bialystok who

---

13   Biography by Idelovitch, CZA A192/110; Tidhar, II, pp. 854–855; Avitsur, *Inventors*, pp. 133–136.
14   Papo was probably selected for training by Netter, who knew him personally from Mikve Israel. It is noteworthy that Rothschild sent him to France before he met with either Mohilewer or Feinberg. Upon his return, Papo was paid a salary of one hundred francs per month as a drilling supervisor. See Rothschild's letter to Hirsch, 6 April 1883, in Yavne'eli, II, p. 81.
15   Idelovitch, p. 482; Scheid, pp. 205–206.
16   Tidhar, I, p. 517; Aaronsohn, Officials, p. 169 (no. 63).

Agronomists and Technicians

Rishon le-Zion wine cellar and some of its technical workers, 1898

settled in Petah Tikva in 1883 and opened a textile factory in Yahud, began working at the winery in 1889. Rothschild sent over an anonymous French barrelmaker in March 1890, while a Rumanian Jewish chemist, Bruchiner, was taken on in the summer of 1890 to head the laboratory. After a year or two, he left to manage the new perfume refinery in Yesud ha-Ma'ala.[17]

Hayim Moses Slor, a silversmith from Jerusalem who came to Petah Tikva in 1878, joined the Rothschild staff as an assistant surveyor in 1885. In 1890, after years of experience under Mordechai Lubman (see p. 160 below) and two German surveyors in Petah Tikva and Hadera, he became the official surveyor of the Rothschild administration and carried out measurements in at least ten settlements, first for Rothschild and later for the Jewish Colonization Association and other bodies.[18] (Maps 4, 5 and 9 are based on his surveys).

This core of technicians increased appreciably over the next decade as jobs in infrastructure, construction, and other occupations opened up. With the establishment of industrial plants in Rishon le-Zion, Zikhron Ya'akov, Rosh Pinna, Yesud ha-Ma'ala and Tantura (near Zikhron Ya'akov) in the 1890s, the technical sector of the Rothschild administration came to bear as much weight as the others. However, while the technical workforce was expanding, fewer agronomists were being hired, thereby highlighting the gradual shift toward industrial processing as a chief source of income — a trend that germinated in the Rothschild colonies in the late 1880s.

---

17 Hirsch's letter to the secretary of the AIU dated 19 March 1890 (French manuscript), AIU Archives, France, b322/5; Tidhar, II, p. 761; Yaari-Poleskins and Harisman, pp. 252–254.
18 Ibid., p. 205.

Agronomists and Technicians 145

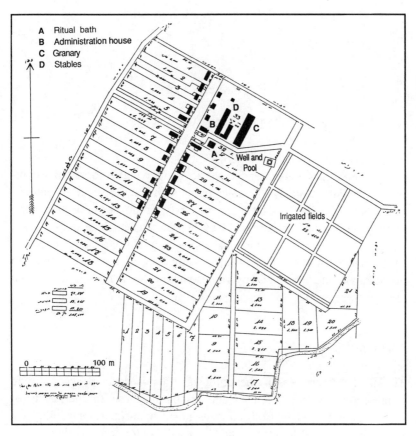

Map 5: Plan of colony of Be'er Tuviya, 1896
Source: Slor, Plan of Be'er Tuviya, 1896
(JNF map 924, Hebrew University map collection)

CHAPTER SIX

COMMUNAL WORKERS

Public employees who extended services to the entire community comprised the largest body of wage earners in the Rothschild colonies. Records for the 1880s point to at least sixty employees in this category, which included medical staff (doctors, pharmacists, medical aides, nurses, midwives), educators (teachers, principals, school supervisors), religious functionaries (rabbis, cantors, ritual slaughterers, circumcisers, ritual bath attendants), watchmen, colony representatives (*mukhtarim*), and minor assistants.

Medical Staff

The medical services in the colonies did not develop according to a pre-conceived plan, but as an ad-hoc response to the needs of the community. When Rothschild assumed financial responsibility for the colonies in 1882-1883, no licensed doctor was available and professional medical assistance was sought in the nearby cities.[1] As Rothschild's involvement grew between 1884 and 1887, clinics were opened in the three major colonies and a resident pharmacist-medic dispensed drugs. The European doctors hired by Rothschild did not reside in the colonies, but they were qualified, experienced practitioners who made the rounds every week, and earned a monthly wage of one hundred francs.[2] Towards the end of that period, a resident doctor was

---

1 On the medical services available to the colonists in the cities, see Aaronsohn, *Baron*, pp. 136–137.
2 Ibid., pp. 137–138. These were doctors trained at well-known European universities (Paris, Zürich, Berlin and Heidelberg).

The medical staff of Rishon le-Zion, c. 1890

appointed in each of the regional colonies whose duties included making the rounds of the minor colonies once or twice a week and supervising the work of the pharmacists.

At the end of the decade, small hospitals were established in two of the regional colonies and the pharmacies were modernized and stocked with expensive drugs. More paraprofessionals were taken on, among them women colonists who worked as midwives (earning ten francs per delivery) and nurses in the infirmaries. Pharmacies were opened in the smaller colonies, both those sponsored by the baron as well as those on an independent footing. The pharmacists, their aides and midwives were all in Rothschild's employ, and his doctors cared for the sick in every Jewish settlement in the area.[3]

Moreover, from 1887 onwards, Rothschild instructed his staff to provide free treatment and drugs to all the Arabs who came to the colony clinics. When, at some point, one of the doctors was dismissed and

---

3   For more information and references, see ibid., pp. 138–140.

ordered to leave the colonies, his Arab patients showed their gratitude by approaching the district kaymakam (local Turkish governor) and pleading on his behalf. The physician of Rishon le-Zion reported that in addition to seven Jewish communities, where he examined 6,722(!) patients in less than a year, he provided medical care to nine Arab villages.[4]

During the third stage of Rothschild's involvement, 1887–1890, the baron's medical service was thus open to Jews and Arabs alike, not necessarily colonists, and provided for the region as a whole. It had such a good reputation that people came in for treatment from as far away as Jerusalem.[5] On the other hand, the independent farmers had no alternative. Outside the colonies, doctors' fees ran from five to ten francs a visit, and in special cases as much as fifty, which was more than the average worker earned in a month. Hence the free care available to Jewish settlers was indispensable not only from a medical point of view but also from a financial perspective.

The medical staff members, especially doctors, were distinguishable from the other public employees in three respects. Firstly, more than other Rothschild employees, they tendered their services over a widespread area, bringing them into contact with more people outside the colonies. Secondly, medicine was the only sphere in which the Turkish authorities set professional standards and required official licensing. Medical institutions were regularly inspected and action taken against anyone found practicing without a license. Thirdly, doctors were highly regarded and consulted in affairs outside their profession. They helped to settle disputes between colonists and administrators, advised the colonists on religious matters, and offered their opinion on development plans. The pioneers were well aware that physicians were crucial in their struggle for survival and treated them with the utmost respect.[6]

---

4   D'arbela, p. 90; Scheid, pp. 88–89; Samsonov, pp. 164, 194; Hissin, *Journey*, p. 127.
5   Hissin, op. cit., p. 131.
6   A special trip to Constantinople was needed to arrange a medical license for one of the colony doctors. See CZA A51/3b. Similar cases not connected with the colonies are mentioned by Gera, p. 38, and Livingstone, p. 61. On the doctors' community involvement, see Aaronsohn, *Baron*, pp. 142–143.

Teachers and Educators

In the sphere of education, two facts stand out: first, that the foundations of modern learning and the centrality of the Hebrew language were established in the 1880s; and second, that Rothschild's teachers, principals and inspectors played a critical role in shaping the school curriculum and putting it into practice.

On the heels of his agreement to rescue Rishon le-Zion from collapse in mid-1883, Rothschild wrote of establishing a school, preferably one that would teach farming, as befitting the needs of a new agricultural settlement.[7] A school for the children of the colonists did not materialize in Rishon le-Zion, but the idea resurfaced two years later in the form of an agricultural training program for six young Hovevei Zion members brought over from Russia. Within another two years, the *arbeitershule* in Zikhron Ya'akov opened its doors to laborers and new immigrants. Both these programs offered supervised work in the fields under the guidance of Rothschild's agronomists rather than frontal classroom teaching.

In the early years, no changes were made in the educational framework in the colonies. Children attended the traditional *heder* (religious elementary school) which operated out of a private home. Classes were taught in Yiddish by an orthodox *melamed* (traditional tutor) The only difference was that Rothschild took over financial responsibility and paid the teachers' wages. During the second stage, 1884–1887, the traditional format continued side by side with a more modern type of school, the *talmud torah*, which offered foreign languages in addition to religious study. The talmud torah was an integral part of the community services provided by the Rothschild administration. It was housed in a public building, usually another wing of the synagogue, and its teachers, either colonists or officials who taught as a sideline, were paid by Rothschild. Talmud torah students studied French and Arabic, as well as Hebrew, which was a totally new concept.[8]

---

7   Rothschild's letter to Hirsch, 22 June 1883, in Yavne'eli, II, p. 84.
8   On the Hebrew, Arabic and French classes, see Schub, *Ha-havazzelet* 16 (1886), no. 11, p. 985; and Rabinowitz, Foundation Stone, p. 985. On the directors and officials who worked as teachers, see Rabinowitz, ibid., and Rothschild's letter to Hirsch, 9 April 1885, CZA J41/72.

This was a fluid, dynamic period as far as education was concerned, combining old and new. Old-fashioned tutors and erudite colonists often worked together in the same school. In 1886, the children of one colony learned under a local rabbi and a tutor from Tiberias. In another colony, two tutors offered religious instruction and a French teacher who served as headmaster also taught arithmetic, geography and history.

Rosh Pinna's school headmaster with family, 1887

From 1887, the educational system in the colonies became truly modernized. The schools were reorganized, special classes were opened for girls, a broader syllabus was introduced, qualified teachers were employed and educational supervisors were appointed. The greatest change was in the level of the teachers, who were dedicated, highly-trained professionals, though their background was not necessarily in the field of education. The girls' classes organized in 1887–1889 were taught by women from the colonies, either colonists' wives or daughters, none of them formally trained. From 1890, those who showed an aptitude for teaching were sent to the AIU teachers' seminary in Paris.

Around this time, educational supervision was introduced. Headmasters were appointed, and the schools were inspected by local and regional supervisors. The result was a tri-level pedagogic hierarchy that was similar to the scale in other professional spheres in the colonies, apart from the fact that it stopped at the regional level. In education, as in health, there were no national supervisors or executive chiefs in Paris. On the other hand, there was only one supervisor on the regional level throughout the 1890s, compared with several in the sphere of medical services. Neither the headmasters nor the supervisors enjoyed the virtual autonomy of the doctors; they were responsible to the regional colony directors. Teaching salaries, however, were high and determined on an individual basis. Outside the colonies a tutor might earn 20–30 francs a month; under the baron, even a novice received double that sum, and a headmaster earned 150 francs or more in addition to housing and other benefits. The principal of the school in Zikhron Ya'akov, which ran four regular classes and one preparatory class in 1890, was paid 150 francs a month plus forty francs for the "rental" of a room.[9]

Religious Functionaries, Watchmen and other Public Employees

The Rothschild administration also employed religious officials, watchmen, colony representatives (mukhtarim), and a variety of minor clerks and assistants. The religious functionaries — rabbis, ritual slaughterers,

---

9   Eliav, *First Aliyah*, II, pp. 201–207; Idelovitch, pp. 225–226; Hissin, *Journey*, p. 314. More data and references in Aaronsohn, *Baron*, pp. 145–148.

cantors, *mikve* (ritual bath) attendants, synagogue beadles and circumcisers — made up the largest sub-group. There were some, such as the circumcisers and occasionally the beadles, who did not draw a regular monthly salary. Others performed a dual function; for example, rabbis and ritual slaughterers who taught in the colony schools or led services in the synagogue, or a ritual bath attendant who did office work.[10]

The first religious functionaries hired by Rothschild were the slaughterers. Considering that ritual baths were among the earliest communal structures in the colonies, some built prior to Rothschild's involvement, it is curious that so little is said about bath attendants. Perhaps they were employed only part-time or the baths were run by volunteers in that same way that certain synagogue-related duties were performed without pay.

After the slaughterers came the rabbis, whose responsibilities included "settling religious questions, overseeing *kashrut* [ritual lawfulness of food], the ritual bath and the *eruv* [one of the Sabbath laws], sermonizing on Sabbaths, settling personal disputes and writing letters..."[11] In addition, many of the rabbis spent three to six hours a day in the classroom. In light of the piety of the majority of the colonists, the position of rabbi was clearly an important one. Among the later religious employees of the Rothschild administration were four kashrut supervisors who were taken on when the winery was opened in Rishon le-Zion.

Like the medical staff, the duties of the religious functionaries often extended beyond the borders of the colonies. The ritual slaughterers in particular served the needs of the small independent colonies and urban Jewish communities lacking a slaughterer of their own. As of 1888, Rothschild employed a rabbi to supervise religious affairs in Petah Tikva.[12] However, unlike the doctors, religious functionaries occupied a low rank in the administrative hierarchy. Many of them worked in a dual capacity, and their salaries and employment conditions were inferior to that of other Rothschild officials. Moreover, the colony directors from

---

10 Hada Hu, p. 220; Pukhachewsky, Feuilleton; and Idelovitch, pp. 98–100, 386–387.
11 Jawitz, letter of 18 August 1890, in Eliav, *First Aliyah*, II, p. 203.
12 Hissin, *Journey*, p. 159 (for the period up to 1890); *Ha-melitz* 28 (1888), no. 80; Scheid, p. 228. More on rabbis and religious functionaries in Aaronsohn, *Baron*, pp. 149–150.

whom they received their instructions did not always treat them with due respect.

Domestic security throughout the country being poor in those days, the colonists had no choice but to keep sentries posted around their homes and in the fields to keep out thieves and marauders. Thus another group of Rothschild employees were full-time watchmen. In the early days, before Rothschild's intervention, the colonists did their own guard duty in addition to hiring outsiders. This state of affairs continued when Rothschild stepped in: the colonists rotated among themselves, and Jewish and Arab watchmen were brought in as reinforcements. Every night fourteen colonists in Zikhron Ya'akov kept an eye on the grounds while four mounted guards patrolled the fields.[13] The sources refer to a number of Jews employed by Rothschild in this capacity, but the majority seem to have been Arabs. The Arabs were paid a regular wage calculated on a monthly or yearly basis, but they were not "Rothschild officials" in the ordinary sense because of the hiring procedure. They were recruited by an Arab notable from one of the neighboring villages who gave them orders and distributed their pay.

Finally, Rothschild paid the salaries of minor clerks and assistants who performed various unskilled jobs in the colonies, such as a Christian Arab housekeeper and cook, a Jewish coachman, an Arab boy who assisted the colony doctor, and an elderly Jewish spinster employed as a clerk.[14]

---

13 Epstein, *Ha-maggid* 30 (1886), no. 12, reports that the watchmen in the fields were paid in wheat.
14 Aaronsohn, *Baron*, p. 152 and references.

CHAPTER SEVEN

OTHER EMPLOYEES

Not all the employees of the Rothschild administration fell into the category of monthly wage-earners. Perhaps they were not "officials" in the sense defined above, but they were no less crucial for the development of the colonization enterprise and were instrumental in bringing many of the baron's plans to fruition.

On one end of the scale there were temporary employees such as craftsmen and laborers who worked by special contract or for a daily or weekly wage, and on the other, there were associates of Baron de Rothschild and the Alliance Israélite Universelle, who received no salary at all and performed their duties on a voluntary basis. The former occupied the bottom rung, taking orders from those above them, whereas the latter were higher on the scale of authority and gave the orders themselves. The laborers and craftsmen represented the last link in the long line of workers who toiled to make Rothschild's dreams a reality. The volunteer advisors and supervisors were the indispensable bridge between Rothschild and his administrators in Eretz Israel. Our understanding of the colonization enterprise would be incomplete without a thorough study of both these groups.

Advisors and Supervisors

Much of Baron de Rothschild's efforts in the sphere of colonization would have been for naught without the assistance of his advisors in France, Michael Erlanger and Rabbi Zadoc Kahn, and his supervisors in Eretz Israel, Samuel Hirsch, Levi Emil Franck and Abraham Moyal. Erlanger, a wealthy merchant born in Alsace, played an active role in the Parisian Jewish community as an executive member of the Consistoire Central des Israélites de France and vice-chairman of the Alliance Israélite Universelle. When Dr. Albert Cohn died in 1877, he was appointed administrator of charities of the French Rothschilds.[1] As the patron of the Russian Jewish community that emerged in Paris in 1880, Erlanger probably engineered the meeting between Rothschild and Rabbi Samuel Mohilewer, who arrived in Paris at the end of 1882. It was this encounter which eventually led to the founding of the colony of Ekron. Shortly afterward, Erlanger arranged for Rothschild to meet Joseph Feinberg, the representative of Rishon le-Zion. Until his death in 1893, Erlanger worked without remuneration to further the baron's undertakings in Eretz Israel. He helped Rothschild reach important decisions, was Rothschild's liaison man in dealings with the AIU, brought together Rothschild and the Hovevei Zion movement in Russia, and served as his chargé d'affaires in the colonies. Erlanger gained an intimate knowledge of the issues confronting the pioneers, mainly by correspondence, but also through visits to the colonies and meetings with colony officials and settlers who came to Paris.

Through a weekly exchange of letters with Samuel Hirsch, Erlanger forwarded instructions and arranged for money to be transferred to the colonies from Rothschild and Hovevei Zion. It was to Erlanger that the colonists turned, whether to complain about ill-treatment by colony officials or to request further aid. They wrote to him, traveled to see him in Paris (hoping to meet Rothschild as well), and deliberated with him during his two or three trips to the Holy Land. Throughout the decade, beginning in 1883, all Rothschild's property was registered in Erlanger's name, and any contacts between the colony officials and the Turkish authorities were carried out in his name.[2]

Zadoc Kahn served as chief rabbi of Paris for twenty-three years before becoming chief rabbi of France. He was the honorary president of the AIU and very active in Jewish communal affairs.[3] As a rabbi and a close friend of the Rothschilds, Kahn was consulted on virtually every

---

1   On Erlanger, see Idelovitch, pp. 148–149.
2   Erlanger wrote hundreds and possibly thousands of letters in French on the subject of the colonies, preserved in the CZA manuscript files J41/43 to J41/46. More on the registration of land and buildings in Erlanger's name in Aaronsohn, *Baron*, p. 154, nn. 2–3. Rothschild's name was used after Erlanger died in 1893.
3   On Zadoc Kahn, see above, p. 53, note 7, and Idelovitch, pp. 150–151.

Rothschild's aides: M. Erlanger, S. Hirsch, C. Netter

important issue connected with the colonization enterprise and served as a valuable contact in the baron's dealings with the Hovevei Zion movement. Unlike Erlanger, however, he had little to do with the day to day administration of the colonies.[4]

Much has been written about the influential positions of Erlanger and Kahn and their role in firing Rothschild's interest in Jewish colonization in the early 1880s. Less attention has been devoted to their contribution as advisors, especially that of Erlanger. The continuous guidance in the management of the Jewish colonies provided by these figures throughout the 1880s was no less important than their actions in 1882. Thus, although their work was voluntary and based in Paris, they were very much a part of the Rothschild administration. Three other volunteers — Hirsch, Franck and Moyal — were stationed in Eretz Israel, and the offices where Hirsch and Franck operated rose to the status of national administrative centers by the end of the decade.

Rothschild's chief resident representative in Eretz Israel in the 1880s was Samuel Hirsch, (pp. 122ff. above), who headed a number of AIU schools in the Mediterranean basin before assuming his post at Mikve Israel in 1879.[5] Hirsch played a crucial role in the administration despite the lack of any formal title or duty and the deterioration in his status as

[4] Rabbi Kahn's correspondence with Hirsch has been preserved in its entirety in CZA J41/71 and A51/3.
[5] Idelovitch, pp. 149–150; Tidhar, II, p. 746; Druyanow and Laskov, I, pp. 582–583.

the most powerful figure on the local scene, first in relation to Scheid —
who stepped in as director of the colonies at the beginning of 1884 —
and then to Franck, who arrived in mid-1887.[6]

Hirsch's strength lay in his position as director of Mikve Israel,
the country's sole source of agricultural manpower and knowhow, his
ties with AIU leaders in Paris who figured prominently in the Jewish
community and mingled with Baron de Rothschild, his background as
a native of Alsace steeped in French culture, and his personal qualities
as a disciplined, hardworking and highly capable man. Hirsch's major
efforts on the baron's behalf were in the spheres of manpower and
financial management, in which he had no peer. He nominated candidates
for various positions in the administration, supervised their work, and
coordinated most of the baron's financial affairs in the colonies. Among
his duties were distributing funds from the AIU in Paris in the form of
promissory notes and personally supervising expenditures.[7]

Levi Emile Franck, a Jewish banker and shipping agent in Beirut,
became involved in the colonization enterprise though his work with the
AIU in Lebanon. Late in 1882 he was asked to oversee the development
of the colony of Zammarin, later Zikhron Ya'akov, by the Central
Committee of Hovevei Zion in Galatz, Rumania.[8] In this capacity,
Franck was responsible for transferring Rothschild's early contributions
to Zammarin in 1883, and accompanying Elie Scheid on his first visit to
the northern colonies at the end of that year. Franck continued to offer
valuable assistance in the years to come, although he received no salary

---

6   Aaronsohn, *Baron*, p. 155. Hirsch was criticized by the colonists for having excessive power, particularly during the first half of the 1880s, but many of his detractors later became admirers.

7   See Hirsch's letters in the AIU archives in France, Mikve Israel files E120/a to E120/g, for example, letters of 14 March 1883 and 7 April 1884 (manuscripts, French), b721/9, b5966/5 respectively. Evidence of his prolific correspondence with Rothschild's officials and leading colonization activists in Eretz Israel and overseas may be found in the thousands of letters preserved in the Mikve Israel files of the CZA (J41). Also see the replies to Hirsch's recommendations and instructions drafted by Erlanger (CZA J41/43-46) and Rothschild (CZA J41/72).

8   Klausner, *Hibbat Zion*, pp. 38, 113, 131–136 (and elsewhere, using index); Aaronsohn, Est')lishment, pp. 16–17ff.

and operated without a formal title or specific authority.[9] Unlike Hirsch, who was closely involved in the smallest details of life in the colonies, Franck was able to maintain a distance from the administration which lent him the aura of a detached, unbiased observer in the eyes of the colonists. In this respect, Franck was closer to a supreme court judge or an arbitrator than an ordinary supervisor.

Abraham Moyal, a distinguished merchant and banker from Jaffa, assisted the pioneers of Rishon le-Zion in the purchase of land in the summer of 1882 and had the property registered in his name.[10] His supervision was sought by the Rothschild administration for short periods of time, for example, when Ekron was in the process of establishment. Although both Moyal and Franck offered their services without pay, there is evidence that they did enjoy certain benefits as a result of their activities.

The five personalities described above had much in common. They were all active in the Alliance Israélite Universelle, all financially established (prosperous merchants or dignitaries), all experienced in Jewish community work, and all brought up on French culture. As already noted, all but one were natives of the province of Alsace.

Interestingly, these features crop up time and again in people chosen by Baron de Rothschild to represent him and his interests. A prime example is Elie Scheid, whose key role as chief supervisor of the colonization project has already been discussed. Another was Nissim Behar, headmaster of the *Torah ve-Avoda* school established in Jerusalem by the AIU in 1882. There was little direct contact between Rothschild and Behar, apart from one occasion when Behar escorted Rothschild around Jerusalem. Behar's instructions were usually issued by the AIU headquarters in Paris and passed on to him by Samuel Hirsch. A colleague of Behar's who was also involved in the colonies was David Arieh, a member of a distinguished Jerusalem Sephardi family who was active in AIU affairs. Arieh kept the books for Torah ve-Avoda and substituted as headmaster when Behar was away. The building permits for Yesud ha-Ma'ala and Castina bear

---

9 See Franck's letters to Hirsch, CZA J41/69.
10 Smilansky, *Family*, II, pp. 125–128; Tidhar, III, p.1185. Also see Moyal's letters to Hirsch, CZA J41/28/11.

his name.[11] Less well-known but no less important was Isaac Fernandez, a Jewish merchant and engineer in Istanbul who may have represented Rothschild in dealings with the central government as early as 1883. As head of the Jewish community and vice-chairman of the AIU in the Ottomen capital Fernandez was instrumental in securing building permits for the colony of Zikhron Ya'akov in May 1884. He continued to volunteer his services as the baron's unofficial liaison man in the years to come along with the secretary of the AIU, Felix Bloch.[12]

Among Rothschild's advisors and supervisors were a number of French technical advisors, some of them permanent staff members and others hired for a specific job. One of the advisors of the second category was Lippmann, a hydraulic engineer who supervised the excavation of artesian wells in five colonies between 1883 and 1889, and took in one of the colonists as a trainee in his firm.[13] Others were Professor Gayon, a Bordeaux wine specialist; Leroy, an agronomist who guided the colonists until Ermens' appointment as agricultural supervisor in 1888;[14] Guntz who was Rothschild's "treasurer for colonization affairs" in 1890 and appears to have been on his secretarial staff since the early 1880s; and Charles Mortier, a French Christian who managed the Château Lafite winery at the baron's estate in southern France, and offered advice on winegrowing in the colonies from 1885.[15]

---

11 Biographical data on Nissim Behar in Gaon, II, pp. 151–159; Triwaks and Steinman, pp. 239–248; Tidhar I, pp. 75–76. On David Arieh, see Benschimol's letter of 20 June 1888 (French) in Druyanow, *Documents*, II, p. 549; Izraelit, p. 2; and correspondence with the AIU leaders in Paris in 1887–1889 (manuscripts, French) in Molcho files, Yad Ben-Zvi Archives, Jerusalem, 6/4/1–1.

12 Fernandez and Bloch's letter to AIU headquarters in Paris, 17 July 1884, in Idelovitch, p. 122.

13 See references to Lippmann in Rothschild's letters to Hirsch (Yavne'eli, II, pp. 71,77), Erlanger's letters (ibid., pp. 234, 246, 247) and elsewhere; professional opinion sent to Scheid on stationary of Lippmann's firm, 24 March 1888 (manuscripts, French), AIU Archives in Paris, f1835/4; and Papo's letter to Hirsch, 17 January 1888, ibid., f4934/3.

14 See reference to Leroy in Erlanger's letters cited in Yavne'eli, II, pp. 234–245.

15 Ever-Hadani, PICA, p. 211.

Professional Experts and Craftsmen

The Rothschild administration entered into four types of work agreements with its professional experts: contracts for a specific one-time service, contracts for construction and related trades; contracts for the regular supply of goods and services; and contracts for special services rendered as needed.

Architects, engineers and surveyors commissioned by the administration signed a short-term contract, as in the case of Mordechai Lubman, the country's first Jewish surveyor. Lubman received his diploma in Russia in 1876 and was sent to Eretz Israel by Hovevei Zion in 1884. That same year, Rothschild took him on as a surveyor in the Jewish colonies and he drew the earliest known map of Zikhron Ya'akov (see Map 1).[16]

Building contractors and craftsmen in construction-related trades were employed by the project. Of note were the carpenters, some of whom settled permanently in the colonies and earned their livelihood there. A certain number of colonists had skills acquired in Europe, and Rothschild did not hesitate to employ them in their fields of expertise. Reports from the mid-1880s show that thirteen colonists out of a group of seventy engaged in their former occupations: two shoemakers, three blacksmiths, two tinkers, one saddler, one barrelmaker, two carpenters and one baker. During the early years, their services were sought for specific projects and they continued to work on their farms. In the 1890s, however, some of them abandoned agriculture in favor of a monthly salary.

The building contractors and their workers were usually non-Jews, with a large percentage of Christian Arabs and a smaller number of Europeans. There is evidence that German Templers from Haifa were among the builders of Zikhron Ya'akov in 1885–1888 and Bat Shlomo in 1888–1889. On the other hand, we know of several Jewish construction workers freelancing in the urban and rural sectors who were commissioned by the Rothschild administration, and a group of Jewish builders who hired themselves out as a team.[17] A number of German Templers and colonists worked as wagoneers, transporting loads with their horse-drawn vehicles.

---

16   Tidhar, I, p. 432; Idelovitch, pp. 225–226; Druyanow and Laskov, I, p. 589.
17   Information and references in Aaronsohn, *Baron*, pp. 162–164.

Thus we see that Rothschild tapped whatever sources of local manpower were available to him, including Jewish and non-Jewish workers from outside the colonies, skilled workmen who lived in the colonies, and pioneers who had learned a trade in Europe.

The suppliers signed a long-term contract to ensure regular delivery of basic commodities and services to the colonies. There were bakers, for example, who worked exclusively for Rothschild. Also in this category were the hired watchmen who assisted the colonists in guarding their property. Not all of them were Arabs, but the Arab watchmen as a group, and particularly the Arab notables who acted as contractors, played a role of special importance. Towards the end of the summer of 1888 Rothschild paid the sheikh of a neighboring village a monthly wage of sixty francs to find two villagers who would safeguard the wheat fields and livestock of one of the colonies.[18]

In the last category were colonists and residents of nearby towns summoned occasionally to perform some service in return for a predetermined fee. This was the employment arrangement reached with several demobilized soldiers stationed in the outlying colonies. As trained horsemen and marksmen familiar with the terrain and well-versed in the customs of the local Arabs, these former soldiers, three of whom were living in Rosh Pinna in the 1880s, were employed as translators, escorts, financial couriers, messengers and intermediaries in contacts with government officials. When they were not needed, however, their pursuits were those of the ordinary farmer and pioneer.

Another group called upon when needed were the midwives. Little is known about the women who provided this service, but the sources indicate that midwives were available in every colony and should rightly be included among the employees of the Rothschild administration.

Finally, there was a small circle of Rothschild agents, most of them respected members of the urban Jewish community, who were hired by special contract to deal with the Arabs and the Turkish authorities and arrange matters pertaining to visas, land registry, title deeds and building permits. Attesting to the unique relationships common in those days, a regular salary was even paid to a certain Muslim "holy man" who

---

18 Ibid., pp. 164–165.

Some of the first administration buildings, Zikhron Ya'akov c. 1899

had been mediating between the administration and the local Arabs ever since his assistance in clearing up a land dispute in 1886.[19]

Day Laborers

The problem of Jewish versus Arab labor, which developed into a full-blown controversy in the early twentieth century, was already in evidence during the first decade of Jewish colonization. It was an issue contended with by Rothschild and his officials, and by the two categories of colonists — both the financially dependent and the "independents" who employed their own workers.

Employment of Arab labor in the 1880s was a necessity of life, even though the baron and the colonists were united in their preference for Jews. Behind this preference lay ideological, philanthropic and nationalist motives which led to Jewish employees being paid more and to Jews manning most of the permanent jobs. However, a large proportion of the work in the colonies was seasonal, and hundreds of extra hands were required for short intervals at certain times of the year.

19   Ibid., pp. 165–166.

Temporary employment of this type may have been a disadvantage for Jewish workers, but for the Arab peasants and Bedouin it offered many benefits.[20]

In consequence, during those periods when large numbers of workers were unnecessary, the labor force in the colonies was mostly Jewish. Aside from the slack agricultural seasons, this was also true for several years in the mid-eighties, after the settlers had mastered the farming techniques they learned from the local peasantry but had not yet begun to plant on a massive scale. Nevertheless, whenever a new tract of land was prepared, a large field sown or a building erected, the demand for workers rose temporarily and the colonists relied on Arab labor to meet their needs. These day laborers were usually hired by an Arab contractor affiliated with the Rothschild administration.[21]

When Rothschild ordered the beginning of large-scale planting in the winter of 1890, the employment of day laborers reached a peak. Between 300 and 1,000 workers were needed in each of the major colonies, and there was no choice but to hire Arabs because the Jewish labor force consisted of no more than 100–150 per colony. The total number of Arab laborers employed by the administration is difficult to ascertain. During the first decade, the figure was probably in the hundreds; as extensive plantations were introduced at the turn of the century it seems to have swelled to several thousand.[22]

As for Jewish labor, many immigrants reached the shores of Eretz Israel without sufficient means to establish themselves as farmers. In order to earn their livelihood, they usually ended up at one stage or another as hired hands of the baron. No written documentation has come down to us concerning those who worked on an irregular basis and for brief spans of time. On the other hand, we do know of three special types: exemplary workers who stayed on for long periods and eventually received farms of their own; workers who went home to the cities or rural settlements from whence they came; and organized groups.

---

20 Yellin, pp. 82–83; Kollat, p. 342. Rothschild's insistence on the employment of Jews is mentioned by Ben-Yehuda, Settlement, and Benschimol, letter of 9 June 1887 (French), CZA J41/49.
21 "Special Expenditures" notebook of Rosh Pinna, 1885, 1889–1890 (manuscript, French), CZA J15/6354.
22 Kollat, pp. 337–382; Braslavsky; Aaronsohn, Baron, pp. 167–168.

Perhaps the most well-known group was that of the Bilu pioneers employed in Rishon le-Zion in 1882. They planted mulberry trees, toiled in the fields, prepared hay, dug wells and did construction work, for which they earned the standard fee for Jewish laborers at that time — one franc a day. Most of them went back to Mikve Israel after six months and others took their place. Nine of the original group founded the colony of Gedera at the end of 1884. The five who remained in the baron's service until mid-1884 were given tracts of land and later became farmers in their own right.[23]

Although the Bilu pioneers were motivated by a very definite ideology and were unlike the other pioneers on a personal level, they failed to leave any special mark on Rishon le-Zion. As farmhands, it seems there was little difference between them and other hired workers of the Rothschild administration.

Another organized group was sent to the colonies by Hovevei Zion late in 1885. Under Rothschild's sponsorship, six young trainees attended a two-year agricultural program which required them to work in the colonies as day laborers. The same was expected of the farming school students in Zikhron Ya'akov, of whom there were sixty at the end of 1887. As part of their training, they cleared land, planted trees, paved roads and dug wells in Zikhron Ya'akov and the daughter colonies.[24]

The Jewish laborers were generally young, indigent Hovevei Zion pioneers without farms of their own. An exception were the colonists who worked as day laborers while waiting for their vineyards to bear fruit. These made up a large portion of the labor force in Rishon le-Zion in 1886–1887 and imparted a special character to the local workers' association which emerged at this time. "Agudat ha-Poalim," as it was called, was the first organization of workers in the country and enjoyed the full support of Baron de Rothschild. Its aims were to improve the professional and economic status of its eighty members through training programs, unemployment benefits, job referrals, inexpensive meals and housing, and mutual support. Some of the members worked in the "independent" colonies where only Jewish labor was employed, and others worked for the Rothschild administration, which had a deliberate

---

23 Laskov, pp. 120–123, 347–362; Salmon, Bilu, pp. 117–140; and Na'aman.
24 Aaronsohn, *Baron*, pp. 170–171.

policy of preferring Jewish labor to Arabs. Despite the help extended by Rothschild officials in organizing a communal dining hall and living quarters, members of the "Aguda" took an active part in the colonists' revolt. As a result, the association was disbanded, the administration became more wary of Jewish workers and the employment of Arabs increased.[25]

The most important group of Jewish workers emerged in the 1890s when two wineries opened and a one more wave of immigrants reached the country. However, momentum in the development of the colonies was evident even before the immigrants arrived. During the first half of 1890, an upswing in building, agriculture and industry created an urgent demand for workers that swelled the ranks of the Jewish proletariat and brought thousands of Arab laborers into the colonies — all of them employees of the baron.

Who Ran the Colonies?

Having described the vast network of officials entrusted with the management of the Rothschild colonies, we must ask ourselves if the administration was indeed the controlling factor. Did it wield genuine power, or was it merely a tool in the hands of Baron de Rothschild? Were the colony officials in a position to act independently or were they mere proxies? Who made the final decisions in each sphere?

As we have seen, the hierarchy was operative on a local level, too. The top echelon in each colony was the colony director, and all the other officials stationed in that colony reported to him.[26] We have also seen that, in principle, the daily activities of the administration closely reflected the policies laid down by the baron himself. A high level

---

25 Barzilai, Memories, no. 41, p. 4; Braslavsky, p. 77 and references.
26 Scheid to one of the agronomists: "You are of the opinion that administrators should not intervene in your affairs... [but] the administrator represents the views of the patron... The baron himself has determined that matters will be decided from above — to keep the agronomists and winegrowers from acting on their own initiative" (Undated quote in Ever Hadani, Vinegrowers, p. 49). The statements of a headmaster, a rabbi and a doctor working in the colonies indicate that this practice applied equally to professional employees, all of whom reported to the colony director.

of correspondence was maintained between Rothschild and those who carried out his instructions by means of a centralized, rigidly structured hierarchy in which areas of responsibility were clearly defined, reports were conscientiously filed and supervision was exercised on a continuous basis.[27]

However, in spite of Rothschild's forcefulness as the man at the top of the pyramid, and his occasional involvement even at the lowest levels, the actions taken by his officials did not always mesh with his articulated policies. When inconsistencies of this sort occurred during the first two stages of his work in the colonies, prior to 1887, they were probably a function of the "trial and error" approach which he initially embraced. However, after this period the sanctioned experimentation ceased and any inconsistent actions had to be the product of independent decision-making on the part of a particular official. Thus the personal views of the administrators cannot be ruled out as a factor in colony management.[28] But this was not the general rule and despite differences in style, Rothschild's officials operated remarkably alike wherever they were stationed, demonstrating that they were indeed an instrument in Rothschild's hands.

The administration exercised control over its employees and the inhabitants of the colonies in various ways. If an employee did not follow orders, he was fined, and the sum deducted from the salary paid him by the colony director. If he was found incompetent, or showed signs of rebellion, he would be relieved of his duties altogether, generally by Elie Scheid, or lower down the scale (manual laborers, for example), by the regional director.[29]

---

27 "The baron... himself knew of, acted and resolved all issues, and not his administrators," Erlanger's letter to Mohilewer, 8 Elul 5649, in Druyanow, *Documents*, II, p. 761.
28 A case in which Rothschild officials were given free rein is mentioned in Erlanger's letter to Hirsch, 19 September 1884, in Idelovitch, p. 131. A few cases of officials acting without the knowledge of their superiors are cited in Scheid's letter to Hirsch, 9 July 1885 (manuscript, French), CZA J41/74, and Erlanger's letters to Hirsch, 25 March 1887 and 8 June 1888, CZA J41/46.
29 More on fines and dismissals as reported in various sources, especially the Hebrew press, in Aaronsohn, *Baron*, pp. 174, 175, nn. 5 and 6.

Table 3
Direct aid from Rothschild to settlers, 1890
(in francs)

A. Regular Payments to Dependent Families (Rishon le-Zion)

Type of Aid	No. of Recipients	Average Monthly Payment (per person)	Annual Total
Personal Support	17	58	12,000
For Cultivation of Vineyards	17	20	4,000
To Feed Horses	a few	?	1,000
Total	17	83	17,000

Source: Hissin, *Journey*, pp. 146–147.

B. Monthly Payments to Families (Zikhron Ya'akov)

Type of Aid	Family X Details	Payment	Family Y Details	Payment
Personal Support	for 3 persons	42	for 14 persons	168
Wages	To father as the *Mukhtar*	50	To daughter as a teacher	150
Rent[1]	For 1 room	50	For 2 Rooms	90
Temporary Aid[2]	To sick mother	30	For a wet nurse (for twins)	20
Total		172		428

Source: Hissin, *Journey*, pp. 306, 314.

1 Rooms rented out to the baron's employees in homes of these families
2 One-time sums were also granted for the holidays, to new mothers, etc.

The colonists were often manipulated by having their financial support withheld. Rothschild distributed income subsidies based on family size amounting to ten to twelve francs a month, kept the colonists' horses fed, and reimbursed the sums spent on cultivating vineyards, usually for hired labor. Special gifts were made around holiday time, and to new mothers and the sick. The colonists received these payments, totalling 40–160 francs per family, at regular weekly or monthly intervals.[30] If an individual colonist refused to cooperate, one of the pressure tactics applied by the administration was to withhold this money or deduct fines from it at the discretion of the colony director.[31]

Other methods were used to control the "independent" farmers and hired laborers. Though farmers did not receive financial support from Rothschild and their land belonged to them, they were totally reliant on the public services provided by Rothschild, which included legal assistance, water, medical care, education, religious services, and so on. Moreover, the administration monopolized all the markets and labor resources. santions against Consumers, which produced the quickest results, were used frequently in the 1880s to impose the baron's will on the so-called independent farmers. If a colonist's wife was refused medical care or his children kept out of school, he could not resist for very long. Sanctions in the productive sector, which had long-range effects, were increasingly resorted to in the 1890s when much of the land was planted with vineyards and the colonists, both dependent and independent, sold their produce to the baron's wineries.[32]

Authority over the hired laborers was exercised indirectly, through pressure on the permanent inhabitants of the colonies. All laborers, even

30   Pukhachewsky, Founders, no. 42, p. 13; Smilansky, *Memoirs*, II, p. 22; Hissin, *Diary*, p. 56, and elsewhere.
31   See Belkind, p.94, on Benschimol's threat to fine any colonist found hosting an undesirable guest. Also see reference to fines amounting to "half the *halukka*" in Pines, I, p. 179, and Hissin, *Diary*, pp. 56, 68.
32   An independent farmer who was lax in doing guard duty was fined, and his family prevented from receiving medical care in Rishon le-Zion until he paid the fine. In another instance, an independent farmer was told that public services would no longer be open to him if he transferred ownership of his property. See Aaronsohn, *Baron*, p. 176, n. 9. Another source cites the case of an independent farmer whose grapes were boycotted at the Baron's winery in 1890. See Smilansky, *Memoirs*, II, pp. 20–21.

those hired by the "independent" farmers, required work permits from the colony director. No colonist could accommodate or employ a worker without one. The absence of direct control over the hired laborers was a weak spot in the network, but the power of Rothschild's officials was considerable even in this sphere, especially at the end of the 1880s when the bureaucracy was firmly entrenched.

The true strength of the Rothschild administration was put to the test when the officials were faced with the uprising of a whole group of farmers. These "rebellions" followed a similar course in each colony: the colonists protested against the poor management and condescending attitude of the administrators, their complaints were rejected by the top echelons in Paris, and an open battle ensued over the colonists' demand that the administrators in question be removed. At this point, Rothschild would cut off financial support, withhold public services, and even call in the authorities. The colonists responded by organizing and trying to manage on their own, which usually lasted no more than a few months until the money ran out and infighting among the colonists weakened their resolve. Finally, they would give in and accept authority, consenting to the expulsion of the ringleaders. At some later date, it was common for Rothschild to replace the offensive officials in an effort to placate the colonists and restore their confidence.[33]

In the face of insurrection, the Rothschild administration would also take advantage of the baron's legal status as landlord or official owner of the colonies. Rothschild would order the organizers of the rebellion off his land; if they refused, he summoned the authorities. In extreme cases, he would stop paying the colony's taxes. Unable to pay the thousands of pounds they owed and surrounded by enforcement officers, the colonists were only too ready to end their fight.[34] Added pressure on the rebels came from the leaders of the Hovevei Zion movement who feared for the future of the colonization enterprise if Rothschild withdrew. Hovevei Zion believed that the colonists were morally obligated to

---

33 For a description of five rebellions and seven minor disputes, see Aaronsohn, *Baron*, p. 177, nn. 12–13 and references.
34 On the use of mounted police to evict the rebels, see Samsonov, pp. 138, 164, 166, 170. On tax collection with the help of the military, see ibid., p. 168, and Schub, *Memories*, p. 116.

tone down their opposition, and expressed their belief that Rothschild's intentions were good. Implicitly, they recognized the inferiority of their own organization and acceded to the baron's supremacy in the sphere of Jewish colonization.[35]

In short, Rothschild was in complete control of the colonies. He reigned both directly and indirectly over an impressive array of communal workers, dependent and independent farmers, and temporary workers through his ownership of real-estate and production resources (land, buildings, water), his monopoly over public and consumer services, his financial support of the colonists through wages, income subsidies, credit, etc., and the social pressure of outsiders and peers who encouraged the rebels to give in.

In the literature, the dominance of the Rothschild administration has been portrayed most negatively. We read about heartless officials who acted without the baron's consent and to the detriment of the colonization enterprise. The administrators did in fact make strict demands upon the colonists and sometimes disregarded their rights as individuals. The motive, however, was not personal aggrandizement or hunger for power but a sincere desire on Rothschild's part to further the cause of Jewish colonization. The harsh measures employed were not a form of tyranny; in Rothschild's eyes they were bureaucratic imperatives. The imposition of fines, for example, and the threat to cut off public services, was the only way to convince the independent farmers to participate in a scheme designed to bring them closer to self-sufficiency. Similarly, the need to obtain consent for the transfer of private property was not an injustice; it was, and still is, an accepted practice in organized rural cooperatives. In many respects, the Rothschild administration acted as any settlement committee or community steering body might have. Indeed, similar methods were used by other organizations involved in colonization both in Eretz Israel and elsewhere.[36]

---

[35] Letters of Lilienblum and Pinsker exerting moral pressure on the rebels of Rishon le-Zion, in Barzilai, *Memories*, no. 21, p. 5. Also see entries in Meerovitch diary for June 1889, CZA A32/18.

[36] Compare measures taken by Hovevei Zion (reported by Hissin, *Diary*, p. 71, and Friedenstein), and the contracts signed by the colonists of the Jewish Colonization Association in Argentina.

It may well be that the severe paternalistic approach adopted by Rothschild was colored by subjective factors such as his own personality and upbringing, and that ideology, too, played a part. Many European intellectuals of the day held social beliefs which implied that a successful colonist was one who obeyed the rules, lived a well-regulated life and shared in communal responsibilities.[37]

Thus we find that the operational methods of the Rothschild administration were the combined product of ideology, necessity and practical experience. Furthermore, the seemingly heavy-handed control over all aspects of life in the colonies, so intriguing both to Rothschild's contemporaries and to students of history, was only an instrument: it was no more than a bit part in the major drama unfolding in the Jewish colonies.

---

37 See Kellner, *Revolt*, p.4, who claims that Hovevei Zion and the Jewish aid societies in Europe and America subscribed to the theory of social Darwinism developed by Spencer. Little concrete testimony is available regarding the beliefs of Baron de Rothschild, and his own writings are too laconic to provide many clues.

PART III

THE JEWISH COLONIES IN 1890: THE MARK OF THE BARON

Introduction: The End of a Decade

By the summer of 1890, the Jewish colonizing venture in Eretz Israel was in its eighth year. Although the colonies were young and still beholden to Edmond de Rothschild, a careful examination will show that the major developmental trends and distinguishing features were clearly visible even at this early stage. In 1890, social and settlement processes were fully under way, yet the door was opening on a new chapter in the history of Jewish colonization. Thus 1890 is the perfect juncture for a review of the beginnings of the colonization enterprise and the contribution of Baron de Rothschild. The following chapters will be devoted to three central aspects of the farm settlements established by the early Zionists: physical environment, agriculture and industry, and lifestyle.

In our study of the physical environment, emphasis will not be on the entire colony but on the built-up area. This occupied only a small percentage of the land, which was chiefly agricultural, but its spatial and functional layout were crucial in determining the character of the colony and its imprint on the Palestinean landscape.

The second chapter surveys the economic infrastructure created by 1890. Agriculture and agro-industry were the chief sources of livelihood, given the fact that the colonies were envisioned at the time as farm communities first and foremost. However, non-agricultural pursuits did have a place as Rothschild took over and created a network of employment opportunities in the spheres of trade, commerce and services.

The final chapter depicts the social and cultural milieu of the colonies. We will discuss demography, class differences, communal services, education (including the emergence of the Hebrew language as a leading manifestation of nationalism), religion, cultural activities and social events, all of which came together to form the spiritual landscape of the Jewish settlements within a decade of their inception.

CHAPTER EIGHT

LAYOUT AND ARCHITECTURE

Orderly vs. Free-style Colonies

By evaluating building density, uniformity of appearance and external contours, we discern certain distinct settlement patterns followed by the Jewish colonies in the 1880s. On the one hand, there were orderly settlements arranged in a compact, homogeneous manner, and on the other, free-style, sprawling settlements characterized by lack of contiguity and farms of different sizes. In 1890, Zikhron Ya'akov, Ekron, Be'er Tuviya and Bat Shlomo belonged to the former, as did Shefeya and Yesud Ha-ma'ala in later years. Gedera, the only Hovevei Zion colony existent in 1890, was also of the first type. All these colonies were laid out with great regularity, as enclosed compounds with evenly-divided plots and uniform housing in neat rows. By World War I, there were twelve more Jewish colonies of this style. Petah Tikva, Rishon le-Zion and Rosh Pinna were of the second type.[1]

In much the same way, the Jewish colonies in 1890 followed contour plans that were typically linear or non-geometric. The linear settlements were arranged along one central axis with residences and farmhouses on either side and the entire colony circumscribed by a wall. Ekron, Yesud ha-Ma'ala, Bat Shlomo and Gedera were arranged in this type of linear pattern, also known as the *Strassendorf* model or street-village. Zikhron Ya'akov formed a T-shape, in a variation on the Strassendorf model. Petah Tikva, Rishon le-Zion and Rosh Pinna lacked a clear geometric

---

[1] A similar differentiation between orderly and free-style colonies is made by Ben-Artzi, *Jewish*, pp. 257–261. Much of this chapter was inspired by his work, which examines settlement patterns in general and draws comparisons between types of settlement in Europe and Eretz Israel prior to 1914. However, he does not examine all the colonies, and those of the 1880s are often disregarded entirely.

pattern in 1890, although their overall shape was squarish or rectangular.[2] Thus we find that patterns of settlement and contour plan overlapped, and that two clear-cut settlement types were evident even in the early years of Jewish colonization.

Of all the orderly colonies, as we shall call the first type, the most systematically organized was the newer section of Zikhron Ya'akov developed by the Rothschild administration at the end of 1883. The new site, selected before Rothschild's sponsorship, was an elongated, flat-topped hill west of the low-lying slope occupied by the Arab village of Zammarin.[3] The colony was T-shaped, its main street crossing the hilltop from north to south and intersected by a shorter road. The land on either side of the main street was parceled out into seventy lots in keeping with the number of farmers. Each lot measured 20 meters across, with the length ranging between 150 and 200 meters (3–4 dunams). The other residents — craftsmen, Rothschild officials and civil servants — were given lots on the intersecting road, where the public buildings were also located.[4]

Zikhron Ya'akov was built in two principal stages. While the question of land ownership was being contested in the courts and the Ottoman authorities imposed a ban on the construction of housing, fifty prefabricated wooden cabins were shipped over from Rumania and reassembled along the main street. The work was carried out by contractors from the Templer colony in Haifa under the supervision of the Rothschild administration. At the same time, permanent buildings of stone were constructed on the intersecting street for a school, pharmacy, offices and synagogue which had previously been housed in temporary quarters.[5] Thus the general character of the colony, with its T-shape and symmetrical arrangement of cabins and farms, was the product of a year of intensive construction during 1885.

2   Ibid., pp. 200–201, 207, 210.
3   Aaronsohn, Establishment, p. 62. The site was selected around March 1883 either by Franck, the colony supervisor appointed by the Central Committee in Galatz, or by an engineer commissioned to prepare building plans (Brill, p. 179).
4   Scheid, p. 69; compare Maps 2, 4 and 5.
5   Ibid., pp. 81, 220–221; Samsonov, pp. 96, 99, 120. For a detailed account of the synagogue dedication ceremony during which the colony was publicly called Zikhron Ya'akov for the first time, see Wissotsky, pp. 144–146.

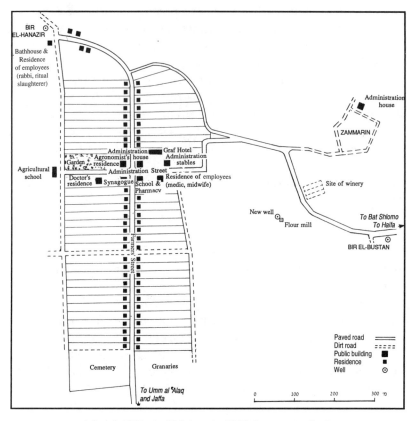

Map 6: Zikhron Ya'akov in 1890 (reconstruction)
Sources: Schumacher, Plan de la colonie Zicron-Jacob et ses environs, 1887; Soffer, Zichron-Ya'aqov et Meir Shefeiya, 1941 (PICA map); Scheid, pp. 81–83, 86, 106–113; Samsonov, pp. 96–110, 120, 194–195

The next stage began a short time after the cabins were up and the last of the families residing in Haifa settled in the colony. Now that the legal problems had been sorted out and the necessary permits received for construction, the wooden houses were gradually replaced with permanent structures of stone. The work took close to eight years (terminating in 1893) because it was carried out by individual families as their finances permitted rather than by the Rothschild administration. A stone house was built either beside the cabin, which was then used as a warehouse or barn, or on the same spot, after the cabin was dismantled.[6] During this period, an agricultural school and dormitory were built, nine houses were added and large-scale growth took place in the number of farm buildings, especially barns and granaries. Plans were discussed for a winery and a well was excavated in early 1890 to furnish water for the new site (see Map 6).[7] Building activities in Zikhron Ya'akov continued into the nineties, but the basic pattern of settlement established before 1890 remained intact and can still be discerned today.

Zikhron Ya'akov was the first Rothschild colony to follow a master plan, but Ekron was already existent when work began there at the end of 1883. As in Zikhron Ya'akov, the pioneers of Ekron were faced with serious legal problems and until these were resolved, building was limited to an area of two dunams. As a result, Ekron, too, developed in stages. In 1884, four row houses containing a total of fourteen apartments were built in Ekron, two on each side of the road. Two centrally-located public buildings — an administration house and a synagogue that also functioned as a school — were erected at the same time.[8] Barns and other farm structures were added in the common yard behind the houses after a lapse of about two years. When another permit was received in 1888, ten single-family units were built in the colony, which was renamed Mazkeret Batya following Rothschild's visit in 1887.[9] These homes of uniform design sat on small plots of ground on either side of the road, lined up with the row houses. At some later date, an enclosure was built around the colony, joining up with the back walls of the farmhouses.

Another orderly, Strassendorf-type colony was Be'er Tuviya. At the end of 1888, Rothschild's carpenters hastily assembled a total of thirteen cabins, prefabricated in Rishon le-Zion, on the land selected for the new

6   Hissin, *Journey*, p. 319; Ben-Artzi, Documents, p. 59.
7   Expense book of Zikhron Ya'akov administration, January 1887–December 1892, CZA J15/5956; Zikhron Ya'akov accounts, October 1888–January 1891, CZA J15/5960 (especially builders' accounts on pp. 28–29, 40–41); Kantor, Through, p. 40.
8   Hissin, *Diary*, pp. 74, 81, 208; Wissotsky, p. 97; Rabinowitz, Foundation Stonoe, pp. 986–987.
9   Rothschild to Zadoc Kahn, 15 September 1889, in Druyanow, *Documents*, II, p. 782. Also see etching of the colony in Oliphant, p. 182.

settlement of Be'er Tuviya. After this initial effort, which took only a few days, construction slowed considerably. By 1890, Be'er Tuviya consisted of one street, approximately twenty-two identical cabins, and two or three wooden buildings that served as a school, office, stable and warehouse. Hereafter, the colony disbanded and the homes stood half empty for several years. When Hovevei Zion took over in 1896, little was changed apart from the addition of a number of stone buildings (see Map 5).[10]

The first seven houses were built in Bat Shlomo in 1888/89, again following a simple linear pattern. No sources are available for the timetable of the rest of the construction, although we know that there were sixteen houses by the turn of the century, including three public buildings (a synagogue, school and ritual bath). The date of completion of the enclosure that surrounded the colony and stood out as a dominant feature of the landscape, is also unknown. Nevertheless, this enclosure played an important role in preserving the original contours of the colony and accentuating its kinship with the Strassendorf model.[11]

The early settlers of Shefeya, ten bachelors from Zikhron Ya'akov, moved to the site of their new colony late in 1889 after occupying an abandoned building in the vicinity.[12] The construction of eight permanent houses commenced in 1890 and reached completion the following year (1891 being consequently mistaken for the year of establishment) (see Table 1). By World War I, Shefeya also had three public buildings, but again, the pattern of settlement established in 1890 remained basically unchanged.

10   Map 5 shows the colony in December 1896. As in the case of Ekron and Shefeya, not all the maps have been published and it is difficult to know precisely which buildings were standing in 1890. A few of the larger buildings, one of the wooden stables, the warehouse and the ritual bath may have been built later. The only change in residential housing between 1890 and 1896 was the construction of another room in many family homes.
11   Bronstein, p. 2; Samsonov, pp. 180–189, 212; Hershberg, *Oriental Lands*, pp. 137–138. Compare with Ben-Artzi, *Jewish*, map; and photograph in Raffalovich-Sachs, p. 25.
12   See entry on Shefeya in Zikhron Ya'akov administration book, CZA J15/139; Samsonov, p. 190; Hissin, *Journey*, pp. 332–333. The eight "houses" were actually eight apartments in four two-family houses.

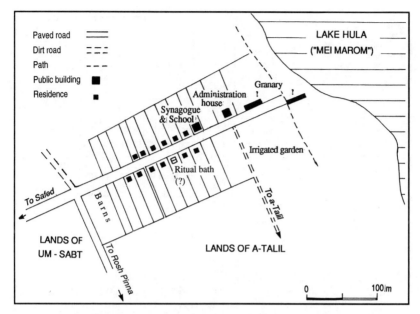

Map 7: Yesud ha-Ma'ala in 1890 (reconstruction)
Sources: Schub, *Yesud*, p. 4; JNF map 3055, Hebrew University; Shub, *Private Farms*, p. 21; Hissin, *Journey*, pp. 409–415

To a certain extent Yesud ha-Ma'ala was another Strassendorf settlement, although the pioneers spent more than five years living in an old granary and mud-and-straw huts in Bedouin fashion. The situation changed when the land was properly registered and building permits were received in 1889. Rothschild took over financial responsibility for the colony later that year and commissioned plans for permanent housing and settlement infrastructure. The land along the main street was divided into sixteen lots, and in early 1890, the first stone buildings were put up to serve the needs of the community: an administration house, a ritual bath and synagogue, a school, and a pharmacy. By the end of the year, the main street was graced by a dozen private homes (see Map 7) and this figure doubled in the coming decade. The property lines were not entirely straight and the lots were somewhat irregular in size and shape, but a general linear pattern was dominant

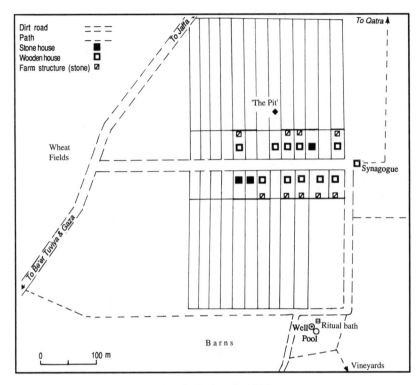

Map 8: Gedera in 1890

Sources: Plan of lands of Gedera in 1885 (JNF map 6072, Hebrew University); Hissin, *Journey*, pp. 180–187; Ariel, pp. 44–47; Laskov, pp. 286–288

until the turn of the century when a new street with five homes was added slightly north of the colony.[13]

The colony of Gedera followed the Strassendorf model more strictly. It contained sixteen rectangular plots of one dunam each on either side of the main street, forming a perfectly geometrical pattern. Gedera was the only settlement planned by Hovevei Zion rather than the Rothschild administration, but the same guidelines were used as in the design of Zikhron Ya'akov and other Rothschild colonies. Although Hovevei Zion

---

13 Ibid., pp. 409ff. (including description of cornerstone-laying for the first houses on 11 May 1890); Ben-Artzi, Galilee Colonies, p. 410 and diagram 3.

funded the construction of three stone buildings, ten stone barns, and ten wooden homes by 1890, nothing could have been done without the preparatory work of Rothschild's officials in handling the legal aspects of land ownership and building rights in 1888.[14] In fact, years later, when the plans were fully implemented, there was little visible difference between Gedera and the colonies developed under Rothschild's auspices (see Map 8).

Of the seven colonies described above, the only one that deviated somewhat from the compact, uniform arrangement characteristic of the street-village was the T-shaped Zikhron Ya'akov. A totally different layout was evident in Petah Tikva, Rishon le-Zion and Rosh Pinna — the "free-style" colonies, as we shall call them. Development work did not begin in a new site when Rothschild stepped in to aid these colonies, but continued around the existing core of settlement. Furthermore, Rothschild was not the only developer and the various parties at work in the colonies in question failed to coordinate among themselves or appoint a central overseer. In consequence, the original plans were invariably disregarded and these colonies expanded haphazardly in every direction, with no thought given to contiguity or uniformity of appearance.

In 1879, when Petah Tikva was emerging as a colony, the founding fathers established by-laws that provided for a methodical, clear-cut arrangement of streets and farms. In 1884, an engineer from Jerusalem was commissioned to draw up blueprints and a surveyor was called in to measure the land. According to plan, the colony was to be square in shape. However, the erratic course of development throughout the decade and the absence of a central body to supervise construction and impose uniform standards obscured the original pattern.[15] Moreover, a growing shortage of land and spiraling property values towards the end of the decade prompted the settlers to carve up plots and disregard building regulations. As a result, both building density and heterogeneity increased. Other influential factors were the partial financial support

---

14   Ariel, p. 47; Hissin, *Journey*, pp. 181–187. See two interesting photographs of Gedera in Raffalowich and Sachs, pp. 14–15.

15   The square design of Petah Tikva is thought to have been copied from the Jewish neighborhoods outside the walls of Jerusalem, for example, Mea Shearim, which was the hometown of many of the colony's founders. Others detect the influence of the Jewish towns of Eastern Europe. See Cassuto, p. 256.

184   Chapter Eight

of Baron de Rothschild and the accelerated pace of development. In 1890, the colony of Petah Tikva constituted a melange of makeshift shelters, handsome private homes, and large public institutions.[16] This

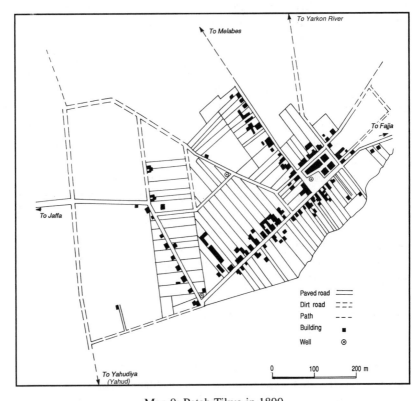

Map 9: Petah Tikva in 1890
Sources: Slor, Map of Petah Tikva in 1890 (in Tropeh, *Beginning*, p. 114); Shapira, *Petah Tikva*, maps on pp. 14a, 74a

---

16 Petah Tikva Archives, file 10 (misc.) p. 1; Yaari-Pokskin and Harisman, pp. 386, 444; Hissin, *Journey*, pp. 260, 267. Estimates for the number of houses in 1890 range from twenty to eighty. The discrepancy is probably due to certain estimates referring to residential buildings only as opposed to all buildings, or stone buildings as opposed to buildings of a temporary nature. See ibid, p. 252; Slor's map in Tropeh, *Basic*, p. 114.

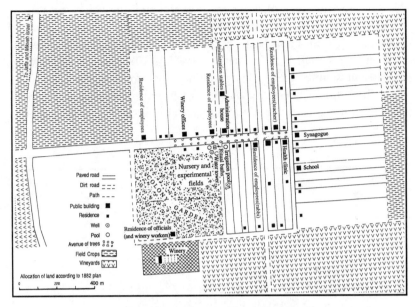

Map 10: Rishon le-Zion in 1890
Main Source: Aaronsohn, *Baron*, p. 193

same diversity and lack of symmetry continued to characterize the colony not only at the turn of the decade but in the years to come (see Map 9).

In many respects, Rishon le-Zion and Petah Tikva were alike. Although Rishon le-Zion had a master plan drawn up by its founders prior to the intervention of the baron, construction activities during the first stage (end of 1882 and first part of 1883) were carried out by individual settlers without outside supervision. As the years went by, a tendency towards heterogeneity persisted due to the presence of independent farmers, demographic growth and economic developments that spurred the building of new roads, subdivision of plots and construction of temporary structures. Yet unlike Petah Tikva, where Rothschild stepped in only at the end of the decade, Rishon le-Zion was administered by a central authority almost from the beginning. Rothschild's officials kept an eye on construction in the colony, including projects pursued independently, so that the original plan was not totally obliterated.

186   Chapter Eight

There were still signs of order in 1890 although the colony was more heterogeneous in appearance and built up less densely than the colonies managed by Rothschild from inception. As in the master plan, Rishon le-Zion was rectangular in shape (see Map 10), and the farms were carved out symmetrically, though perhaps not equal in size. Deviation from the original geometric pattern began only in the early twentieth century, whereas this trend was already obvious in Petah Tikva in the 1880s.

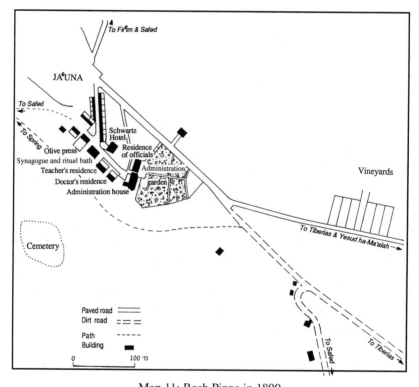

Map 11: Rosh Pinna in 1890
Main Sources: JNF map 68/3, Hebrew University; Schub, *Private Farms*, pp. 8–17; Scheid, pp. 129–130

In 1890, Rosh Pinna bore a greater resemblance to Petah Tikva than to Rishon le-Zion. This colony developed in three separate stages. During the first stage, the founders built fourteen closely-spaced homes of uniform style along one street. During the next stage, under Rothschild's patronage, a second street was added for public buildings and offices. There were seven buildings altogether, with ample room between them in contrast to the earlier type of construction.[17] Finally, toward the end of the 1880s, a third street was built, non-contiguous with the others (see Map 11). This street was divided into thirty lots that were built up over the next decade in the Strassendorf style characteristic of other Rothschild colonies. The focal point of the colony eventually shifted to this area and a fourth street was added. Although it is unclear whether construction commenced in the 1880s, it appears likely that six or seven buildings were standing by 1890.[18] In any case, Rosh Pinna was not a regimented, compact colony but one which was laid out spaciously and leisurely in three different styles.

In summation, when the Rothschild administration drew up preliminary plans for six colonies and these plans were followed through by a central administrative body, the resultant colonies were well-organized, enclosed entities that retained a compact, uniform appearance throughout the decade. On the other hand, in those three colonies where Rothschild was not involved from the outset, the original design envisaged by the founders was generally lost in the flow of development. By 1890, they were amorphous, sprawling settlements laid out in an irregular pattern featuring open spaces and heterogeneous building styles. The sole Hovevei Zion colony, Gedera, was modelled after the Rothschild colonies and closely resembled the Strassendorf village with its linear, tight arrangement of houses and farms.[19]

---

17 Schub, Private Farms, pp. 9–10; Ben-Artzi, Galilee Colonies, p.409.
18 E. Taubenhaus, *Ha-maggid* 35 (1891), quoted in Niv, p. 133; and veiled references to planning and preparatory work in the summer of 1889 in "Letters from Eretz Israel," *Ha-maggid* 33 (1889), quoted in Niv, p. 127.
19 It was too early to discuss layout in two other Jewish settlements of the 1880s: Bnei Yehuda was not built up yet, and Nahlat Reuven, later-Nes Ziona, consisted of one farmyard.

Architecture

A major feature of the landscape in the Jewish colonies were the buildings: residences, public institutions and farmhouses. Towards the end of the 1880s, the residential buildings were of six different types. The Rothschild administration built private homes of standard design which incorporated a main entrance hall, a kitchen, and two bedrooms (see below). The kitchen was a direct extension of the entrance hall, and the bedrooms were situated on either side. Sometimes the kitchen was added onto the back of the house and entered from the back yard (where the toilet facilities were also located). Like most of the other housing in the colonies, these homes had red-tiled roofs imported from Marseilles.[20] Single family units of this type eventually became the most popular form of housing in the colonies, but until the late 1880s they were considered quite unusual. By mid-1890, 51 to 62 homes of this design could be found in five different colonies.

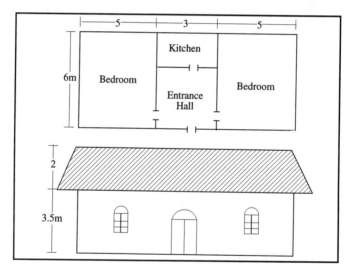

Standard single-family dwelling unit in the Rothschild colonies
(Source: CZA J15/2274)

---

20 Ben-Artzi, *Jewish*, pp. 127–131, 146–147. The interiors of various homes in 1890 are described by Pukhachewsky, Founders, no. 40, pp. 11–12; Hissin, *Journey*, p. 121; Kantor, Through.

The Rothschild administration also built another type of housing that was very similar to the first but accommodated two families. Again, the interior consisted of three rooms and a kitchen, but each house consisted of two living units, back to back, thereby reducing building costs. The houses measured twelve by thirteen meters (or two units of seventy-eight square meters each).[21] Like the private homes, the duplexes were constructed of local stone, usually *kurkar* (soft limestone), with a concrete floor and tiled roof. Toilet facilities, not included in the original design, were later added in a corner of the back yard.

A third type were row houses such as those built in Ekron in 1884. The interior design was the same, but each building was two storeys high and consisted of three or four living units. Initially, farm animals were housed on the ground floor, and the families lived on top.[22] By the end of the decade, however, barns were available and the ground floor was also used as a residence. The four row houses in Ekron contained a total of fourteen living units.

Apart from uniform stone housing in the three styles cited above, there were three additional types of dwellings common in the Jewish colonies. Although design and building materials varied widely, it is possible to distinguish between them on the basis of permanence. Thus we find two types of temporary structures and another type of permanent dwelling. In 1890, the colonies still retained many of the shelters erected as a stopgap until permanent housing could be completed. Some were old abandoned buildings acquired together with the property, such as large, free-standing stone farmhouses renovated to meet the settlers' needs, or primitive huts of branches, mud and straw left in the fields by Arab peasants.[23] Others were makeshift accommodations built especially for the purpose. Like the Bedouin, and the local fellaheen, the pioneers made use of local materials such as reeds and clay to fashion rough shelters. However, a more popular form of temporary accommodation were the pre-fabricated wooden cabins shipped over from Europe until building permits were

---

21 Ben-Artzi, Documents, pp. 46–48. .
22 Rabinowitz, Foundation Stone, pp. 986–987. Also see above, n. 8.
23 Horowitz, Yesud ha-Ma'ala, pp. 249–250; Samsonov, p. 190; Aaronsohn, Establishment, pp. 54, 60; Brill, p. 182; Scheid, p. 59.

One of the first dwelling huts in Zikhron Ya'akov

issued by the Turkish government. Each cabin, measuring thirty-two square meters (4x8 meters), contained two small rooms. Occasionally, the interior walls were reinforced with fifteen centimeters of filler concocted of local kurkar, sand and mud. Nearly eighty-five cabins of this kind were assembled in the colonies in the 1880s.[24]

Lastly, there were permanent dwellings built independently by the settlers themselves. This appears to have been the largest category, although exact figures are not available. It included any permanent housing, of whatever size or style, constructed without the supervision of a central authority. Surprising as this may seem, unregulated, free-style construction was common in the three major colonies even after Rothschild assumed control. Residential buildings outnumbered public buildings in the colonies, but the imposing physical presence of the latter could not fail to capture one's attention.

The public buildings were the largest and finest architectural specimens in the colony, and served as a social, functional and spatial rallying point. With the exception of a few buildings in Petah Tikva and one in Gedera financed by Hovevei Zion, all the communal buildings belonged to

---

[24] Details in Aaronsohn, *Baron*, pp. 197–199 and references in nn. 32–34, 39–40.

Rothschild — further evidence that public services and the Rothschild administration were virtually one and the same in the Jewish colonies.

From the standpoint of public facilities, the colonies belonged to two categories: the smaller ones with only one or two such buildings in 1890, and the central colonies, boasting schools, synagogues, medical facilities and administration buildings. The buildings themselves were of two types: multi-purpose buildings that combined various functions such as a school and synagogue; and single-purpose buildings such as ritual baths, pharmacies and offices.

The synagogue built in Rosh Pinna in 1885, the colony's first public building, served a variety of purposes. In 1890, the upper storey housed the sanctuary complete with men and women's sections, two classrooms and a pharmacy. A mikve (ritual bath) was located on the ground floor.[25] The imposing synagogue in the center of Rishon le-Zion was completed in 1889 after three years of bureaucratic entanglement. In 1890, a boys' school was operating in the basement after occupying the first floor of the unfinished building since 1886 (the girls' school functioned in

Rishon le-Zion synagogue, c. 1899

25 Hada Hu, p. 219. The school building built in the early 1890s is now a youth hostel.

rented quarters until a separate building was constructed for it around 1890).[26]

The synagogue established in Ekron in 1886 was perhaps the best example of the multi-purpose synagogue-school known as a (shule). This three-storey building was the center of virtually all the communal services in the colony except for administration. The ground floor was a school and the first floor a synagogue and study house. The upper floor housed the women's gallery and living quarters for the rabbi and teacher. Some say there was also a pharmacy on the ground floor.[27] Other multi-purpose buildings in the colonies were the synagogue-school-pharmacy in Yesud ha-Ma'ala, the school-pharmacy in Zikhron Ya'akov, and the synagogue-guesthouse-pharmacy in Gedera, which was not yet in a permanent building in 1890.

By the end of the decade, all the colonies had separate ritual bath facilities. Given the fact that the settlers were Orthodox in their religious observance and that ritual baths could not be housed in temporary structures on account of the special laws involved, the construction of a mikve often preceded that of a synagogue. The ritual bath of Zikhron Ya'akov, built in 1883, was the sole public building to grace the colony before the settlers turned to Rothschild (who later financed its renovation and enlargement). Similarly, the one in Petah Tikva was the one public building funded by Hovevei Zion when the society became affiliated with the colony in 1885. In Gedera, a mikve was the first project embarked upon after the installation of the water pump, and the ritual bath on the ground floor of the first public building in Rosh Pinna was completed before the synagogue on the upper floor.[28]

The planning of ritual baths and synagogues even in the small colonies founded at the end of the 1880s was strong evidence of the importance which Rothschild and his administrators attached to religion. The ritual baths were constructed immediately, but the synagogues in many of the colonies took three to five years to complete, and in more extreme cases,

---

26 Hissin, *Journey*, p. 129. Classes were conducted in the homes of four wealthy colonists until a permanent structure was built.
27 "Ekron," *Knesset Israel* (1886), p. 987; *Ha-havazzelet* 16 (1886), nos. 13; *Ha-maggid* 30 (1887), no. 27–28.
28 Epstein, History p. 976; Wissotzky, p. 188; Yaari-Poleskin and Harisman, p. 386. Further details in Hissin, *Journey*, p. 332.

several decades. Once the plans were realized, the synagogue generally stood out as the largest and most elegant structure in the landscape.

The synagogue in Zikhron Ya'akov, completed in 1885, was an architectural gem. The facade was embellished with iron grillwork and the interior with wood carvings. The sanctuary was lit by tall windows on three sides, and over the entrance was a magnificent rosette-shaped window which later displayed a clock bearing Hebrew numerals. The women's gallery, supported by pillars, ran around three sides of the main hall, in the center of which stood a handsome pulpit. Sections of the ceiling and walls were covered with paintings.[29]

By 1890 there were schools in all the colonies, even the smallest and most recently established. Around this time, school buildings were built under the auspices of the Rothschild administration in the two newest colonies as well as two Hovevei Zion settlements that had lately come under Rothschild's wing.[30] All these schools were small and modest, with the exception of one two-storey building where the headmaster's family occupied the upper floor as was customary in Europe.

The presence of medical clinics and full-fledged hospitals in the regional colonies was a unique feature of modern Jewish colonization in the early 1890s. The clinic in Rishon le-Zion was allotted a one-storey building of its own in a central location opposite the synagogue. It housed a pharmacy, a doctor's office, and living quarters for the pharmacist's family.[31] The agricultural school (*arbeiterschule*) in Zikhron Ya'akov also moved to a separate building in 1887. Containing a single large hall, it was often referred to as "the barracks."[32]

Another kind of public building was the administration house. Such buildings were not planned in the smaller colonies, and in some other colonies office work was carried out in a room of one of the private houses. On the other hand, in Ekron, as in the three main colonies, a separate structure was put up for this purpose: a spacious two-storey

---

29 Field survey. The synagogue interiors were similar in Rishon le-Zion, Rosh Pinna and Ekron, but not as grand.
30 Ben-Artzi, *Jewish*, pp. 160 ff; Hissin, *Journey*, p. 204; Tropeh, *Basic*, pp. 78–79.
31 This building is now the Rishon le-Zion museum. See photograph of the pharmacy interior with medical staff taken in 1889, Gera, p. 37.
32 Student letter written in 1888, in Eliav, *First Aliyah*, II, p. 156; Samsonov, pp. 147–148; Scheid, p. 85.

building.[33] In this building, as in all others built for this purpose, there were living quarters for the officials on one floor (usually the upper one) and offices on another.

In the three main colonies, several administration houses were built in the 1880s rather than just one. In Rishon le-Zion the first administration house (which was the administrative headquarters until 1894) was a two-storey building with an attractive wooden balcony built on the main street in 1884. The second administration house was erected around 1887, almost below the first administration building, opposite the colony garden. The gardener and his assistants lived on the upper floor of the large administration house built at the end of 1890 in the back yard of the first administration house. In addition, at least four residences were sold to the administration as offices (after their tenants left the colony).[34]

In Rosh Pinna a large administration house was built at the end of 1884 or in 1885 at the end of the new road. Other buildings were built along it at the turn of the decade and Rothschild officials such as doctors and teachers lived there. At the end of the 1880s, the baron's agronomist lived in one of the residences of the early settlers on the old road which had previously served as a temporary office.[35]

In Zikhron Ya'akov there were several administration houses in 1890. That in the center of the new colony was one of the first stone houses erected in 1884/5 and served as the residence of the colony director. The first floor of the old administration house on the hill in Zammarin was used as a residence for the gardener's assistants after the opening of the administration house in Zikhron Ya'akov; at least four other houses were used by various officials: the gardener's house, the doctor's house,

---

33 Note 8, above. This two-storey building, formerly the town hall and now the Mazkeret Batya museum, has been preserved in its entirety.
34 For details and references (particularly to oral testimonies), see Aaronsohn, *Baron*, p. 204, and see map 12.
35 Scheid, p. 131 and diagram on p. 130; the agronomist's home is also mentioned in Pukhachewsky, Founders, no. 23, p. 14. The apartment and the administration house were restored (the first was rehabiliated as a model farmer's home; and the second one houses an educational institute).

the living quarters of the medic and the midwife, and another building inhabited by the rabbi and ritual slaughterer.[36]

Farm buildings were another component of architecture in the Jewish colonies. Among them were buildings owned by individual settlers, buildings erected by the Rothschild administration or Hovevei Zion for the use of the entire community, and industrial facilities for the processing of agricultural produce. The farm buildings financed by the administration were an inseparable part of the colony, planned and constructed around the same time as the housing. They were usually positioned around the farmyards in such a way that their rear walls created partitions between one farm and the next or formed part of the outer enclosure that encircled the entire colony. The stables and barns were massively built of stone (which deterred thieves), and had mortar or tiled roofs.[37] Aside from sheltering animals, these buildings were used to store agricultural machinery and personal belongings. It was sometimes odd to see such solid farm buildings in colonies where the housing was flimsy and temporary. Indeed, some families preferred to live in them and use their homes for sheds and storage until permanent housing was available.

The farm buildings financed and constructed by the farmers themselves were less uniform in appearance than those built by Rothschild or Hovevei Zion and presumably stood out in the landscape. However, they were few in number and not often described in the literature.[38] Examples of private building were cow sheds, chicken coops, warehouses and silos, most of them constructed of inexpensive material such as clay or wood, with roofs of tin or tile. On some farms, there were dovecotes and Arab-style baking ovens.

Descriptions of the Rothschild farm buildings, most of them stables, are also hard to find. The finest, an elongated, two-storey structure with an imposing entrance and towers, was built in Rishon le-Zion in 1889. It provided storage for agricultural implements and grain, contained

---

36 Ben-Artzi, Documents, pp. 57–59. Also see Map 16 (the administration house in Zikhron Ya'akov was put to many different uses during the 1890s).
37 Ibid., pp. 49–52; Hissin, *Journey*, p. 187. The barns ranged in size from 8.20m x 4.40m to 10m x 6m, and held six to ten animals.
38 One of the few references can be found in Rothschild's letter of 9 April 1885, CZA J41/72 (French). Also see Smilansky, Uncle, pp. 13–15.

stalls for work animals and horses, and housed the carriages in which Rothschild's senior officials rode. In the 1880s, the baron's employees supervised the construction of a stable in Zikhron Ya'akov and structures serving a similar purpose in at least three other colonies.[39]

The first industrial buildings in the colonies were the wineries in Rishon le-Zion and Petah Tikva, the flour mill in Zikhron Ya'akov and the olive press in Rosh Pinna. The winery in Petah Tikva could not compare with the modern plant founded in Rishon le-Zion in 1890. Although the Petah Tikva winery opened one season earlier, it was small and old-fashioned, and operated in a building that functioned simultaneously as a granary, cow shed, dormitory, office, school and synagogue. The olive press established in Rosh Pinna in 1888 was similar in that it was a small private enterprise reliant on unsophisticated, traditional methods of production.[40]

In contrast, the spacious Rothschild winery in Rishon le-Zion employed the height of modern technology. The first wing was built in 1889–1890, in an undeveloped spot on the outskirts of the colony, using land originally designated for agricultural purposes (see Map 10). From the outset, it was capable of processing the entire Rishon le-Zion grape harvest. By the time the second wing was added in the early 1890s, it was among the largest and most advanced wineries in the world.[41]

Production began in a two-storey building: on the ground floor was a 9 x 43 meter hall with a ceiling height of five or six meters, and on the second floor, another hall of 20.5 x 42 meters. The hall on the ground level was vaulted, and its massive walls were nearly five meters thick (which accounted for the difference in size between the upper and lower halls). The grapes were brought in and fermented on the lower floor. The upper hall, with its straw-lined roof, was known as "the cellar" because it was here that the wine was stored, there being no underground cavern for this purpose. Running along the back of the building from north to south were corridors measuring 6 x 7 meters, and on the same side of

---

39 Pukhachewsky, Founders, no. 38, p. 13; Hissin, *Journey*, p. 398; field survey.
40 On the oil press, see *Ha-melitz* 28 (1888); Bendel, quoted, in Niv, pp. 118–119. On the winery, see Herschberg, *Oriental Lands*, p. 153; and photograph in Raffalowich and Sachs, p. 19.
41 Details and references in Aaronsohn, *Baron*, pp. 207, 209.

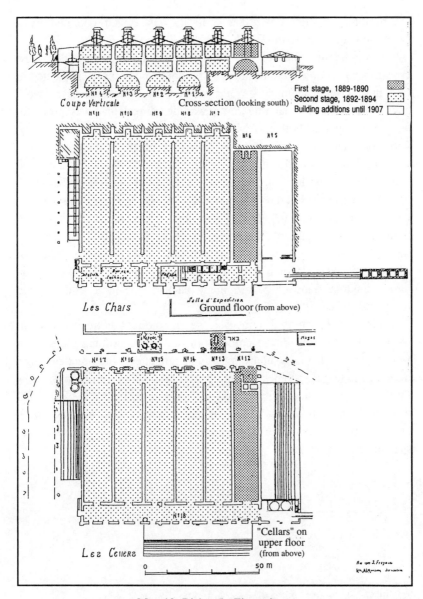

Map 12: Rishon le-Zion winery
Primary Sources: Freiman, I, map between pp. 176–177 and pp. 22–29; Scheid, pp. 202–203; Ideloviteh, pp. 452–453

the building, though not attached to it, was a well operated by a twelve-horsepower pump.

During the first half of the 1890s, twelve halls were added, new corridors and rooms were built on both floors, and access was created to four underground cellars. A water tower was installed over the well, and a sophisticated machine room was developed that was powerful enough to operate both the winery and the flour mill located nearby. Other production facilities were installed separately in the courtyard.[42]

Rothschild's second winery was launched in Zikhron Ya'akov two years after Rishon le-Zion. A site was selected at the end of the 1880s and work was scheduled to begin in 1890. However, other plans seem to have been carried out first. A well was dug there in 1890, and a flour mill built beside it that summer. Construction of the winery itself commenced in 1891. When the work was complete in 1892, the wine cellars of Zikhron Ya'akov covered a larger area than those of Rishon le-Zion during its first stage of development: each of the three underground rooms measured fifty meters in length.[43]

Aside from agricultural industries, we find indirect references to small workshops operating in the colonies in the 1880s. Among the settlers were former locksmiths, blacksmiths and carpenters who practiced their trade in the larger colonies, generally setting up shop in the farmyards. Further impetus for activity of this type was provided by the industrial development in the early 1890s. In the coming years, buildings were put up in the courtyards of the wineries and elsewhere to accommodate specialized workshops.

---

42 Idelovitch, pp. 452–456. Also see Map 18.
43 Building contracts for sections of the winery dating from 1890 onwards, CZA J15/2274/2-5; also see Scheid, pp. 107–108; Samsonov, p. 187; Hissin, *Journey*, p. 314.

Infrastructure and General Appearance

Infrastructure in the Jewish farming colonies of the nineteenth century was by no means infrastructure in the modern sense. There were no electricity, communications, water or sewage lines, but only a network of roads and a few wells. The colonists used steam engines sent over by Baron de Rothschild to supplement manpower and animals in such areas as plowing, conveyance, water supply and irrigation, but this energy could not be diffused and was useful only on the site where it was generated.

Communications and sewage systems were non-existent. Although the telegraph was introduced into Palestine in the 1870s, lines were hooked up only in the major cities. The first telephone in the colonies — which seems to have been the first in the entire country — was installed in the early 1890s to establish contact between the wine cellars and the offices of the Rothschild administration in Rishon le-Zion. Of all the utilities, the water system was the most advanced. In 1890/91, a few lengths of pipe channeled water from the wells in Rishon le-Zion, Zikhron Ya'akov and Rosh Pinna to centrally-located taps. Throughout the 1880s, however, the pioneers had no choice

The first well of Rishon le-Zion (1910)

but to draw water in buckets and store it at home, and sewage flowed into open cesspits.[44]

Wells and a variety of devices for extracting water dotted the landscape in 1890. There were water wheels driven by mules or camels, sloping water channels operated by horses, steam-powered pumping stations, storage and regulating pools, water troughs for animals and even a water tower.

The general layout and contours of the colonies were largely determined by the interplay of streets, but none were paved before 1890. Surfacing and paving stones were introduced later in the decade, and the only preparations made for wagon traffic were the removal of jagged rocks and the addition of earth where necessary.[45] Yet, the impression was quite the opposite of transience, poverty or neglect. The streets were laid out with geometric precision, almost always perpendicular to one another. The housing facing the street was lined up uniformly on either side, usually leaving five meters between the curb and homes. The streets themselves were broad, generally ten, but sometimes as much as twenty-two or even thirty, meters wide. This spaciousness was the result of pre-planning, both in the Rothschild colonies and in the settlements developed by other bodies, and is still evident today. The side streets incorporated in the original plan or added over the years were endowed with similar characteristics, and the sense of width was increased by sidewalks on either side of the street.[46]

The appearance of the streets was further enhanced by decorative elements and greenery. In each colony, an avenue of trees, usually evergreens such as mulberry, sycamore, Persian lilac and eucalyptus, was planted along the main thoroughfare. Houses were separated from the street by attractive fences of unhewn stone, bushes or a combination of stone pillars and wooden slats, and the area in between was planted with

---

44 On the "water conduit" leading from the new well beside the Zikhron Ya'akov winery to the colony in 1890, see ibid., loc. cit.; Kantor, Through, p. 40; Samsonov, pp. 193, 195.

45 Ben-Artzi, *Jewish*, p. 140. Only the mountainous "farmer's road" in Zikhron Ya'akov underwent major resurfacing; see Samsonov, p. 50.

46 Yaari-Poleskin and Harisman, p. 65; Freiman, I, p. 9; Hissin, *Journey*, pp. 42–43, Barzilai, *Beit Halevi*, p. 208.

flowers.[47] In certain colonies streetlighting was installed in the 1880s, and a few featured railings, drinking taps and iron-wrought fountains.[48] The look of the streets differed from colony to colony depending on the number of inhabitants, the topography, and so on. In the colonies designed by the Rothschild administration, the original layout remained basically unchanged at least until 1890, and if any more building was done as a result of demographic and economic developments, the streets simply lengthened.

The approach roads to the colonies left another indelible mark on the landscape. These roads were vital not only for marketing agricultural produce, but for transporting building materials and basic commodities such as water before a regular supply was established. In the early days, and later, too, when the support of the environment was so crucial, the road system created a link with the other colonies and with towns where the authorities were located. Hence one of the very first steps in founding a new colony was clearing the way for a road. Some of this work was financed by the early pioneers, but most by Rothschild or Hovevei Zion.[49]

If the colony had only one approach road, which was the case in Ekron, Be'er Tuviya, Bat-Shlomo, Shefeya and Yesud ha-Ma'ala in 1890, it fed into the main street and did not cut across to the other side of the colony. In this respect, these colonies differed from the classic Strassendorf village. On the other hand, Zikhron Ya'akov, Rosh Pinna, Rishon le-Zion and Petah Tikva possessed more than one approach road and it was possible to leave the colony via another route.

By the 1880s, the colonies were also connected by a network of internal access roads that led from one colony to another or established a link between the old and new sites of the same colony. These roads were evidence of an important geographical phenomenon: the emergence

---

47 Ben-Artzi, *Jewish*, p. 140; on the tree-lined avenues, see Hissin, *Journey*, p. 154; Samsonov, p. 124; and Barzilai, *Beit Halevi*, pp. 32, 36, 40, 47, who describes the lanes of mulberry trees in four colonies.
48 On streetlighting, see Samsonov, pp. 110, 134; Yaari-Poleskin and Harisman, p. 390. Remains of this street finery (similar to that introduced in Paris in the 1870s) can still be seen in Zikhron Ya'akov.
49 Samsonov, p. 59; Scheid, pp. 67–68; M. ben H. Hacohen, *Ha-melitz* 22 (1890) quoted, in Laskov, p. 321.

of regional divisions. Unlike the Judea district on the southern coastal plain, the areas around Zikhron Ya'akov and Rosh Pinna, then known as the Samaria region and the Galilee, suffered from difficult topographical conditions and a paucity of roads. To overcome this problem, the Rothschild administration developed a network of regional access roads. The improvement of the carriage road between Rishon le-Zion and Ekron after Rothschild's visit to the colonies in 1887 was apparently a step in this direction.[50]

In the Shomron district, the administration improved the Haifa-Tantura segment of the coastal highway from Haifa to Jaffa, and a carriage road was built from Tantura to Zikhron Ya'akov. At the end of 1888, carriage roads were laid between Zikhron Ya'akov and its newly founded daughter colonies, Shefaya and Bat Shlomo. Two more carriage roads were built in the Galilee from Safed to Rosh Pinna and from Rosh Pinna to Yesud ha-Ma'ala (partly following the contours of the historical coastal road that progressed northward along the upper Jordan rift and turned east at the Bnot Ya'akov bridge).[51]

No description of the road network in the colonies would be complete without mentioning the field roads that radiated from the colony, generally as an extension of other roads. They were shaped by two factors: the manner in which the farmland was divided and the acquisition of more land. Roads were cleared along the edges of the fields to allow the passage of wagons and agricultural implements, and other roads were built or improved to link up new tracts of farmland.[52] There was a tendency in the 1880s for much of the new building to proceed along these outwardly projecting roads. As such, they played an important role in determining the direction of further growth, and over the years, some of them became an integral part of the colony.[53]

---

50   Barzilai, Memories, 41, pp. 7–8; Epstein to Pinsker, Druyanow, Documents, II, col. 43, also see Map 15. Further details in Aaronsohn, *Baron*, p. 215.
51   H. Falk, *Ha-zvi* 2, no. 41 (1886), p. 165; Hissin, *Journey*, p. 329. For conflicting accounts of the roads in the Rosh Pinna area, see Aaronsohn, Jewish Colonies, p. 295.
52   On the clearing of field roads on a new tract of land readied for planting in Rosh Pinna, see *Ha-maggid* 33 (9 Elul 5649 [1889]).
53   "Carmel Street" in its early years, as a dirt road encircling the built-up section of

"The administrators' street" in Zikhron Ya'akov (aerial photo, c. 1947)

In some colonies, the streets developed around specific functions, such as administration, services, commerce, and industry, which determined the subsequent use of land on that street. This was most obvious in the larger colonies where Rothschild's public buildings and offices were

---

Rishon le-Zion, is visible in a photograph taken around 1898 (Raffalovich and Sachs, p. 23a).

clustered in a particular area. As the bureaucratic mechanism grew, a class-oriented social hierarchy emerged that was accentuated by spatial differentiation. In Zikhron Ya'akov and Rosh Pinna, officials and farmers lived on separate streets. Yet even in those colonies where the social hierarchy was invisible to the eye, or non-existent in the 1880s, the service and administrative center was unmistakable. In Ekron, the two public buildings — a two-storey administration house and a three-storey synagogue and school — were the tallest structures in the colony, dominating the center of the colony's one street. This was true in nearly all the colonies including Gedera, albeit on a smaller scale.[54]

Industrial buildings also tended to be consigned to a separate zone. Two out of three factories operating in the colonies in 1890 were outside the residential area. The winery in Rishon le-Zion was the built in a new site on the colony outskirts, and this was the plan for the Zikhron Ya'akov winery and flour mill. For obvious reasons, both were situated near the main approach road. The only colony with a winery in the center of town was Petah Tikva (the Nahalat Zvi winery on the Lahman estate). Interestingly, the factories built by the Rothschild administration over the next decade in Yesud ha-Ma'ala and Rosh Pinna were also zoned separately, whereas those built by Hovevei Zion in Gedera and Rehovot were not.

Shops and businesses that opened before 1890 were not set apart in a commercial quarter. We know of business ventures operating temporarily out of a room in a private home in at least eight settlements. The hotels and resort facilities offered in a few of the colonies were located in the residential neighborhood, though always in a central spot not far from the public services. Neither was any special district created for the markets that opened in the larger colonies in the second half of the 1880s.[55]

Tracts of land which remained vacant in the main colonies were turned into attractive public parks. In Rishon le-Zion, the land beside the plant nursery (which was used for agricultural experimentation and later became an orchard) was developed into a park. The same was true for the vacant lot at the end of the "public service street" in Zikhron

---

54 Hissin, *Journey*, p. 398; Barzilai, *Beit Halevi*, pp. 46–47.
55 References in Aaronsohn, Jewish Colonies, p. 299, nn. 100–101.

Ya'akov, and the land near the administration house in Rosh Pinna.[56] In these last two colonies, the public park was in the administrative quarter, whereas in Rishon le-Zion, it was in the residential neighborhood.

Another conspicuous feature of the colonies was the network of fences and enclosures that separated between the parcels of land and circumscribed the colony as a whole. Inside the colony, the boundaries were usually defined by rough stone walls reaching the height of a man. Four of the Rothschild colonies, and Gedera, too, were encircled by an outer wall of dressed stone that was taller than a man.[57] It reinforced the farm buildings whose exterior walls formed a natural boundary in the farmyards, and served as protection against the theft of livestock that was common at the time.[58]

The outer enclosure, visible from afar, came to symbolize the Jewish colonies of the nineteenth century in the same way that the water tower symbolized the cooperative settlements of the twentieth century. It lent a final touch to the orderly, "European" look of the colonies and accentuated the sense of compactness and uniformity that were achieved through the meticulous planning and supervision of one central body.

Conclusion: The Spatial Pattern of the Colonies in 1890

The appearance of the colonies at the end of the 1880s was an outward manifestation of intricate processes at work in all areas of colony life. Demographic changes, and especially population growth, were the impetus for founding new settlements, enlarging those already existent, and increasing building density. The inevitable result was deviation from the original plans and greater diversity of appearance. The need for more housing frequently conflicted with objective limitations such as the difficulty in obtaining building permits and the lack of funding, which

---

56 Pukhachewsky, Founders, no. 24, p. 12; Scheid, p. 83; Hissin, Journey, p. 124.
57 Barzilai, Beit Halevi, p. 36; Ariel, p. 47 Also see photographs in Raffalovich and Sach, p. 14, 15, 25.
58 Ben-Artzi, Jewish, pp. 139–141. Ben-Artzi and other sources are not clear about the extent of the walls and fencing built in 1880s. Presumably, the outer enclosure was built at the same time as the farm buildings.

206   *Chapter Eight*

often impeded development for years and led to makeshift building and overcrowded living conditions.[59]

It is important to understand the developments which produced changes in the landscape, or, put differently, the historical factors behind geographical transformations. As we have seen, the primacy or order of occurrence of certain phenomena was particularly decisive. Facts established during the first year, such as Zikhron Ya'akov's status as the largest colony or its simultaneous development in two different sites, had a crucial impact on the physical appearance of the colony for many decades. Similarly, the housing pattern in Rishon le-Zion and Rosh Pinna before Rothschild took over continued to determine their contours in the years to come.

While the development of housing in the colonies passed through several stages, including a period of makeshift building on a temporary site, a period of solid building on a permanent site, and often a period of more elaborate building, the plans of the first year left a lasting imprint. From experience gained over time, the two-family units envisaged in Zikhron Ya'akov during the early days were transmuted by the end of the decade to single-family units. However, the basic design remained unchanged.

The style of building in the colonies was influenced by many outside factors, but cultural and philosophical considerations seem to have held greater sway than pragmatic, socio-economic considerations. For example, the choice of an elevated site in the center of town for the synagogue was apparently dictated by religious sentiment. For the same reason, certain colonies avoided intersecting streets, lest they form the shape of a cross.[60] The Arab influence was minimal and usually the product of necessity rather than a conscious desire to imitate. Arab elements included the use of stone rather than wood as a building material, the construction of mud huts, and early experiments with vaulted rooms and flat roofs. All of these were temporary solutions that were soon replaced.[61] On the other hand, the Templer colony in Haifa was

---

59   On spiralling land costs, the housing shortage and high rents, see Hissin, *Journey*, p. 113; and Pukhachewsky, Founders, no. 38, p. 13.
60   Until nowadays one can trace these phenomena in the old quarters of Rishon le-Zion and Petah Tikva.
61   Hissin, *Journey*, pp. 180, 319; Schama p. 71 and n. 37, attributes these experiments to Rothschild's vision of simple, inexpensive Arab-style housing. Aside from a vague

emulated in a very calculated manner through the employment of German contractors, surveyors and engineers. In addition, Arab contractors and builders from the urban sector brought with them modern influences and building styles fashionable in the cities (most noticeable in the private homes).[62]

Rothschild and his officials played perhaps the greatest role of all in shaping the physical landscape of the colonies. The financial support of the Rothschild administration made possible the drawing up and implementation of an inclusive program of development, and its network of supervisors insured that all building followed a pre-determined pattern and conformed with strict standards of quality control and uniformity. In the absence of such a body, as was the case in certain colonies during the 1880s, the original plans were disregarded and the character of the colony was utterly changed.

Thus we find two types of colonies at the end of the decade: the "administrated" colonies as opposed to the "free-style" colonies. Zikhron Ya'akov, Be'er Tuviya, Bat Shlomo, Shefaya, Yesud ha-Ma'alah and Gedera were in the first category, as were the majority of the colonies established in later years in other parts of the country.[63] The "administrated" colonies were settlements built around a single, tree-lined avenue (with the exception of one, with two intersecting streets). The homes and farms were laid out in orderly rows, with the focus of attention being the imposing public and administration buildings. The entire complex was circumscribed by a wall.

The "free-style" colonies — Rishon le-Zion, Petah Tikva and Rosh Pinna — were built in an unrestricted manner, paying no heed to the original plans. They were designed from the outset as self-contained,

---

reference in Rothschild's letter of 21 October 1884, in Idelovitch, p. 133, I have found no proof of this, even in Schama's own references.

62 On the Germans in Haifa as the builders of Zikhron Ya'akov and Bat Shlomo, see Carmel, p. 42. It is possible that other factors, such as the geographical features of the land or the national origins of the settlers, affected the style of building (Ben-Artzi, *Jewish*, p. 255). However, I have found no evidence of this in the 1880s and travellers' accounts of resemblance to towns in Lithuania or Hungary probably had more to do with the social-cultural milieu than physical similarity.

63 Ibid., p. 225ff.

"The vineyards' street" in Rosh Pinna, c. 1898

geometrically shaped settlements with farms of uniform size set in a straight line or an intersected square. Building activities in the course of the 1880s totally ignored these guidelines, creating an incoherent pattern of homes and farmyards. The streets were also arranged haphazardly, and housing in a variety of styles was clustered in separate neighborhoods without regard for contiguity or the protection of an outer wall. Nevertheless, there was a certain resemblance between the "free" and "administrated" colonies. The "free" colonies were also graced by a large number of public buildings (these, too, built by Rothschild) and building standards were generally high.

The modern appearance of the nineteenth century Jewish colonies contrasted sharply with the Arab villages in the vicinity. They were also quite unlike the small towns of Eastern Europe and France, with their disorganized, huddled look and few examples of public building.[59]

The difference between the "administrated" and "free" colonies hinged on a combination of centralized planning, established building standards, generous investment, use of modern technology, and rigorous supervision and control. These measures led to a high degree of correspondence between the preliminary plans and actual implementation. By means of control over real-estate, finances and day-to-day management, the Rothschild administration was able to stabilize the physical development of its colonies and regulate the use of land.

As we have seen, the Jewish colonies were not all of the same face. Yet a certain physical entity emerged in the course of the 1880s that distinguished the colonies from other forms of settlement. The shaper of this entity was first and foremost Baron Edmond de Rothschild. In his impact on the colonies, he far outweighed even the Ottoman authorities whose negativism towards the settlers posed numerous obstacles. Whereas regional elements played a completely marginal role in developing the infrastructure for Jewish agricultural settlement, the central planning and supervision of the Rothschild administration left an indelible imprint that affected both the physical and human landscape.

---

59 Ibid., pp. 246–248. Ben-Artzi concludes that the Jewish colonies differed from the villages of northern Europe and the Templer colonies in Eretz Israel in two major respects: the multitude of public buildings and the separation of housing and farm buildings. While the aesthetic sense and general notions of physical layout drew upon modern European thinking, Ben-Artzi believes that the Jewish colonies were a more self-styled local product than an imitation of existing settlement models.

CHAPTER NINE

FARM AND ECONOMY

It is commonly assumed that plantations were the only agricultural branch pursued in the colonies of the First Aliya, and that their cultivation was literally forced upon the colonists by Baron de Rothschild. In fact, the agricultural economy was much more diverse, and included field crops, vegetables, livestock farming and a wide range of fruit trees in addition to the vineyards so often described in the literature. On the following pages, we will discuss each of these branches in detail, and consider such factors as land, manpower, and agricultural technology in the development of the early Jewish colonies.

Viticulture

Grapes were destined to become the favored crop in the colonies of Baron de Rothschild, but the transition was far from sudden. In the early days, several varieties of French and Arab grapes were grown at the pioneers' own initiative and expense, always as a secondary crop. The emphasis was on field crops, primarily wheat, and the situation remained unchanged when Rothschild took over.[1] The only difference was that Rothschild's officials began to distribute vines among the colonists and plant small tracts of land on an experimental scale. No one, however, was compelled to substitute viticulture for grain. Eventually vineyards did achieve prominence in the economy of the most important colonies, but a combination of local, physiographic and social factors was responsible

---

1 Further details and references to primary sources in Aaronsohn, *Baron*, pp. 221–222; Aaronsohn, Agriculture.

rather than a fundamental decision by Rothschild. The settlers themselves realized after two failed harvests that the soil was problematic (ranging from rocky to sandy) and wheat was not the dependable source of income they had once envisaged.[2] The question passionately debated from this point was whether to continue with dry cereal farming, which meant fertilizing their fields and purchasing more arable land, or choosing an alternative that was profitable yet less reliant on good quality soil. Among the proposals were raising sheep or cultivating vines and fruit trees.[3]

The debate in the colonies went public in the summer of 1885 when one of the pioneers, an agronomist by profession, published a treatise in support of viticulture.[4] Meanwhile, Rothschild began to take an interest in the colonies. The officials he dispatched to report on the harvests of 1884 were pessimistic about the future of grain and recommended an investment in viticulture. Rothschild heeded their advice and vines were planted that winter in Rishon le-Zion, the first colony to come under his control. Based on the experience of the colonists who had been tending vineyards for two years, common French varieties were distributed among the farmers, together with the tools needed for planting.[5] Viticulture received an added push the following year when Rothschild purchased over 3,000 dunams of land and parcelled out plots to those future colonists who were prepared to plant vineyards on them and sign contracts to that effect.[6]

The very fact that so much land was allocated for vineyards has been perceived by scholars as evidence of a deliberate decision on Rothschild's part. By the end of 1886, viticulture was indeed spreading into other colonies and more land was being purchased to plant vineyards by new colonies specializing in the branch. Yet it was only after Rothschild's

---

2 On the grain harvests and more sober attitude towards the future of dry farming, see Aaronsohn, Agriculture. On the perceptions of the early settlers, see Katz, First Furrow, pp. 87–90.
3 Letter of 22 June 1884 (Russian), in Druyanow, *Documents*, III, pp. 601–602; Belkind, pp. 85, 97; Hissin, *Journey*, pp. 96–97.
4 Meerovitch, *Advice*.
5 Aaronsohn, Vines, pp. 33–34, and references there.
6 Hirsch's letter to the AIU, 3 March 1886 AIU Archives in Paris C/881/2; Ever-Hadani, *Vinegrowers*, pp. 42, 67.

first visit to the country in 1887 that a comprehensive agricultural policy was actually delineated.

In the summer of 1888, Rothschild's chief superintendant arrived for his annual tour of the colonies in the company of a French agricultural expert, who had just been appointed as chief agronomist of the Rothschild administration. The *jardinier* conducted soil tests in each of the colonies and concluded that (a) viticulture was the most suitable crop; (b) the produce should be made into wine; and (c) 5,000 vines could provide ample income for an entire family.[7] To complete the economic plan, Rothschild's advisors urged the immediate establishment of a winery.

From the settlers' perspective, this was the turning point. It was finally clear to them that Rothschild intended to turn viticulture and the production of wine into a major economic branch. In their memoirs, the colonists recall enticing promises made by Rothschild's officials, and their recommendation that the farmers plant more of their land with vines. There was hearsay about the opening of another winery, and a guaranteed annual income of at least one franc per vine.[8] Their imagination fired, many colonists invested all their resources in planting grapes and largely neglected other economic branches.

As it transpired, 1888/89 was a fallow year according to the Jewish calender. During the *shemitta*, which falls every seven years, Jews in the Holy Land are forbidden by religious law to cultivate their fields. The question of whether the rabbis would consider this an exceptional case and release the colonists in Eretz Israel from the obligation was a burning issue throughout the Jewish world. The religious leaders of the Diaspora supported their exemption, but the final decision was made by the rabbis of Eretz Israel who ruled that the laws of shemitta must be strictly observed.[9] The prohibition covered all work in the fields, i.e., plowing, sowing and reaping, as well as planting new trees, but not tending existing plantations.

In consequence, the entire year was devoted to grafting new varieties onto existing vines. Enormous sums of money were invested in grafting

---

7   *Ha-melitz* 28, no. 126 (1888), cited by Druyanow, *Documents*, II, cols. 538–539.
8   Barzilai, *Memories*, 21, p. 6.
9   Klausner, *Kattowitz*, I, pp. 324–347; Kaniel, pp. 129–132; also see references in both works.

finer French grapes on the rootstocks of common Arab and French vines, and the money, of course, came from Rothschild. His agronomists, however, had been arguing with him over which varieties of grapes were most appropriate for the production of wine. There was no argument that French varieties ·should be planted, but Rothschild's chief agronomist felt that common strains were preferable, whereas Rothschild himself set his mind on more excellent ones. Naturally, it was Rothschild who had the final word.[10]

From this point on, priority was given to choice vines originating mainly from the Mèdoc region (such as Cabarnet-Sauvignon, Malbec and Semillion), both for new plantings and grafting. Phylloxera, however, had ravaged vineyards all over Europe and spread to Turkey, prompting the Ottoman authorities to ban the import of vine shoots from Europe into their empire. Circumventing the Turks, rootstocks of choice French vines were found in India, where they had been planted around 1880 by the now chief agronomist of Baron de Rothschild.[11] By the winter of 1890, the planting of vineyards had reached frenzied proportions and even in many of the colonies outside Rothschild's jurisdiction, viticulture reigned supreme.

The cultivation of grapes thus began slowly, as a localized and pragmatic solution in a few settlements where the soil was poor. During these early years vineyards were planted with a mixture of local and French strains. Only towards the end of the 1880s was a comprehensive economic plan developed around commercial agriculture. Large-scale cultivation of choice winegrapes fit in well with this plan and was adopted by all the Rothschild colonies. Eventually a great part of the other colonies were swept up in the momentum and also planted vineyards. By 1890, vines were being grown on over ten thousand dunams, which accounted for twenty-seven percent of the cultivated

---

10 Scheid, pp. 96–98, 202. More on the views of both parties and the connection with viticulture in France and North Africa in Aaronsohn, Vines, and Aaronsohn, *Baron*, pp. 315–316.
11 Pukhachewsky, *Founders*, no. 41, p. 12. Various documents in Hebrew and French compiled by Meerovitch, CZA A32/37. On the restricted import of vines, see Les Archives de Ministère d'Agriculture in the Archives Nationales Françaises, file F10/1622, document dated November 1887.

Vineyards in Gedera, 1898

farmland and nearly fifteen percent of the total area of the colonies.[12] However, while viticulture was certainly important at the end of the 1880s, and became even more so during the next decade, it was not the only branch of agriculture in the colonies.

Other Plantations

Aside from vineyards, Rothschild's officials supervised the planting of various types of trees in the Jewish colonies during their first decade of existence. Nineteenth-century sources refer to many kinds of trees, which may be categorized into three groups: citrus trees, traditional Mediterranean trees and non-fruitbearing trees (the latter were not productive in the agricultural sense, but were grown and tended along with the others). During this period, trees of all three categories, as well as one other

---

12 Gurevich and Gertz, table 30; Ever-Hadani, *Vinegrowers*, pp. 37–38.

type — deciduous trees — were under cultivation in the modern Jewish colonies.[13]

In keeping with Rothschild's decision to promote agro-industry, most of the plantations were of the commercial variety. Again, Rothschild was not intent on developing a monoculture based on grapes, although they were certainly a favored crop. Towards the end of the 1880s and all through the 1890s, an array of industrial crops were cultivated, among them mulberry trees for the support of silkworms, citrus fruit for producing jams, and aromatic plants for perfume. The list of experimental plantations was endless, including castor-oil plants, tea, coffee, spices and cotton.[14] Other experiments involved non-fruitbearing trees such as eucalyptus, cypress, she-oak, ficus, bamboo, etc.[15] Quite a few of the crops were tropical or sub-tropical because Rothschild believed these were appropriate for a "hot climate," and the majority were annuals, as was common on the large plantations in Europe. The perennial crops, however, proved most adaptable.

Among the traditional Mediterranean crops grown in the colonies prior to 1887 were olive trees and a few carobs for animal fodder. After Rothschild's visit, almonds and apricots were introduced on a wide scale, and deciduous fruit trees, such as peaches, apples, cherries, pears and pomegranates, became popular.[16] Citrus achieved major importance only during the first half of the twentieth century. In the 1880s, one of the central Rothschild colonies raised oranges and citrons in an irrigated nursery and grafted cuttings onto wild orange stock (*khushkhash*) in a small orchard nearby. Another colony received thousands of lemon, citron and orange saplings from Mikve Israel, but only a certain percentage took root. The only successful plantation of sizeable proportions was a grove of 10,000 orange trees planted in 1890 as part of a comprehensive development plan in Zikhron Ya'akov.[17]

Noteworthy in the non-fruitbearing category were Australian eucalyptus trees raised at Mikve Israel and replanted in the Rothschild colonies

---

13   Data compiled from contemporary newspapers in Aaronsohn, *Baron*, pp. 231–232.
14   Freiman, I, pp. 21, 23; Zussman, p. 261.
15   Pukhachewsky, Viniculture, pp. 266–269. The experimental fields were usually part of the nursery, and located near the well and fruit orchards. See, for example, Map 10.
16   Further details and references in Aaronsohn, *Baron*, pp. 234–237.
17   Ibid., loc. cit.

to drain the swamps and stabilize the shifting sands (among local Arabs, the eucalyptus was known as the "Jewish tree"). Persian lilacs were planted along the main streets, as were pine trees, mulberries and date palms native to the Caribbean islands.[18]

Initially, mulberries served in a decorative capacity only, but their economic potential became evident after a series of private experiments conducted by one of the settlers. In 1889, this pioneer, an agronomist by profession, traveled to Beirut to study sericulture (silkworm farming), then a leading branch of agriculture in Lebanon. The silkworms that hatched from the few eggs he brought back with him fed on leaves plucked from the mulberry trees along the colony's main street and successfully spun cocoons. This gave him the idea of growing silkworms as a sideline, which won the approval of Rothschild's chief agronomist and resulted in the mass planting of mulberry trees in 1890. Lands belonging to the administration were turned into mulberry plantations, and saplings were also distributed among the farmers in addition to grapevines. More plantings were inspired early in the 1890s by the supervised experiments carried out by school children in the empty halls of the winery in Rishon le-Zion before it commenced operation.[19]

In the context of a multi-year development plan, mulberry trees were also planted in some of the northern colonies. In one colony, 60–80 dunams of land were parcelled out to each settler, 40–50 dunams for vines and 10 dunams for mulberries and fruit trees such as apricot, olive and almond. On Rothschild's instructions, the common land was planted with mulberries, and residents of the nearby town of Safed were employed as silkworm laborers. By the end of the decade, mulberries, olives and vines were staples of the economy.[20] At this point, the Rothschild administration sent two assistant agronomists to Lebanon to specialize in sericulture, spurring the planting of more mulberry trees and the eventual establishment of a silk-spinning factory.

---

18   Pukhachewsky, Viniculture, pp. 266–269.
19   Meerovitch, Planting, p. 250; *Ha-or*, 1, no. 7 (14 August 1891).
20   Hissin, *Journey*, p. 390; Scheid, p. 137.

Rishon le-Zion and its fields (aerial photo, 1917)

Field Crops

Before Rothschild assumed responsibility, the pioneers devoted the bulk of their energy and resources to field crops, especially grain, and refused to be deterred by poor harvests. Even the low germination rate, which was estimated at forty percent in 1883, did not keep the farmers of Rishon le-Zion from planting the greater part of their land in 1884 with wheat, barley, lupine, sesame, and potatoes. Only after the second harvest, which was an improvement but scarcely brought in sufficient income for three months, were the farmers mentally prepared for a transition to viticulture.[21]

However, there are two important points to bear in mind. Firstly, field crops continued to be grown in all the colonies throughout the 1880s and frequently occupied most of the available farmland. Secondly, the ambitious agricultural program prepared by Rothschild and his staff towards the end of the decade provided for the cultivation of wheat and other field crops in addition to industrial plantations.

In none of the colonies was the reliance on cereals greater than in Ekron and Be'er Tuviya, where dry farming was the sole agricultural pursuit. From reports on the harvests in these two colonies in 1890, we learn that Ekron's seventeen farmers cultivated a total of 2,200 dunams of wheat, i.e., an average of 130 dunams per farmer, which yielded an annual net income of 635 francs per household. Over 4,300 dunams of wheat, sorghum, sesame and lentils were tended in Be'er Tuviya that year.[22]

In Petah Tikva and Yesud ha-Ma'ala, field crops were also dominant. In the mid-eighties, the colonists of Petah Tikva grew barley, buckwheat, sorghum, sesame, potatoes, and watermelons in addition to 2,600 dunams of winter wheat and 2,300 dunams of summer wheat. Crops of this type occupied all the farmland in Yesud ha-Ma'ala with the exception of one small irrigated grove. There was no change in emphasis when Rothschild rendered assistance in 1887–1889, or when he took full charge of these colonies later. The economic plan for Petah Tikva presented in September 1889 provided for the cultivation of both wheat and grapes. The twenty-eight farmers receiving aid from Rothschild were split into two groups that were expected to rotate between the crops.[23] The plan for Yesud ha-Ma'ala called for nurseries for aromatic plants. In 1889, several varieties such as geranium rosa, acacia and others were grown in the colony on an experimental basis. Nevertheless, 1,500 dunams of

---

21 Ibid., p. 182; Freiman, I, p. 16; Aaronsohn, *Establishment*, p. 126; Giladi, *Rishon Le-Zion*, p. 135.
22 Barzilai, *Beit Halevi*, p. 31 (Ekron), p. 37 (Be'er Tuviya).
23 Hayim Pinsker, 12 April 1887, in Druyanow and Laskov, V, p. 133; Yaari-Poleskin and Harisman, pp. 413–414; Hissin, *Journey*, p. 268.

wheat were sown in 1890/91, and the grain fields of Petah Tikva extended over 5,700 dunams.[24]

Wheat fields covered most of the agricultural land in Rosh Pinna, too. Each colonist was consigned eight to twelve separate plots totalling forty-eight dunams. However, the colonists could not earn sufficient income from this quantity of land, and farm management was complicated. In early 1889, the Rothschild administration purchased more farmland from the village of Ja'una, and in May 1890, the fields were redivided so that each farmer received a contiguous expanse of land for orchards and dry farming.[25]

Before the shift to plantations in 1889/90, the main crops in Zikhron Ya'akov were wheat, barley, potatoes, hay, vetch, and corn. Throughout the decade, the colony wrestled with problems arising from this agricultural choice. There never seemed to be enough land and the terrain was rocky and steeply sloped. From the very first year, the settlers of Zikhron Ya'akov realized that the only solution was to purchase more land from the surrounding Arab villages. Their efforts bore fruit in the mid-eighties and the new territory was immediately plowed and tilled. When the daughter colonies of Zikhron Ya'akov were founded in 1888/89, dry farming was planned in advance as the major agricultural branch — despite the agrarian reform under way in the older colonies. In Zikhron Ya'akov, the colonists were given a choice between wheat and plantations. Most of them opted for plantations with an emphasis on vineyards, but five chose field crops and each were consigned 300 dunams of land for this purpose.[26]

Cereals were still much in evidence in Rishon le-Zion in the second half of the eighties. 460 dunams of farmland were planted with field crops in 1890/91, and a large proportion of experiments in the Rothschild

---

24 Planning of nurseries for aromatic plants mentioned in Scheid's letter to Pinsker, 9 September 1888 (French), in Druyanow, *Documents*, II, p. 595; list of crops in Hissin, *Diary*, p. 415.

25 Rosh Pinna ledger of expenditures for 1884, CZA J15/6355 (French manuscript, no pagination); Hada Hu, pp. 221, 223; Scheid, p. 138; reports from contemporary newspapers in Niv, pp. 114–115.

26 References and further details in Aaronsohn, *Baron*, p. 241.

nurseries involved field crops such as Bermuda grass, saffron (crocus), asparagus, poppy, cotton, and peanuts.[27]

Given the fact that 25,000 dunams, i.e., over half of all the farmed land in the colonies in the early 1890s, were sown with grain, it is quite likely that field crops ranked first among all the agricultural branches at the time. Contrary to the accepted view, the quantity of land allocated for field crops was more than two and a half times greater than for vineyards.[28] Field crops were virtually the only branch in two colonies and extended over much of the farmland in six others. While the relative importance of an agricultural sector does not necessarily hinge on the number of dunams devoted to it, field crops were clearly far from the bottom of the scale on the eve of the 1890s.

Vegetables and Livestock

Vegetables and livestock were also raised in the Rothschild colonies, generally for local consumption. Although their economic importance remained marginal, a small number of settlers tried their hand at running private farms specializing in vegetables or livestock and dairy products. The cultivation of a vegetable garden supervised by the administration was possible only if an appropriate water source was available, and the site of the garden was determined by its location. In many colonies, vegetables and fruit trees were grown on irrigated land set aside for this purpose. Vegetables were also grown as intercrops between rows of trees. Dugourd's first report from Rishon le-Zion in December 1882, before patronage, recorded the purchase of "twelves kilos of peas, cabbage seeds, cabbage flowers, celery, radish seeds, carrots, etc."[29] An irrigated garden was tended beside the lower well in February 1883, and the following year, forty dunams of irrigated land were planted with summer crops and fruit trees (this was probably the "orchard" mentioned in later sources).

---

27   Ibid., p. 242, n. 75.
28   Calculations based on Gurevich and Graetz, table 30. The division of the land was not entirely clear, particularly with regard to nurseries. Some were used for experimental purposes and contained flowers and field crops in addition to fruit trees.
29   See "Accounts of the Colony of Rishon le-Zion," December 1882, appended to Hirsch's letter, 10 January 1883 (manuscript, French), AIU Archives, b5355/9.

The Rothschild administration also conducted agricultural experiments in this area and utilized it throughout the decade as a vegetable garden. The strawberries grown here were reportedly presented to government officials as gifts.[30]

Some of the land purchased in the Zikhron Ya'akov region after the establishment of the colony was naturally suited for gardening due to its levelness, rich soil and high ground water, tapped by digging a number of shallow wells. By one account, probably exaggerated, the entire tract of 320 dunams was turned into a vegetable garden at the beginning of 1883. At any rate, Dugourd grew cabbage and other vegetables there when the colony came under Rothschild's wing at the end of the year, and the garden remained in use in the coming years.[31]

The vegetable garden in Rosh Pinna was planted in 1886, following the construction of conduits that brought water from a nearby spring. Dugourd also organized plant nurseries and set aside six hectares on the northern outskirts of the colony for gardening, each colonist receiving one dunam. A similar pattern can be traced in Ekron. A vegetable garden and a nursery for fruit trees were established in September 1889 after a well was dug and a water supply system inaugurated. In Petah Tikva and other colonies, home gardens planted with hop, cucumbers, horseradish, turnips, radishes, cabbage, garlic and onions were tended by the farmers' wives and daughters.

"David's Garden" in Sumeil, near Jaffa, was the only known farm that operated as a commercial enterprise. This was a family farm owned by a widow named Sarah Ita Pelman, and was not affiliated with the Rothschild colonies. Pelman and her sons sold their home-grown vegetables and dairy products in town, taking advantage of their proximity to the Jaffa marketplace. In this respect, they were similar to the Templers who settled in the Haifa area around this time.

The Rothschild administration was openly skeptical of such ventures. A colonist from Petah Tikva who applied for a loan to dig a well for his vegetable garden was rejected by Erlanger on the grounds that "...there

---

30 Pukhachewsky, *Founders*, no. 33, pp. 12, 15; ibid., "Our Agricultural Experimentation at the Initiative of Baron Edmond," Idelovitch, p. 269.
31 Dugourd's letter to Hirsch, 1 December 1883 (manuscript, French), CZA J41/51; Hissin, *Journey*, p. 341; Brill, p. 179; Samsonov, pp. 97, 130–131.

is no possibility in the city of Jaffa to sell large quantities of vegetables, and should they be exported to Alexandria in Egypt, not a penny will be left over; the colonists do not need to purchase vegetables because they grow their own, and even if the sowing succeeds, it will amount to nothing because there is nowhere to market..."[32]

The distance of the colonies from urban markets was less problematic in the case of livestock and animal products. The first plans involving cattle, poultry and sheep fell through, but in 1885, Joseph Feinberg succeeded in establishing a dairy farm in Rishon le-Zion and two apiaries began to operate, one in Zikhron Ya'akov (encouraged by Laurence Oliphant) and the other in Nes Ziona (inspired by the Baldenspergers, a German family also engaged in beekeeping).[33]

Two more enterprises involving livestock were launched in 1886. The first was a private scheme, unassisted by Rothschild. One of the independent settlers in Rishon le-Zion took steps to establish a large, modern poultry farm. He built a large partitioned coop in his yard similar to the ones he had seen in Germany and filled it with imported German chickens. Three years later, all the chickens had died and the project was abandoned.[34]

The second scheme, raising livestock for market, was carried out with Rothschild's help. The baron financed the purchase of hundreds of sheep and each of the colonists of Rosh Pinna received a flock of forty to fifty. The total number of sheep in 1887 was estimated at four hundred.[35] This was the only known case of assistance from Rothschild in the sphere of animal husbandry, and was probably motivated by the administration's desire to provide the colonists with a source of supplementary income and a use for their unfarmed land. No other projects of this type were endorsed by Rothschild; on the contrary, his officials seem to have played a part in ridding Rishon le-Zion of a herd of goats owned by a number of colonists in 1885. A "statistical survey of various colonies" at the end of 1889 found no livestock at all apart from eighty cows in Rishon

---

32   Diskin, p. 57 (quotation from a letter written in the 1880s).
33   Barzilai, Memories, 21, p. 4 (dairy); Samsonov, p. 102 (apiary); Smilansky, *Family*, I, p. 226; Hanauer, p. 127.
34   Smilansky, Uncle, pp. 13–15.
35   Hada Hu, p. 23.

le-Zion and oxen used in the fields. On the other hand, in March 1890 the Rothschild administration established a dairy, poultry run and rabbit hutch in Rishon le-Zion to keep its own employees supplied with fresh milk, eggs and meat.[36]

Honey from the apiaries operating at the end of the decade (there were 162 in 1890/91) was produced on a commercial scale by the Lehrer family of Nes Ziona, who introduced sophisticated, modern techniques, and on a more limited scale in Zikhron Ya'akov, Bat Shlomo, Rishon le-Zion and Petah Tikva, where production followed traditional lines.

An inventory of livestock at the close of the 1880s lists a total of 380 cows and 258 calves,[37] while the cultivation of vegetables encompassed only 280 dunams. These figures testify that the scope of both branches was small and — in contrast to other areas of farming — Rothschild played a very minor role in their development. The hesitation and lack of interest of his officials probably resulted from their perception of these sectors as minimal in importance. Nonetheless, they did leave a mark on the landscape and for a small number of farmers they were a valuable source of income.

Agricultural Manpower and Technology

The Jewish colonies suffered no lack of manpower or agricultural expertise, although the literature seems to infer otherwise. The sources were many, and Rothschild drew upon them all: indigenous (the colonists and their families), local (Arab peasants, members of the urban Jewish community, new immigrants), and foreign (from neighboring countries and Europe). Each of these categories provided both skilled and unskilled labor as well as a reservoir of agricultural knowledge and experience.

When Rothschild became involved in the Jewish colonizing effort,

---

36 Hissin, *Journey*, p. 133; Belkind, 19 June 1885, in Druyanow, First Days, I, p. 10; Pukhachewsky, Founders, no. 44, p. 3. Many families kept a milk cow (sometimes two) and a few fowl for their own consumption.

37 Figures based on Gurevich and Gertz, table 30. Rosh Pinna, Zikhron Ya'akov and daughter colonies were not included in the inventory. According to pasture records (manuscript, French; CZA J15/5979), a total of fifty-five cows were owned in these colonies by thirty-eight farmers.

he found 130 men "fit for work" in Zikhron Ya'akov, not including youngsters who did chores from the age of twelve or thirteen, and wives and grown daughters who provided extra hands, especially during the harvest season. Few of the colonists were seasoned farmers, but at least one person on every colony had some prior agricultural experience or theoretical knowledge. In some colonies, European or locally trained farming experts (from Mikve Israel) were hired to help out during the first year, so that the presence of the professional agronomists sent in by Rothschild at a later stage was not a total innovation.[38]

Over the years, the Rothschild administration employed a growing number of agronomists trained at Mikve Israel or in the colonies themselves. In addition, the children of the colonists returned from local and European farming schools equipped with knowhow and preferences that had an effect on agricultural life in the colonies.[39] The number of trained farmers varied from year to year and from one colony to the next, but their importance was overwhelming by the end of the decade.

A vital source of manpower in the colonies were the laborers from the surrounding Arab villages. Hiring Arabs was a fact of life for the early pioneers, although their employment was to become a major bone of contention in the twentieth century. In their dependence on local workers, the colonists of Eretz Israel were no different from their counterparts in other parts of the world. Their approach was to utilize whatever resources were available to them, irrespective of high-minded doctrines such as self-reliance.

With hundreds of Arabs on its payroll, the Rothschild administration appeared to encourage the use of Arab labor. The baron himself felt otherwise judging from remarks about the benefits of hiring Jews that he was heard to make during his visits to the country.[40] Indeed, most of the Arab workers in the 1880s were seasonal laborers taken on during

---

38 Memoirs of Alter Ashkenazi, Yad Ben-Zvi Archives 4/8/10/12; Hirsch, 26 December 1883, AIU Archives in Paris, b322/5; Dugourd's letter to Hirsch, 18 September 1885 (manuscript, French), CZA J41/51, etc.

39 Dozens of references to the children of colonists who studied at Mikve Israel can be found in the AIU Archives in Paris. See, for example, the list of students, f3435/2, dated 17 June 1889, and g9974 (for 1889/90).

40 Rothschild to Hirsch, 19 February 1885, CZA J41/72; Dugourd to Hirsch, 23 December 1883, CZA J41/51; Benschimol, 9 June 1887, CZA J41/49.

harvesting or for specific chores such as weeding and threshing. However, the advantages of cheap temporary labor became clear at the end of the decade when extensive tilling and planting were carried out in all the colonies and the pool of Jewish workers proved insufficient to the task.

This demand for working hands had repercussions outside the colonies and even in other countries. Graduates of the Mikve Israel agricultural school made plans to work in the colonies (rather than leave for the French colonies in North Africa, as was the custom earlier in the decade), workers crossed the border from Lebanon to prepare the land for planting in Rosh Pinna in 1890, and peasants from Arab villages near the colonies, such as Sarafand al Kharab on the outskirts of Rishon le-Zion, flocked to the colonies in droves.[41]

If we evaluate Arab labor not simply as a pool of working hands but as a source of agricultural knowhow and experience, there were two groups of Arabs at opposite ends of the scale. Lowest in influence were the Arab tenant farmers. These were not directly employed by the Rothschild administration, but they cultivated large tracts of land by contract, usually during the first season after a new piece of land was purchased. Most influential were the Arab farming instructors. Such instructors were hired even before Rothschild stepped in, but the trend continued throughout the decade and Arabs were still employed in this capacity at the end of the 1880s.[42]

The Rothschild administration also employed many of the destitute Jewish immigrants who reached the shores of Eretz Israel, and further widened the circle of local manpower by bringing in workers from the urban Jewish community (mainly Safed) and organized groups of young people.[43] The colonists themselves were frequently hired by Rothschild to do various jobs. During the early years, they transported loads or

---

41 Compare Hirsch's report of 26 October 1883, AIU Archives, b322/5, with that of 19 September 1888, ibid, f/1481/4; Grazovsky's letter to Eisenstadt (Barzilai), 18 December 1889, in Druyanow, *Documents*, III, pp. 66–67; ledger of "workers wages" for 1889/90, CZA J15/5957.
42 Oliphant, p. 5 (entry for 12 December 1882); CZA J15/5960, pp. 24, 30; Hada Hu, pp. 221–222.
43 Testimony in Niv, pp. 112–124; Pukhachewsky, Founders, no. 29, p. 15. The Rothschild administration continued to employ laborers from Safed throughout the 1890s.

worked as unskilled construction workers; later, they were taken on as seasonal farm hands or employed in trades they had practiced in Europe. This provided the colonists with an income when they were earning little from their farms, and the administration with a ready source of labor.

In the sphere of farming techniques and work implements, as in manpower and knowhow, the colonies were open to both foreign and local influences. Consequently, the decisions of the upper echelons in France (Rothschild and his advisors) were not always echoed in the actions of the colony administrators and colonists. As the colonization enterprise entered its second decade, we find that the agricultural orientation of the Jewish colonies was not strictly French-European or strictly Mediterranean as some are inclined to believe. Neither was there any clear transition from primitive to modern.[44] Reality was much more complex, involving the use of agricultural techniques and implements from both worlds in a selective manner. Furthermore, a perusal of the sources indicates that all the Jewish colonies were subject to this duality, whether they were sponsored by Rothschild or autonomous.

The plows and plowing methods in the colonies illustrate this point.[45] Even before Rothschild, the settlers used both traditional and modern European implements. We hear of heavy iron plows of French, German, Hungarian, Rumanian and Russian manufacture being drawn by horses, as was customary in Europe, and then being replaced by the more traditional oxen after a few weeks in the fields. This combination of old and new remained in force after Rothschild took control. Although European plows were standard in the colonies throughout the 1880s, the traditional wooden plow was used occasionally, and Rishon le-Zion's blacksmith succeeded in developing a cross between the two in the form of a lightweight iron plow.

Aside from European plows, the colonists employed a variety of simple farming tools produced in Europe such as hoes, mattocks and sickles, and expressed an interest in more complicated machinery. However, genuine mechanization took place only later, when Rothschild's administrators introduced steam-powered harrows, reapers, and threshers. Under the tutelage of the colony agronomists, the colonists

---

44 Giladi, Agronomic, pp. 175–189.
45 Avitsur, Plow. For more details, see Aaronsohn, *Baron*, pp. 249–250 and references.

Agricultural implements in Castina, 1898

learned modern farming technologies, experimented with new crops and raised seedlings in sophisticated nurseries and greenhouses. In one colony, the farmers' sons worked as apprentices in the nursery, gaining practical experience by assisting the agronomist in his duties and theoretical expertise by studying professional literature from France.[46]

European tools and methods of cultivation were most visible in the plantations and vineyards. In their early efforts, the pioneers had imitated the haphazard planting style of their Arab neighbors with total disregard for spacing or crop differentiation. Rothschild's agronomists inaugurated a more rational approach that featured even rows, careful selection and separation of grape varieties, summer plowing, pruning, and disease prevention.[47] They also introduced methods of soil improvement that were new to the region, such as utilizing the organic fertilizer that piled up on the outskirts of the Arab villages and growing intercrops as green manure. By 1890, all the colonies were fertilizing their fields to increase

---

46 Ibid., p. 251.
47 Pukhachewsky, Founders, no. 32, pp. 12–13; Levontin, p. 99; Freiman, I, p. 173, 186–193; Hissin, *Journey*, pp. 105, 138–140.

yields (and income) per dunam and compensate for the shortage of arable land.[48]

The emphasis on European technology varied from branch to branch and may have been connected with the perception of some agricultural pursuits as more being "European" than others. Vineyards and nurseries, for example, were perceived as overwhelmingly European, whereas dry farming was traditional. Some colonies broke with tradition by employing a combination of modern equipment pulled by oxen, but on the whole, the cultivation of wheat was done in the old-fashioned way.

Water supply, with its indirect bearing on agriculture and cardinal importance to colonists in all parts of the Mediterranean basin, was relatively modern in the Jewish colonies. Drills and steam pumps were imported from France, the wells beside the wineries in Rishon le-Zion and Zikhron Ya'akov were equipped with twelve-horsepower engines, and in some of the colonies, water flowed through metal pipes. Yet amid all this technological progress, old-fashioned waterwheels, animal-drawn buckets and pulleys, and windlasses were still very much a part of the landscape.[49] Water management was thus another dimension in which local and foreign elements existed side by side.

Land, the most basic of all agricultural resources, was more than a means of production. It was the root of conflict with the neighboring Arabs, a means for exercising control over the colonists (by the government, Rothschild and Hovevei Zion), a pretext for expansion rather than intensive development, and a source of loan collateral. Valuable historical insights can be gained from the manner in which land was classified, measured, parcelled out and registered, or from such phenomena as the concentration of land holdings in the hands of wealthy local Arabs, which had important ramifications for the colonization enterprise.[50]

In the colonies, where arable land was scarce, the success of a farm depended on high yields from a relatively small parcel of land. When the colonists grew wheat as their major crop, most farms were no larger

---

48   Raab, p. 127; Ariel, p. 42; Hissin, *Journey*, pp. 36, 172, 189, 235; Barzilai, *Beit Halevi*, p. 36.
49   Dugourd, 12 March 1884, CZA J41/51; "From the Land," *Ha-zvi* 2, no. 24 (1886).
50   Ben-Artzi, *Jewish*, pp. 99–100. For a detailed case-study see Kark.

than 80–150 dunams. They soon found, however, that they could not support themselves unless they cultivated at least 200–300 dunams. In the mid-eighties, the colonists began to consider other alternatives, preferably crops that produced enough to support a family on 20–50 dunams. Crops that were not negatively influenced by sandy or rocky soil and could be grown without subdividing the land into many small strips were also advantageous.[51]

When Rothschild set out to establish plantations as a major economic branch in the Jewish colonies, the size of the farms was an important consideration. His plans could not be implemented without radically changing the layout of the agricultural sector. Among the necessary steps was repossessing the land that had been apportioned to the colonists, redividing it, and marking out tracts for plantation. Before redistributing the land among the individual farmers, the administration supervised the planting of vines and trees in the designated areas, and hired the colonists as temporary workers to assure them an income and enable them to gain familiarity with the new crops.

As often happens in agrarian reform, social costs were high. Abrogating private property to enable large-scale plantings and relegating the farmers to the status of day laborers sparked fierce antagonism in the colonies. On the other hand, the reform prompted further advances in agricultural technology. The colonists formed work teams specializing in either dry farming or plantations, agronomists were appointed to head different sectors, and new machines were brought in to improve efficiency.[52] As the use of European technology became increasingly widespread in the early 1890s, the scales tipped once and for all in favor of modernization.

---

51 Precisely how much land was needed was debated frequently in the colonies. For the colonists' point of view, see, for example, Avitsur, Agriculture, p. 231; for the administrators' point of view, see Scheid, pp. 79–80, 158–159.

52 On the agricultural experts, see ibid., loc. cit.; on locomobile and horse-driven plows, (manège), see Pukhachewsky, Founders, no. 44, pp. 12–13.

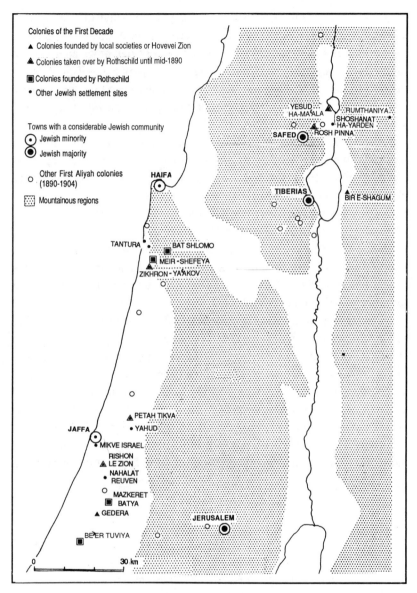

Map 13: Jewish settlement in Eretz Israel, 1882–1890
Sources: Data in this volume; Aaronsohn, Building, p. 83; Ben-Arieh, Settlement, pp. 83–143

Conclusion: Agriculture and Other Economic Factors

In the Jewish colonies as a whole, over fifty percent of the land was under cultivation in 1890. Wheat was the largest crop, accounting for 25,000 of the 40,000 dunams of farmed land. There were also 10,000 dunams of vineyards and nearly 3,000 dunams of fruit-bearing trees such as almonds and olives. Most of these lands, including the vegetable gardens, plant nurseries and experimental fields that made up the remaining percentage, were cultivated using the newest tools and techniques.[53]

Baron de Rothschild's contribution to this state of affairs cannot be overstated. The proportion of farmed land in his colonies was close to ninety percent and he was the driving force behind most of the technological progress. His vision of a modern market-based plantation economy to replace the traditional grain crops was nothing short of revolutionary and changed the face of Jewish colonization for years to come. Rothschild was the instigator of agrarian reforms that tapped the country's scarce natural resources (land, water), exploited its wealth of human potential (labor, expertise) and invested heavily in intensive, specialized plantations grown for industrial processing and commercial export. From 1885, the new economy revolved around the cultivation of grapes, later focusing on the French varieties from which fine wines would be produced. After the establishment of the first wineries toward the end of the 1880s, even the Hovevei Zion colonies and the independent farmers found themselves caught up in the frenzy and rushed to plant more vines.

Despite this flurry of activity, viticulture was not the only agricultural branch pursued in the Jewish colonies. Grain farming was still being developed under the encouragement of the Rothschild administration, especially in the newer colonies, and several types of trees, mulberries in particular, were being planted in large numbers. By 1890, there was a visible shift toward industrial crops of various kinds. Alongside the expansion of vineyards and wineries, factories were established to process local produce, among them a silk-spinning and textile mill, a

---

53 Figures based on Gurevich and Gertz, table 30: Jewish crop yields in 1890/91. Compare with Avitsur, Agriculture, pp. 225–226.

perfume refinery, a drying plant for raisins and a factory for jams and jellies.[54]

A question that begs attention is why Rothschild chose viticulture. Why not watermelons, for example, which were more profitable than grapes and brought in twice as much as grain? This crop was well known to the colonists given the fact that the Arabs cultivated thousands, if not tens of thousands of dunams of watermelons in the 1880s. The same could be said for olive trees and livestock. And why not citriculture, which had so many points in its favor? Citrus fruit was an intensive, specialty crop grown for market. It was associated in the minds of the colonists with "progressive" agriculture and the capitalistic sector, and had expanded rapidly since the 1860s, especially around the Jaffa area. By the 1880s, it ranked second among the country's export products.[55]

No definite answers are provided by the literature. Perhaps Rothschild was wary of the high initial outlay involved in cultivating citrus. Given the low rainfall and rapid evaporation rate, citrus groves required constant irrigation, a network of wells and pumps, and regular tilling of the soil. Above all, citriculture demanded large parcels of land with a high groundwater level, which involved a great expense and were hard to find. Other possible deterrents may have been the Templers' unsuccessful orange-growing scheme in Haifa (as opposed to their success in viticulture) and the problems in overseas shipping faced by Mikve Israel in the mid-eighties.[56] Personal factors seem to have been involved, too. The experience amassed by Rothschild and his agronomists in the vineyards of southern France and Algeria no doubt created a subjective preference for the crop they knew best.

---

54 Avitsur, *Daily Life*, pp. 342–344; Herschberg, *Way*, pp. 75–94, 116; Schama, pp. 108–110. All these factories had been planned in the 1880s. Other proposals such as the manufacture of candy from apricots and dyes from peaches, were never implemented.

55 See Avitsur, Watermelons; ibid., *Jaffa Port*, Charts 8 and 13; citriculture surveys on 26 December 1883 and 23 March 1884, AIU Archives, Paris, b322/5, b721/9.

56 Hirsch, 5 January 1884, 26 March 1884, AIU Archives, b721/9, c3295/7; Brill, p. 194. Contemporary sources reveal that a dunam of land for citrus groves was three times as expensive as the same amount of land for vineyards. Citrus also required an initial outlay that was four times higher than other plantations, and the yearly investment until the first harvest was six to seven times higher.

An important point to bear in mind is that farming, in spite of the obvious strides in this sector, provided only a small fraction of the colonists' income. The inhabitants of the Jewish colonies depended first and foremost on Baron de Rothschild, who invested some six to ten million francs in their personal and collective betterment by 1890 (compared with a quarter of a million francs from Hovevei Zion).[57] The steady cash flow from Rothschild amounted to thousands of francs per month, not to mention the enormous sums budgeted for major projects that boosted the economy of the entire region, such as the Rishon le-Zion winery in which he invested half a million francs in less than a year.[58]

The farmers received monthly stipends based on family size that covered living expenses, animal fodder, and the upkeep of vineyards, especially wages paid for hired labor. Special sums were distributed at holiday time, on the birth of a child, and in the event of illness. If a family member worked for the administration or a room in the house was rented to a Rothschild official, payments were even higher.[59] Aside from the money paid to the farmers as individuals, Rothschild laid out the funds for community expenses such as construction, public works, cultivation supervised directly by the administration (experimental fields, nurseries, plantations on communal land), and general expenses such as salaries of officials, operation of communal services, taxes and land purchase.

Revenue from agriculture, which was minimal in any case, was literally eclipsed by the baron's financial support. Gross income from wheat amounted to eight francs per dunam, and net income to no more than four or five. Colony records indicate that dry farming profits totalled 350-850 francs per annum (depending on farm size and other independent variables), which worked out to an average of 630 francs per annum, or 52.5 francs per month.[60]

---

57 Hacohen, Land, p. 13; Ever-Hadani, PICA, I, p. 168.
58 Receipt book for Rosh Pinna, J15/6355; AIU Archives 2510/13–13, 2 January 1887; Hissin, *Journey*, pp. 147–146.
59 Bachelors received a monthly stipend of thirty francs, a married couple — thirty-six francs, a family of three — forty-two francs, a family of four — forty-eight francs, and each additional family member — twelve francs (Hissin, *Journey*, p. 314). Also see table 15.
60 Figures in Barzilai, *Beit Halevi*, pp. 31, 37, 38–39. See table 17. For recorded income

The wineries of Zikhron Ya'akov, c. 1895

Grapes, subsidized by Rothschild and sold to the wineries at a fixed rate of 23 francs per kantar (288 kilograms), brought in three times that amount — 28 francs per dunam, or as much as 840–1,400 francs per annum and an average of 93 francs per month.[61]

Yet these sums were a drop in the ocean compared to the amount of aid received directly from Rothschild, regardless of individual productivity. Unfortunately, dependence on outside assistance weakened the colonists as a group and decreased their motivation. The work ethic in the colonies suffered because virtually all the services were operated and paid for by the baron. Although a system was devised to assure that the colonists

---

from wheat, see ibid., p. 31; Meerovitch, Castina, p. 6; Hissin, *Journey*, p. 149; survey of Rothschild administration in Zikhron Ya'akov, 1900, in Ever-Hadani, *Vinegrowers*, p. 46.

61 Figures based on Hissin, *Journey*, pp. 146–147. In the 1890s, Rothschild continued to subsidize the farmers' grapes but prices were adjusted according to variety.

paid their share of community expenses — the administration kept an account of their debts and annual yields — they bore little communal or personal responsibility for the economic future of the colony.

On the other hand, the stipends received by the colonists were important from a socio-psychological point of view. The steady income helped them through the uncertainty of the early years and enabled them to withstand the rigors of pioneer life. Furthermore, the massive injection of capital into the productive and industrial sectors during the second half of the 1880s created the foundations for continued economic development in the 1890s. Translated into financial assets, this capital investment made it possible for the colonists to free themselves from Rothschild in the early twentieth century and operate the public service infrastructure independently.[62]

The Rothschild administration served as a conduit through which the baron transferred funds to the colonists for public and private use, but it was also a decisionmaking body with definite ideas about how to best expend these funds. Just as it shaped the appearance of the residential sector, it was instrumental in giving form to the agricultural sector and producing a distinctive blend of town and farm that stood out as a lush and verdant entity in the local landscape. Visitors were impressed by the stately avenues of trees, the neat flower gardens and vegetable patches around the homes, the plant nurseries and experimental fields geometrically intersected by irrigation ditches, and the large, contiguous tracts of land planted with vines and fruit trees, all carefully spaced in the "European" mode. Finally, the Rothschild administration was responsible for introducing an element conspicuously absent from the Palestinian landscape in the nineteenth century — which was shade. Thanks to the leafy plantations, gardens and trees of the Jewish colonies, the parched and barren land of Eretz Israel described in contemporary literature was changed beyond recognition.

---

62 On the sense of security generated by Rothschild's support, see Hacohen, Land, p. 13. The Rothschild administration also provided the colonists with alternate means of earning a livelihood, by hiring them as day laborers (see Hissin, Journey, pp. 268, 327, 332, 335, etc.) and in other capacities (ibid., pp. 83, 85, 118, 134, etc.).

CHAPTER TEN

SOCIETY AND CULTURE

The social and cultural landscape of the modern Jewish colonies in Eretz Israel was highly attuned to developments in the physical and agricultural sectors and vice versa. Economic needs, for example, increased along with the population, and farms were successful or not depending on the composition of the labor force. Similarly, the imposing synagogue and school buildings were physical evidence of the the primacy of religion and the emergence of a modern educational system.

Demography and Social Structure

Our ability to provide accurate population figures for the Jewish colonies in the 1880s is severely hampered both by the absence of reliable censuses in the Ottoman Empire during the nineteenth century and by the diversity of the estimates that appear in contemporary sources. With the colonies in a general state of flux as groups of pioneers and laborers moved from place to place, population turnover in the rural sector was extremely rapid, even in the smallest outposts and over very brief periods of time. The problem was exacerbated by the immigrant make-up of the population, and the fact that the colonies were still in an early stage of development.[1] In consequence, the emphasis will be on demographic features and patterns rather than on figures.

---

[1] Even a contemporary source commented that "it is impossible to determine absolutely who is a permanent resident and who is temporary" (Hissin, *Journey*, p. 132). In one case, three different population totals were reported for the same colony within the span of two months.

Table 4
Population of Jewish colonies circa 1890

Source	Klein, 1899		Luncz, 1891		Barzilai, 1890–91 (in Gurevitz and Gertz)			
Colony	Families	Persons	Families	Persons	Farmers	Laborers	Others	Total
Petah Tikva	69	412	94	446	250	20	217	487
Yahud	12	50	—	—	—	—	—	—
Rishon le-Zion	35	90	59	226	219	60	80	359
Ness Ziona[1]	11	30	12	—	54	39	13	106
Mazkeret Batya	18	185	18	200	167	—	48	215
Gedera	15	87	13	—	37	6	12	55
Zikhron Ya'akov	86	515	80	400	—	—	—	570
Daughter-colonies			30	—	—	—	—	
Rosh Pinna	32	178	54	300	—	—	—	500
Yesud ha-Ma'ala	15	65	14	—	69	15	39	123
Be'er Tuviya	5	50	—	—	—	5	35	40
Bnei Yehuda	—	—	—	—	—	—	—	—
Mikve Israel	—	—	—	about 60[2]	76	49[2]	5	130
Total	298	1,662	374	(2,037)[3]	—	—	—	2,585

Sources: Klein, p. 35; Hissin, *Journey,* throughout work; Luncz, *Guide*; Gurevich and Gertz, Table 30.

1 Called in the source by its initial name: Nahalat Reuven.
2 Students of the agricultural school.
3 Total includes estimates for colonies with partial figures.

The population of the colonies was basically divisible into three classes: enfranchised "citizens," permanent residents and temporary workers. The citizens were landowners who constituted the core of the colony. They were the policymakers, entitled to vote for and be elected to various committees and associations.[2] Most were farmers, but there were also craftsmen and civil servants who had gained sufferage after having completed a set period of residence in the colonies and having aquired some land. In the second category were the landless permanent residents who had no voting rights, such as craftsmen living in rented quarters and civil servants dwelling in public buildings. The permanent residents of the Rothschild colonies were nearly all employees of the baron.[3] In the lowest class were Jewish and Arab laborers who were perceived as temporary residents although many remained in the colonies throughout their lifetimes.[4] In the 1890s and possibly earlier, certain Arab families were reported living on the land of the farmers who employed them, but they were not accounted for in population surveys and their social status is unclear.

From the demographic data at our disposal, families in the colonies averaged about 5.3 persons per household. However, this varied considerably in different colonies and social groupings. In one colony of seventeen farmers, all married, the average family size was closer to ten, and in another, where four of the sixteen farmers were bachelors, the average was less than three.[5] Households of ten or more persons were not at all unusual. Often, several related families lived together — parents, grown children, their spouses and offspring, in-laws, and sometimes even grandparents — forming a *hamula* or extended family. The original core of settlers remained relatively stable throughout the 1880s and 1890s. Hence the population growth evident in most of the

---

[2] On the permanent residents and their rights in society, see Giladi, Citizens, p. 148.
[3] Thirty-two officials were counted in Rishon le-Zion in 1891, "not including their apprentices and servants, and those who supervised the laborers." In another colony, sixteen of the thirty-three family heads were "residents" in the hire of the baron — twelve officials and four craftsmen. See Barzilai, *Beit Halevi,* pp. 21, 32.
[4] On the Jewish workers who lived in the colonies for eight years or more, see Barzilai, *Beit Halevei,* no. 1.
[5] Figures based on Barzilai, *Beit Halevi,* pp. 19–21, 30–31.

colonies was largely dependent on natural increase, which was slow but steady, and the surplus of new members over departures.[6]

Table 5

**Demographic development of Petah Tikva
1882–1890**

Year[1]	Arrived	Left	Immi-gration Balance	Births	Deaths	Natural Increase	Total
1882	66	—	—	—	—	—	66
1883	130	—	+130	—	1	− 1	195
1884	95	5	+ 90	3	3	0	285
1885[2]	91	20	+ 71	3	4	− 1	352[2]
1886	39	19	+ 58	8	4	+ 4	376
1887	41	14	+ 27	10	4	+ 6	409
1888	66	17	+ 49	14	6	+ 8	466
1889	39	36	+ 3	19	7	+12	481
1890	40	25	+ 15	25	11	+13	503

Source: Herschberg, *Way*, p. 134.

1 The original years at the Hebrew source aims at the Jewish calander, which does not overlap exactly the Julian calander (e.g., the year 5642, which appears here as 1882, is actually Sep. 1881 to Sep. 1882).

2 The figures for 1885 are quoted directly from the source, despite the miscaculation in it.

---

6   More on demographic development in Aaronsohn, Cultural, pp. 148–153.

Table 6
Mortality rates in Rosh Pinna, 1883–1890

Category[1] Year[2]	New Borns	Babies M	Babies F	Children M	Children F	Adults M	Adults F	Elderly M	Elderly F	Total
1883	1	2	1	—	2	—	1	1	—	8
1884	1	—	—	—	3	—	—	—	—	4
1885	1	1	1	—	—	1	—	—	1	5
1886	—	—	—	1	—	—	—	1	1	3
1887	2	—	3	—	—	—	—	1	—	6
1888	1	1	3	—	—	1	—	—	1	7
1889	5	3	6	1	3	—	1	—	—	19
1890	5	1	4	3	1	—	—	—	—	14
Total	16	8	18	5	9	2	2	3	3	66
		26		14		4		6		
%	24.2	39.4		21.2		6.1		9.1		100

Source: Adopted from CZA A25/9 ("List of deceased in the colony of Rosh Pinna...," pp. 231–233).

1   Newborns — up to one month old; babies — one month to a year; children — ages 1 to 15 years; adults — ages 15 to 59 years; elderly — ages 60 years and over (the distinction between adults and elderly was added here; the other categories appear in the original).
2   See note 1 table 5 about the years.

The social cohesion and sense of community vital in all settlement ventures, especially in the rural sector, was even more essential in Eretz Israel. Many of the difficulties encountered by the farmers could only be resolved by cooperative effort, thereby prodding them into alliances that were initially voluntary. In time, however, group affiliation became mandatory and the decisions of the community obligated all its members. Many different societies were founded and social activity, both organized and spontaneous, gave shape and form to communal life. Responsibility for organized social programs was in the hands of settlement committees, societies that were ever-present in the colonies, and ad hoc committees to meet specific needs. In certain cases, the settlement committee was disbanded after the colony became a holding of the Rothschild estate. However, this did not prevent bodies of a similar nature from emerging later with the full support of the administration. Thus at the end of the century both the Rothschild and Hovevei Zion colonies provided fertile ground for organized social activity, despite the absence of a general organization empowered to represent the comprehensive interests of all the colonists.[7]

The various societies established in the 1880s were specialized associations, each assigned to a specific task or the welfare of a given

A local committee, Rishon le-Zion, 1897

---

7   Ibid., pp. 161–162. For examples of comprehensive social organizations, see Aaronsohn, *Baron*, pp. 262–272.

sector of the community. The literature mentions as many as seventeen during the period in question, all located in the Rothschild colonies. Some were traditional organizations of the type common throughout Jewish communities world-wide. At least eight societies of this kind, devoted to religious study, guest accommodation, care of the sick, and burials, etc. were active in the colonies during the first decade.[8] In addition, there were ad hoc alliances such as the group of Zikhron Ya'akov farmers who banded together in 1889 to redistribute the land as specified by Rothschild in his plan for agrarian reform, and the committee responsible for sanitation in Rishon le-Zion.[9]

Another type of social organization made an appearance in the colonies as modern ideals such as self-help and social action gained currency. For example, societies of watchmen were set up by colonists who stood guard in rotation, and labor unions were organized to promote the welfare of local workers through vocational training, job referrals, and mediation between workers and employers. The unions also furnished a socio-cultural framework for the laborers, and brought them together for evenings of music and song.[10]

Among the societies fired by a social cause were the nationalist Hebrew language and land purchase associations. In 1888, a group of Rishon le-Zion farmers established a society to promote the use of Hebrew in the colonies, and a Jerusalem association of Hebrew speakers, *Safa Brura*, opened a branch in Rosh Pinna in 1890.[11] In the summer of 1889, the *Keren Kayemet* society was founded in Rishon le-Zion to purchase land in bulk and expand Jewish colonization by private means. The founders included teachers in the hire of the Rothschild administration as well as laborers and independent farmers. As a non-regional association, its

---

8   See reports in contemporary newspapers, for example "A Pleasant Sight," *Ha-havazzelet* 18 (1888), no. 17, pp. 132–133; "May Lying Lips be Sealed," *Ha-melitz* 28 (1888), no. 113, pp. 1195–1196; Bronstein, p. 2. Also see primary sources such as burial society and hospitality society record books in Zikhron Ya'akov archives, pp. 1–13 and pp. 3–6 respectively.
9   Hissin, *Journey*, p. 100 (Rishon le-Zion) and p. 313 (Zikhron Ya'akov).
10 Aaronsohn, *Baron*, pp. 271–272.
11 Ben-Arieh, *Ha-zefirah* 17 (1890) (pertaining to Rosh Pinna); Ben-Yehuda, *Ha-zvi* 4 (1888), no. 19, (pertaining to Rishon le-Zion). The introduction of Hebrew in the schools was probably the incentive.

headquarters were in Jerusalem and new members were recruited with some success among the "enlightened inhabitants of Jerusalem and Jews from overseas." Four years were spent in raising funds and increasing membership, but no land was ever purchased and the group eventually disbanded.[12] Nevertheless, the idea caught on, and other *Keren Kayemet* societies were established, first in Jaffa, and then the association known worldwide as the Jewish National Fund (JNF), established by the Zionist Organization in 1903 and still active today.

Education

At the end of the 1880s, education in the colonies was a mix of traditional and modern. Traditional religious schooling of the heder and talmud torah variety was available for boys only, under the tutelage of instructors brought in from the urban sector. The classes, conducted in Yiddish, were similar in spirit and format to the Jewish schooling common in Eastern Europe and the established orthodox Jewish community in Eretz Israel. This was the framework introduced in the colonies during the early days of settlement, but as Rothschild became increasingly influential, the seeds of a modern educational network were also sown. The new schools founded by the Rothschild administration were staffed with qualified teachers and supervised by principals and inspectors. They also differed from the traditional schools in that they offered a broader curriculum, accepted girls and operated in more attractive physical surroundings. At the end of the decade, the children studied in large, airy classrooms with benches, blackboards, maps, nature charts and even a podium for the teacher. Uniforms were worn, and the pupils were well-supplied with notebooks, textbooks, pens and inkwells. The same teachers taught both boys and girls, but in separate classes (some sources refer to the girl's classes as "schools" in their own right). Sometimes a special teacher was employed to teach

---

12 "Founders of the Keren Ha-kayemet," Druyanow, *Documents*, III, p. 55; undated letters of Idelovitch and Grazovsky, ibid., p. 56, n. 1. On the society charter, see ibid., pp. 56–57, and Idelovitch, pp. 509–510; also see remnants of documents, including a receipt book from 1889, in CZA A192/193.

School gymnastics in Rishon le-Zion, 1897

the girls handicrafts or vocational subjects. The typical girls' classroom was reportedly spacious and pretty with a sewing machine in the corner.[13]

The curricular changes were perhaps the most important of all. In addition to religious studies (and languages, which had been introduced earlier), the Rothschild schools offered academic subjects such as geography, history, arithmetic and science, and enrichment such as handicrafts, singing and gymnastics. The girls were taught weaving and sewing, and even the boys learned various crafts.[14] Textbooks and bound notebooks were imported from France, and teachers followed a pre-planned course of studies developed for ages 6-13 that became standard in all the Rothschild schools at the end of the decade.[15]

13 Descriptions of various colony schools in the memoirs of Yoel Freiman, CZA A192/139; Neiman, p. 57; Hada Hu, p. 221; *Ha-melitz* 27 (1887), no. 115.
14 On geography and history studies, see, for example, Jawitz, *Dew*, pp. 4, 91; Schub, *Memories*, p. 119. On vocational subjects, Kantor, Through; Hada Hu, p. 200; *Ha-melitz* 27, (1887), no. 115, p. 220; Hissin, *Journey*; p. 128.
15 On the bound notebooks sent from France, see Neiman, p. 57; on the grammar,

Other innovations were the revival of certain Biblical celebrations and the scheduling of regular nature hikes. Bearing in mind that the children were the sons and daughters of colonists, emphasis was laid on physical fitness, the return to the soil and forging ties with the Holy Land. The study of geography was combined with expeditions and outdoor learning, and many hours were devoted to biology. For the first time, the majority of the subjects were taught in Hebrew, possibly beginning with arithmetic. From 1888, Hebrew language classes shifted to the "immersion" method rather than translation into Yiddish (which was still the colloquial language in the colonies).[16] Although the teachers were not accustomed to using Hebrew as a spoken language and there were no Hebrew textbooks, the principles of teaching in Hebrew were gradually formulated and discussed at pedagogic conferences convened in Rishon le-Zion in the early 1890s.

The elements introduced by Rothschild totally revolutionized the educational system in the colonies. Apart from introducing modernity to a society of immigrants turned farmers, they sparked the beginnings of nationalist education that germinated in the coming years.[17] Of course, the schools were not without their share of problems. The reliance on teachers steeped in French culture came in for much criticism on nationalist grounds. There were accusations that a takeover by French culture and civilization was being staged through the schools, and that the girls sent to teachers' seminaries in Paris were part of a plot. The Rothschild administration was criticized for "the sin of contaminating the children's souls and teaching them the customs of France...neither

---

history and geography books sent to Rosh Pinna from Frankfurt via Paris in 1886, see Schub, *Memories*, p. 119; on the curriculum, see Jawitz, *Dew*, pp. 89–92.

16 See various sources cited in Kimhi, pp. 59, 151; also see Walk, p. 420.

17 Walk's study on the emergence of national education in the colonies cites three consecutive stages of development: the inauguration of secular and Hebrew language studies, the use of Hebrew as the language of instruction and the adoption of Sephardi pronunciation, and the fostering of ties to the land and agricultural training. Walk centers his discussion on the 1890s and early twentieth century. Our sources indicate that each of these developments was introduced in the school system in the 1880s, and furthermore, not in stages but simultaneously.

the teachings of our sacred Torah nor the Hebrew language are visible in the schools..."[18]

This was not entirely true. French was indeed taught as a first foreign language in all Rothschild schools, but the study of Hebrew was one of the network's declared educational goals. The baron stated as much when he visited the country on various occasions, and his administrators received clear instructions in this regard.[19] In fact, all the noted teachers of Hebrew were brought to the colonies and their salaries paid for by the Rothschild administration.

Hebrew classes and the use of Hebrew as the language of instruction in Jewish studies had an immediate impact on the young people. Even the adults, most of whom were literate in Hebrew as a sacred tongue, began to be conversant in the language and to speak it on a daily basis.[20] Rothschild's support of the Hebrew language was also evident in his willingness to finance the publication of Hebrew textbooks. The lack of material in Hebrew was felt as soon as the schools began teaching in that language in 1888–1889. The first Hebrew text was written by two teachers working for the Rothschild administration. Other texts were compiled and published with the aid of the baron in the 1890s.[21] In a similar fashion, Rothschild assisted Eliezer Ben-Yehuda, the father of modern Hebrew, to compile and publish his famous dictionary and operate a library in Jerusalem at the end of the 1880s (Rothschild apparently paid the librarian's salary and/or the rent). From 1887, Rothschild supplied

---

18   The remark about the French-mannered farmers' daughters, often taunted as "princesses," in Kostitsky, pp. 47–48; criticism of the French orientation of the schools in Rokeah, Matters, p. 98. The academic level of the schools and the pedagogic abilities of the teachers were also criticized.
19   Jawitz's letter in Eliav, First Aliyah, II, pp. 205–207; Rabinowitz, Review, p. 203; Ben-Yehuda's report in Druyanow, Documents, II, p. 227.
20   Hissin, Journey, p. 129; Lubman's letter to Lilienblum in Druyanow, Documents, II, p. 621; Ha-melitz 29 (1889), no. 185, p. 2.
21   See dedication in honor of the bar-mitzvah of Armand de Rothschild's son, Benjamin, on inside cover of Grazovsky's book Beit ha-Sefer le-Bnei Yisrael, Jerusalem 1891. Also see bibliography appended to Ofek, pp. 113–116, which shows that twenty-nine of the fifty-three children's books published in Eretz Israel before 1900 were written by teachers employed by the Rothschild administration.

Ben-Yehuda with regular funding for his Hebrew newspaper, *Ha-zvi*, for which the later was often ridiculed by his journalistic colleagues.[22]

Under Rothschild, the educational network in the colonies was expanded to include evening lectures for the benefit of the laborers and kindergartens for the young children. In preparation for the opening of the first kindergarten, a teacher was selected and sent to Paris to specialize in modern preschool education. It is noteworthy that these innovations took place in the Rothschild colonies, whereas heder and talmud torah remained the only educational options in the settlements supported by Hovevei Zion. Even in the Rothschild colonies, however, the rise of the new schools did not mark the disappearance of the traditional frameworks. In 1890, old and new operated side by side. Yet the building blocks of a progressive system were now firmly in place and capable of supporting the modern educational structure that was to be built upon them.[23]

Religion and Culture

At the heart of cultural life in the agricultural colonies of the 1880s was Judaism and the Jewish way of life. This may sound like a sweeping generalization, but it was true of all the colonies existent at the time, even Rishon le-Zion and Gedera with their non-religious minorities. The only social groups in the colonies that were admittedly non-observant were the *maskilim* (enlightened Jews) in Rishon le-Zion and the Biluim in Gedera, and perhaps a small number of farmers, laborers and Rothschild employees. All the others were strictly Orthodox, and the cultural activity in the colonies was very much colored by this.

Rothschild's national and regional supervisors were not religious men, but they followed his lead in scrupulously respecting the Orthodox

---

22 Ben-Yehuda's letter in Druyanow, *Documents*, II, p. 113; on payment (monthly?) of two hundred francs and an additional grant of fifty francs to Ben-Yehuda see Erlanger's letter to Hirsch, 26 May 1887, CZA J41/46. On the library in Jerusalem, see Y. Ben-Arieh, *Jerusalem in the Nineteenth Century — The New City*, Jerusalem 1986, pp. 418–419.

23 Further details in Aaronsohn, *Baron*, pp. 278–279. Also see ibid., on the issue of education in general and Rothschild's contribution in particular.

lifestyle of the majority of the inhabitants.[24] The centrality of religion in the 1880s was clearly demonstrated by the men's conscientious attendance of morning, noon and evening prayers, their study of religious texts every day during the agricultural slack seasons,[25] and the joyous celebrations that accompanied the completion of the study of a portion of the *Mishna* (traditional collection of oral religious laws) or the dedication of a new Torah scroll. The latter was marked by a public procession to the synagogue in wagons and on horseback, with musicians playing and shots fired in the air. Afterwards, the community met for a festive banquet, public singing and speeches.[26] Colonists who tried to break out of this mold were sharply criticized in the Jewish community.

Even agriculture and economy were dictated by religion. Work in the fields was halted every seven years in keeping with the laws of shemitta (sabbatical year). Grapes were sold commercially only after the third year in observance of *orlah* (fruit in first years of planting), and special religious inspectors were employed in the vineyards and wineries to guard against *nesekh* (libation wine) which was forbidden to Jews. The laws of *kila'yim* (cross-breeding) restricted the planting of intercrops in the fields and orchards, and the pairing of different kinds of animals, such as oxen and donkeys, in a team. Large portions of the harvest were set aside as *terumah* and *ma'aser* (tithes on produce). For the pioneers, observing these commandments was not a hardship but a fact of life. Moreover, many of them had settled in the Holy Land and gone into farming precisely because they sought an opportunity to fulfil the religious laws associated with agriculture. On the whole, the rabbis were able to find ways of facilitating their observance and minimizing the detriment to the farmers.[27]

---

24 Kaniel, p. 122. Rothschild issued strict orders in 1885 regarding Sabbath observance in Zikhron Ya'akov. Violaters were threatened with expulsion.
25 Mordechai Hacohen, *Ha-melitz* 30 (1890), no. 22; Neiman, p. 70.
26 Ibid.; Bar-Mazla, *Ha-melitz* 27 (1887), no. 129; Belkind, ibid., no. 123; Bronstein, p. 1.
27 Salmon, Confrontation, pp. 43–77; Kaniel, pp. 123–127, 129–132. For references on the subject of shemitta, see ibid., p. 129, n. 1. For primary sources on religion and agriculture, see Aaronsohn, *Baron*, p. 281, n. 21.

Synagogue and the agronomist's house, Zikhron Ya'akov c. 1899

Religion in the colonies had a visible side, too. It affected the appearance of the farmers and buildings, and the rhythm of life as a whole. Most of the colonists had curled earlocks and dressed in traditional Eastern European garb — long black coats and ritual fringes. *Mezuzot* (parchment scroll affixed to the door post) were attached to all the doors, and one of the first buildings erected in each colony was a ritual bath. No work was done on the Sabbath and holidays, and the religious festivals were marked by special ceremonies. The synagogues were a center of community life and the imposing buildings that eventually housed them were the gathering place for a variety of social and cultural functions, among them committee meetings, religious study, receptions and parties.[28] The synagogue premises usually incorporated a school, and the rabbi also functioned as a teacher.

Just as religion was virtually inseparable from education and social life in the colonies of the 1880s, it is difficult to speak of secular culture as a separate category. Elements such as Hebrew and nature walks were as much a part of education as of culture, and the fundamental differences voiced by the colonists were just as strong in the cultural

---

28 Oral testimony of Amihud Schwartz, Rosh Pinna, and Zerubavel Haviv-Lubman, Rishon le-Zion.

arena as in the educational and religious spheres. Those who aspired toward a high level of culture, in which work and a vibrant intellectual life flourished side by side, were pitted against those who yearned for a simple farmers' life devoid of "nightly debates over liberty, wellbeing and other such principles that keep [us] from working during the day."[29] While members of the latter group were satisfied with religion as a solution to their cultural needs, others worked throughout the decade to create a cultural milieu outside the religious realm, usually enjoying the support of the Rothschild administration unless they encroached upon its authority or disregarded its basic tenets.

Modern, non-religious culture eventually gained a foothold even in the most Orthodox colonies. The administrative headquarters in Paris received complaints about parties featuring music, singing and even mixed dancing, and a wedding where the colonists danced to the music of a band.[30] While most of the social events had some connection to religion and the celebration of Jewish holidays or life cycle events usually followed a time-honored format familiar to Jewish communities all over the world, a distinctive note was often added that made the festivities unique.

In addition, two holidays unknown in the Diaspora were introduced in the 1880s: *Tu Bishvat* (the "New Year of the Trees"), which was marked by tree-planting ceremonies conducted by the schools, and a twelve-day autumn harvest festival celebrated with feasting, song and dance.[31] Both were manifestations of the pioneers' renewed ties with the land and agriculture on the one hand, and the revival of Jewish nationalism, on the other. Furthermore, each colony observed a special holiday of its own, usually on the anniversary of its establishment. On that day, guests were invited from out of town, children were off from school, and the colonists paraded through the streets, singing and dancing. Rishon le-Zion's third anniversary was celebrated with a community banquet, speeches, fireworks, salvoes of gunfire, and a bonfire. For the first time, a blue and white flag emblazoned with the Star of David was flown at

---

29 Hissin, *Journey*, pp. 91–92.
30 On music, dancing, song-writing and literary activity, see Aaronsohn, *Baron*, p. 282.
31 Jawitz, Education, p. 59; Neiman, p. 117. Another celebration that may have been revived at this time was *Tu Be'av* (the holiday of love).

the head of the procession as a nationalist symbol.[32] Zikhron Ya'akov's annual holiday coincided with *Lag Ba'omer* (a traditional feast day), the day of Rothschild's visit to the colony in 1887. In 1889, the celebrations included a public prayer service and a banner-waving procession of marchers and horsemen.[33]

Rothschild's tour of the colonies in 1887 was the incentive for a particularly dazzling round of receptions and ceremonies. Aside from determining the economic future of the colonies, his visit was perceived as a social occasion in its own right. For ten days, the colonists feted him with assemblies, speeches, music and song, parades, torch-bearers, flags and fireworks. As Rothschild and his entourage left one colony, he was escorted to the next by members of the previous colony. The festivities in Rothschild's honor were attended by invited Jewish and Arab guests, as well as representatives of the Turkish government.[34]

Other visiting dignitaries were welcomed with receptions on a more modest scale; for example, delegates of the Ottoman government who frequently stopped by the colonies, and the Pasha, whose visit at the end of 1889 was marked by a dinner and an evening of community singing.[35] Cornerstone-layings and dedications of public buildings were another reason for festive gatherings. Even grander were the ground-breaking ceremonies for new colonies. At least three took place in the 1880s, one of them attended by 150 persons.[36] Such events were held as soon as the establishment of a colony was decided upon, even before the commencement of building. The program consisted of a mass procession to the site, choral and community singing, speeches and a banquet in the presence of distinguished local and foreign guests.

The colonists also participated in spontaneous celebrations. Some

---

32 Report in *Ha-melitz* 25 (1885), no. 63, and Belkind's letter, 2 September 1885, in Druyanow, *First Days*, I, pp. 40–41; Hissin, *Ha-melitz* 26 (1886), no. 2.
33 Hissin, *Journey*, pp. 313, 342; Samsonov, p. 181.
34 Neiman, p. 92; Samsonov, pp. 140–144; Pukhachewsky, Founders, nos. 28–29.
35 Kantor, Through. On the official visits to the Judean colonies of the governors of Jerusalem, see, for example, *Ha-zvi* 4, no. 31 (29 February 1888); 5, no. 6 (9 August 1889).
36 Samsonov, pp. 180–181; Nephesh, *Ha-melitz* 30 (1890), no. 72; M. Taubenhaus, *Ha-melitz* 30 (1890), no. 115, p. 480 and continuation in nos. 116, 117; Hissin, *Journey*, pp. 409–411.

were of a religious nature, such as those honoring a new Torah scroll or completion of the study of a tractate of the Mishna; others were family events such as circumcisions, engagements and weddings. These parties were organized along similar lines and were usually joined by residents of other colonies. Somewhat more unusual was the impromptu rejoicing that accompanied the harvesting of Rishon le-Zion's first grape crop in 1887. As an event directly related to the return to the soil, the celebrants — independent farmers, agronomists and Rothschild officials — were acutely aware of its national significance.[37]

The excursions and hikes that were popular among the colonists bolstered this new-found sense of nationalism. Their visits to the neighboring colonies may have been nothing more than courtesy calls, but they helped to strengthen the kinship between them. Trips were also organized to cities throughout the country and various historical sites. We know of a group of thirty colonists from Zikhron Ya'akov who visited the antiquities in Atlit, ten of them on horseback and twenty more riding in two wagons. The settlers of Rishon le-Zion made a custom of visiting Jerusalem or another colony on important holidays. One source provides a detailed account of an excursion to Jerusalem. The thirty colonists rode in three wagons, singing nationalist songs, firing shots in the air, and conversing in Hebrew. Upon reaching the city, they visited the historical sites, attended a play in Hebrew and met with important local figures. Their presence as a large group of Hebrew speakers apparently attracted much attention.[38]

Conclusion: Social and Cultural Landscape in 1890

Within the span of eight years, the Jewish colonies of Eretz Israel enjoyed a rich, constantly evolving social and cultural life. By 1890, 350 families had settled within them, bringing the population to 2,000. It was already possible to distinguish between different groups on the basis

---

37 For discussion and references, see Aaronsohn, *Cultural*, pp. 158–159; Aaronsohn, *Baron*, pp. 283–286.
38 Nephesh in Druyanow, *Documents*, III, pp. 11–12; Hissin, *Journey*, p. 86; idem, *Diary*, p. 81; Kantor, *Basic*, p. 1197.

of socio-economic status (farmers, craftsmen, laborers, officials), length of residence (new immigrants vs. old-timers) and cultural heritage (by country of origin). Less clear at this stage, but gradually taking shape, was the polarity between Orthodox and enlightened Jews. In the 1880s, only two minority groups and a few individuals considered themselves non-religious. The phenomenon was certainly not as widespread in the 1890s, but the stirrings of a new trend were felt as the secular branch of Hovevei Zion increased its activity and a non-religious nationalist culture developed in Eretz Israel.[39]

Each of the components of social life in the colonies — social status, demography, formation of societies, education, religion and culture — was shaped by a synthesis of old and new, local and foreign. In terms of character and size, the farmers' families differed little from traditional households in Eastern Europe. However, the laborers and grown children belonged to subclasses of their own. Another subclass was created by the young bachelors who joined the colonization effort in the 1880s and were especially numerous in the three larger settlements. Members of this group comprised the entire population of two new colonies founded in the course of the decade. Certain blocks of settlements and clusters of pioneers could thus be distinguished in 1890 by demographic composition.

Social activity in the colonies was pursued on two levels. The settlement committees, or in their absence, executive bodies which coordinated the work of several societies, were responsible for comprehensive social planning that involved the entire community; societies devoted to a particular cause sponsored activities on a smaller scale. Committees of the executive type operated sporadically in most of the colonies throughout the decade, but the traditional societies that organized burial, religious study, hospitality, etc. remained the focus of social activity until 1890 and long afterwards.

In the social sphere, the pioneers themselves were the organizers. There was no fundamental difference in this respect between the colonies controlled by Rothschild or Hovevei Zion. Settlement and executive committees were allowed to operate in both types of colonies within

---

[39] Weintraub, pp. 38–48; Friedman, Social, pp. 455–479; Salmon, Confrontation, pp. 43–77.

certain limits. Societies, on the other hand, were basically given free rein.

Other forms of public involvement began to take shape during the decade in response to immediate needs (watchmen societies) and social ideologies connected with Jewish national revival (Hebrew language and land purchase societies). The banding together of modern, enlightened Jews, especially in the Rothschild colonies, commenced in the 1880s and gained momentum in the 1890s. The colonists themselves were the initiators, of course, but the Rothschild administration contributed to this development, first by its silent acquiescence, and secondly by the readiness with which certain Rothschild officials and employees joined in the enlightened nationalist activities.[40]

Education in the colonies was again a juxtaposition of old and new. The influence of the enlightened minority is not easily assessed, although certain members of this group were employed in the schools. On the other hand, there is no mistaking Rothschild's influence in the educational domain. The emergence of a modern school system offering a broad program of academic and vocational subjects, many of them taught in Hebrew, was virtually exclusive to the Rothschild colonies. Yet all this was an outgrowth of the religious heder and talmud torah network that flourished in the early days of the colonization enterprise and remained intact in spite of all the change going on around it. In 1890, these two educational streams — the traditional school found in all the colonies and the progressive school in the Rothschild colonies only — coexisted side by side.

Religion was still at the core of cultural life at the end of the decade and was an inseparable part of daily affairs. Most of the holidays, social gatherings and celebrations were religious, or at least traditional, in character, and constituted a direct extension of the way of life the pioneers had known in their home countries. Nevertheless, culture of a modern, non-religious variety began to evolve in the 1880s. A secular library was established, dancing parties with band music were not uncommon, and traditions that were uniquely fitting for Eretz Israel and the farming colonies came into being, such as agricultural holidays, ground-breaking

---

40 More details in Aaronsohn, *Baron*, pp. 285–287.

ceremonies, excursions to sites of national and historical interest, and singing in Hebrew.

Table 7
Inventory of the Jewish colonies circa 1890

Colony	Area (dunams)	Houses	Stables	Livestock	Vines (units)	Fruit Trees (units)
Petah Tikva	15,078 (b)	42 (b)	27 (b)	384 (b)	350,000 (a)	3,000 (a)
Yahud	160 (a)	11 (a)	2 (a)	108 (a)	2,000 (a)	200 (a)
Rishon le-Zion	7,000 (b)	40 (b)	30 (a,b)	200 app. (b)	800,000 (b)	25,000 (b)
Ness Ziona	1,500 (a)	10 (a)	3–5 (a,c)	42 (a)	60,000 (b)	8,000 (a)
Mazkeret Batya	4,090 (b,c)	18 (a,b)	18 (a)	144 (b)	—	1,500 (a)
Gedera	3,000 (a)	15 (a)	15 (a)	50 (a)	100,000 (b)	2,000 (a)
Zikhron Ya'akov[1]	10,000 app. (a,b)	100+ (b)	86 (a)	288 (a)	100,000 (a,b)	15,000 (a)
Rosh Pinna	5,600 (a)	32 (a)	32 (a)	350 (a)	18,000 (a)	3,000 (a)
Yesud ha-Ma'ala	2,400 (a)	18 (c)	10 (a)	37 (a)	—	100,000 plants (c)
Be'er Tuviya[2]	6,400 (b)	24 (b,c)	5 (c)	10 (a)	—	26,400 Plants (c)

Sources: (a) Klein, unnumbered table on p. 35 — for 1889;
(b) Hissin, *Journey,* passim (and some others) — for Mar.–Apr. 1890;
(c) Barzilai, *Colonies,* passim; Gurevich and Gertz, Table 30 — for 1891.

Note: For additional data and explanations see Aaronsohn, *Jewish Colonies,* I, p. 423. For population figures see Table 4 here.

1 Including Zikhron Ya'akov daughter colonies.
2 Called in the source by its old name: Castina.

The first eight years of the colonization enterprise were crucial in the formation of the new social structure and culture emerging in Eretz Israel. During this short interval, the foundations were laid for a multifarious cultural life in which traditional elements transported from the communities of Eastern Europe mingled with the seeds of a new indigenous national culture. Rothschild's contribution to the development of this culture was no less vital than his assistance in the economic and physical spheres. Furthermore, by helping the colonies establish a unique cultural identity, he provided the Jewish community with the ideological underpinnings of what was to become the "New Yishuv."[41]

---

41 Residents of the colonies were also involved in social activity outside the *moshava*, thereby contributing to the development of the "New Yishuv", the modern Jewish community emerging in the cities.

EPILOGUE

EARLY JEWISH COLONIZATION: FIGURES AND FEATURES

The questions posed in this study fall into three categories: those dealing with tangible aspects of Jewish colonization in the 1880s such as size, scope, and major developmental trends; those dealing with Baron de Rothschild's contribution, such as the nature of his control over the colonies, the degree of his personal involvement, the operational methods he employed, and his importance to renewed Jewish settlement in the Holy Land; and those dealing with the first decade of Jewish settlement as a colonization enterprise, compared to other colonizing efforts.

Jewish Colonization in the 1880s

Dimensions and Importance
In 1882, the one Jewish rural settlement on the map of Eretz Israel was the Mikve Israel agricultural school. By 1890, there were twelve more. Ten were active colonies in various stages of development, one was partially abandoned, and one was a private farm that became a colony in 1890. Numerically, the Jewish rural sector remained very small. In mid-1890, 350 households and a total of 2,000 persons were settled on 85,000 dunams of land.[1] From a spatial aspect, Jewish settlement was also negligible — to the extent that some contemporary sources overlooked its

---

1 See Tables 4,7. A frequently cited source claims that there were 14 settlements with a population of 3,000 and an approximate area of 75,000 dunams (Gurevich and Gertz, pp. 31, 32, Table 30). One basic reason for the discrepancy is that these figures relate to the beginning of 1891.

existence entirely.[2] Nevertheless, the 1880s and its achievements were of paramount importance: it was during these years that a Jewish presence was re-established throughout the country and the foundations were laid for development on a larger scale.

In a landscape dominated by traditional Arab villages featuring clusters of buildings in a hodgepodge of styles without greenery or shade, the Jewish colonies were a striking feature. They were carefully planned in the European mode, with attention to orderliness, space and high building standards. Hundreds of uniform housing units were erected and, unlike the Arab villages, there were dozens of large public buildings such as synagogues, schools, offices, ritual baths and medical facilities. By 1890, the building count had reached 550. The residents of the Jewish colonies enjoyed a diverse social and cultural life with emphasis on education and the increasing use of Hebrew as a spoken language. A network of internal and connecting roads was laid, and industrial zones were set aside for the Rishon le-Zion and Zikhron Ya'akov wineries.

Of particular note were the broad stretches of land designated as public domain, especially the "green" zones that constituted a new land use. There were flower gardens, nurseries and experimental fields, all irrigated, and dozens of unfamiliar crops that had never been raised in the country before. Employing modern techniques and farm machinery, nearly 13,000 dunams of vineyards and other Mediterranean plantations were cultivated in 1890. Greater modernization was also introduced in the wheat fields which covered an area twice as large as that devoted to fruit farming.

European colonization was not entirely new to Palestine. The German Templers had been living in the country for twenty-one years in colonies that bore a visible resemblance to the Jewish colonies. However, Templer settlement was much smaller in scale, and incorporated at this time only four colonies and fewer than 1,400 persons. Furthermore, they lacked certain unique features of the Jewish colonies, such as bathhouses

---

[2] In dozens of volumes of political, consular and commercial correspondence of the French Ministry of Foreign Affairs concerning Palestine in the 1880s, we found only four brief references, all pertaining to Jewish colonization in the north. Of these, two references to Baron de Rothschild and only one to a "Jewish colony." For details see Aaronsohn, Jewish Colonies, appendix 1, pp. 470–473.

The entrance to Rosh Pinna (1918)

and pharmacies housed in separate facilities, standardized residential units, and blocs of land set aside for nurseries and agricultural experimentation.

Independent Jewish farms had been absent from the country for many hundreds of years.[3] As such, the new colonies were of importance chiefly for what they stood for. They were noteworthy for the ideology surrounding their establishment and development, for the agents of settlement that offered assistance, for the economic climate they generated, and for their contribution to the emergence of new organs of social and organizational activity. All these factors came together by the end of the decade to create a new center, a counterpoint to the traditional hub of Jewish life in the "holy cities" of Jerusalem, Safed, Tiberias and Hebron. At the same time, the volume of Jewish settlement was not without significance given the fact that close to six percent of all Jews living in Palestine in the early 1890s were residents of the colonies.

---

3   On Jewish activity in the rural sector that followed the traditional pattern, see ibid., p. 397 and nn. 3–4.

Both aspects were put into sharper focus as the years went by. Not only did the Jewish colonies continue to expand and multiply during the Ottoman period to the point where they left the Templer colonies farther behind and could no longer be ignored, but they even competed with Arab settlement in certain parts of the country. Ideologically, the next generation of Jewish colonists emerged as a component of the "New Yishuv." The colonies thus became a further counterbalance to the "Old Yishuv" in the cities and went on to achieve a leading role in the cultural and political development of the Jewish community as a whole.

Hence the colonies of the 1880s represented both the physical and spiritual backbone of the colonization enterprise in the First and Second Aliya periods and the early Zionst movement.

Major Trends

The most notable trend in the colonies of the 1880s was constant development. This was a decade characterized by uninterrupted growth in the number of settlements, the size of the population, the total area and the proportion of cultivated land, the scope of economic and cultural activity, and the standard of living of the inhabitants. The actual rate of growth tended to fluctuate, but the increase was straightforward and consistent throughout the period. It was nurtured by two outside sources: the largesse of European Jewish benefactors (especially Edmond de Rothschild) and the incessant stream of Jewish immigrants.

Many of the hardships encountered during the early stages of colonization could be traced back to a single origin: the shortage of capital. From an economic perspective, Baron de Rothschild's major contribution lay in the provision of a steady supply of funds that created momentum and eventually enabled the economy of the colonies to "take off" on its own. Over the years, Rothschild stepped up the volume of financial aid and rendered assistance not only to the colonies established under his aegis, but to those of Hovevei Zion, and other needy parties.

Jewish immigration continued throughout the 1880s at a relatively steady pace. Excluding the peak year of 1882, when some 4,000–6,000 Jews reached the shores of Eretz Israel, an average of 1,500–2,000 Jews arrived annually.[4] As a result, the older settlements increased in

---

4   Figures based on reports of consular agents in Palestine, such as a letter of the French

population and new ones were founded. The farmers, craftsmen and laborers who settled in the colonies stimulated the economy both by joining the labor force and by adding the private capital they brought with them to the funding contributed by various Jewish organizations.

Immigration and the injection of capital resources were external stimulators of growth in the colonies. A third factor was internal population growth, as the children of the early pioneers reached adulthood and began families of their own, and the larger colonies took in more and more newcomers, especially laborers, in the mid-1880s. Neither group had means of their own, a state of affairs which created pressure on the colonies to expand their production resources, especially through the purchase of additional land. The settlement network thus grew spontaneously as private farms were founded near the colonies, and officially, as the Rothschild administration sponsored the establishment of new colonies.

Although Jewish colonization was yet in its infancy, most of the developmental processes were discernable by the end of the first decade, for better or for worse. How this pertained to the economic structure and spatial layout of the colonies will be discussed below. Socially, one of the negative features obvious from the start was the lack of cohesiveness or clear organizational identity — notwithstanding the involvement of centralist elements such as Hovevei Zion and Baron de Rothschild. Historical-ideological factors may have been at the root of the problem, such as the individualistic nature of settling the land or the absence of binding socialist principles. The farmers' material reliance on elements outside the colonies, i.e., Hovevei Zion and Rothschild, may have also contributed to social interaction that remained on the local level, not developing into an all-embracing national federation. The lack of unity that was evident in the 1880s continued to typify the colonies in later years and constituted a factor in their relatively minor social and political importance, both nationally and within the rural sector.

Another general trend in the colonies was rapid change. Throughout

---

consul, Ledoulx, stating that 10,000 Jews immigrated to Palestine over six years, 1885–1890. French Ministry of Foreign Affairs, Political Correspondence: Turkia — Jerusalem 22, letter of 8 July 1891, p. 205.

the decade, the pattern of activity was brisk, almost frenzied, in an effort to keep pace with internal affairs in Palestine and Europe, and the vicissitudes of the Ottoman Empire. Among the catalysts were the mass migration of Jews from Eastern Europe that brought a steady stream of immigrants to Eretz Israel in the 1880s, and the frequent changes introduced by the Turkish authorities in the regulations governing Jewish settlement, land purchase and construction.[5]

Spatial Features

A glance at the map of Jewish settlement in 1890 points up four major spatial-geographical features associated with the development of the colonies: (a) preferential locations chosen on the basis of external, political and economic factors; (b) the site of previous settlement as a spatial determinant; (c) the availability of land as a spatial determinant; (d) the emergence of a hierarchy of colonies shaped by the Jewish settlement establishment.

a) Choice of Sites in the North and Center

The attraction of the northern region probably derived from local political conditions. Those involved in furthering Jewish settlement assumed that the authorities in the north of the country, which was part of the *sanjak* of Acre, would be less opposed to colonization than those in the center and south, which were provinces of the *mutessariflik* of Jerusalem.[6] This assumption was basically justified, as demonstrated by the closure of the port of Jaffa and the expulsion of illegal immigrants by Rauf Pasha, the governor of Jerusalem, whereas the governors of Acre and Beirut, despite explicit orders from the Sublime Porte, turned a blind eye towards Jewish settlement activity.[7]

While the idea of colonizing in the north sounded fine on paper, the center of the country was preferable, both economically and historically

---

5   See Mandel, pp. 1–31 and references; Karpat.
6   On the prior settlement of the Galilee, see, for example, Ben-Yehuda, *Ha-havazzelet* 12 (1881), pp. 33–34; Wissotsky to Pinsker, 28 Heshvan 5646 in Wissotsky, pp. 247–248.
7   Subtle differences seem to have existed between various districts (*aqadiya*) in the same region depending on the attitude of the kaymakam toward Jewish settlement and his willingness to accept bribes. See Hissin, *Diary*, pp. 74–75.

Early Jewish Colonization: Figures and Features 263

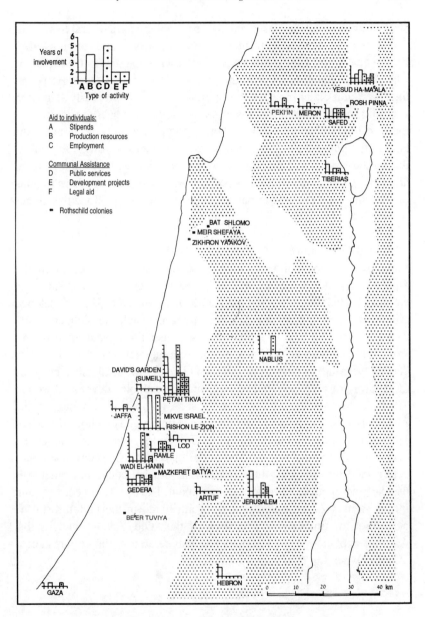

Map 14: Rothschild's projects outside "his" colonies
Source: Aaronsohn, Jewish Colonies, I, p. 406a, Table 25

(Jaffa and its environs was already considered the agricultural heartland, and Jerusalem was the epicenter of Jewish national and religious life). By the end of the 1880s, there were five Jewish colonies in the sanjak of Acre, and an equal number in the mutessariflik of Jerusalem. However, they were not equal in size and importance. Even at this early stage, the centrally located colonies enjoyed a clear advantage over the colonies in the north (see Map 13), which then encompassed only portions of the land in the plains and valleys that became the focus of Jewish settlement during the British Mandate period. There was no Jewish colonization at all in the 1880s in the sanjak of Nablus (Shechem), the southern regions of Palestine, and the greater part of Transjordan (except along the fringes of the Golan Heights).

b) Spatial Distribution

Three major blocs of settlement emerged during this period in the Upper Galilee ("Galilean colonies"), the southern Carmel ("Samarian colonies") and the Jaffa region ("Judean colonies"). They developed around existing Jewish population centers to which the pioneers could turn for socio-cultural support (there was usually a group of residents from their hometown in Europe) and commercial ties. The first such centers were Jaffa, Safed and Haifa, and later — the established colonies of Zikhron Ya'akov and Rishon le-Zion. A fourth bloc developed around Tiberias towards the end of the First Aliya period, linking up the early colonies which had blossomed from tiny outposts into full-fledged settlements, and creating the S-shaped contour of Jewish rural settlement known in Mandatory times.[8] The initial layout of the colonies was thus determined by proximity to a functioning Jewish community that was basically compatible with the new settlement. The absence of colonization in the vicinity of Jerusalem has been attributed in the literature to the perception of this city as a bastion of the "Old Yishuv" and its ills. Another explanation, as we shall see, was related to the circumstances of land ownership.[9]

---

8 Reichman, *Foothold*, pp. 50–55.
9 Ben-Arieh, Aspects, pp. 87–91.

c) Availability of Land

Colonizaton in Eretz Israel took place on land that was peripheral in those days for a combination of spatial, economic-legislative, and agro-technical reasons. With Arab villages occupying the hilly regions of Judea, Samaria and the Galilee, most of the land acquired by the Jewish colonies, apart from the lands of Zikhron Ya'akov and certain portions of Rosh Pinna, were in the lowlands. In the 1860s and 1870s, many Arab peasants responded to economic and legal developments in the Ottoman Empire (such as the passage of the 1858 Land Law) by placing their land in the hands of wealthy city-dwelling Arab effendis, who subsequently put up large tracts for sale, especially in the lowlands, which, security-wise, were the country's weak points.[10] As group settlements with extensive land needs, the Jewish colonies bought up whatever was being sold. In effect, the availability of land determined the distribution of Jewish settlement. Thus another reason for the absence of Jewish colonies in the Jerusalem and Mountanous Hebron regions was the fact that land was not for sale there.

From an agricultural standpoint, none of the sites selected for the early colonies offered much promise. The land was either sandy, rocky, swampy or bone-dry, and had been cultivated extensively or not at all.[11] The Jewish pioneers were able to overcome these geophysical limitations through capital investment and the introduction of modern farming methods and technology. Fortunately, this technology was most effective on the large, contiguous stretches of land with which the Arab effendis were willing to part. Hence the availability of the land and its natural features were instrumental in shaping the spatial distribution of Jewish settlement in Eretz Israel.

d) Hierarchy of Colonies

In the early years of the colonization enterprise, the hierarchy of colonies was identical to the operational and spatial hierarchies of the Rothschild administration. In general, the difficulty in distinguishing geographically between Rothschild's contribution and the colonization movement as a whole is symptomatic of Rothschild's dominance. As we shall see, the

---

10 Granovsky; Avneri, pp. 53–63.
11 Ottoman survey for 1871, in Avneri, p. 253; Aaronsohn, Establishment, pp. 164–165.

perceptions of his individual contribution as the leading developer and of all colonizing efforts in Eretz Israel have tended to overlap. Indeed, no separate hierarchy was evident in the 1880s among the three Hovevei Zion colonies; they were small associate colonies on the lower rungs of the Rothschild hierarchy. The one colony still supported by Hovevei Zion at the end of the decade (like all the settlements operating in 1890 without Rothschild's assistance) was also marginal in importance and influence.

Speaking of hierarchies, Rishon le-Zion was not the chief colony in the 1880s, although this may have been the case on the eve of the twentieth century. In effect, there was no such colony at the time, and Zikhron Ya'akov and Rishon le-Zion where contesting that status (see Tables 4, 7). Their competition was based on the sum of natural advantages over disadvantages and the mobilization of resources, which was often a test of the colony administrator's personal fundraising skill and influence with officials in Paris. The sources show that both Rothschild himself and Elie Scheid, the leading executive, were partial to Zikhron Ya'akov. This compensated for the geographical inferiority of the northern colony compared with the strategic location of Rishon le-Zion (the proximity to Jaffa and the highway to Jerusalem was no less advantageous in those days than it is today). True, Zikhron Ya'akov always had the larger population, but this was not a benefit until Rothschild began funnelling in resources, which were translated into extensive land purchases, more employment opportunities and higher income.

In the absence of a chief colony, the hierarchy of settlement in the 1880s was not complete. The spatial interaction between the colonies that was expressed in a continuous flow of manpower, equipment, knowhow and influences did not emanate from a national headquarters and proceed smoothly from core to periphery. In this respect, Rothschild and his officials hindered the emergence in the 1880s of an independent settlement network and a new social entity.

Rothschild's Contribution

Rothschild, Hovevei Zion and Others

There is no question that Rothschild had a hand in nearly all the Jewish colonizing efforts in Palestine in the 1880s. Nine of the thirteen colonies operating at the time were dependent upon him, i.e., 1,900 settlers out of a total of 2,000, inhabiting an area of 59,000 dunams out of a total of 85,000. His investment in the rural sector was enormous, totalling, in our estimation, roughly eight million francs by the middle of 1890 (approximately one million francs a year). This exceeded many times over the sum invested by all other parties combined.

Other investors in the colonization enterprise were the Hovevei Zion movement in Europe (through its central office and individual branches), members of the urban Jewish community who joined local settlement societies, and immigrants who settled in the colonies, bringing with them private capital. Aside from these permanent contributors, occasional assistance was received from Jewish philanthropists such as Baron Maurice de Hirsch and from anonymous donors who contributed through the Hebrew newspapers. Further sources of aid were Laurence Oliphant, a supporter of the Jews, who put up funding at crucial moments, and the Alliance Israélite Universelle (AIU), which assisted indirectly from time to time but never provided outright grants or loans. Of all these, the most effective was the central Hovevei Zion committee in Russia, also known as the Odessa Committee, founded in November 1884. By 1890, this body had invested nearly a quarter of a million francs in the colonization of Palestine, which was approximately one-thirtieth of Rothschild's investment for the same period.[12]

Income from these sources was responsible for the development of the non-Rothschild sector, i.e., the colony of Gedera, the then uninhabited colony of Bnei Yehuda, the settlements of Yahud and Nes Ziona, the farms of Mishmar ha-Yarden, Sumeil, etc., and the private lands in Petah Tikva, Yesud ha-Ma'ala and Rishon le-Zion.

The point that seems to have escaped the attention of modern scholars and is thus worthy of special emphasis is that Rothschild did not own all the land in his colonies, neither in 1890 and nor at any time during the nineties. This was also true of the former Hovevei Zion colonies, Petah Tikva and Yesud ha-Ma'ala (Rothschild supported only 28 households

---

12 Lilienblum, in Druyanow, *Documents*, III, pp. 84–86. Figures based on Kalmanovitz to Hirsch, 12 December 1887 (French), in Druyanow and Laskov, IV, p. 723.

in Petah Tikva).[13] Even in Rishon le-Zion, which had been administered by Rothschild for years, a few of the founding members and a larger number of newcomers (those who purchased land in Ayūn Qāra) held title deeds in their own name. In 1890, many of these landowners received no financial support from the baron and were considered as being autonomous. While their farms were not entirely independent, they constituted a separate unit that operated alongside the communal farm, which was composed of lands cultivated by Rothschild employees and lands cultivated by farmers receiving support, both under Rothschild supervision. In practice, the landowners were not strictly their own masters because they depended on public services such as water supply, health clinics, schools, etc. provided by Rothschild. Rothschild, in turn, took advantage of this dependence to exercise control over their farms and ensure that they kept pace with the others.

The Hovevei Zion pioneers and their colonies also derived great benefit from the tacit assistance of Baron de Rothschild and his officials. Recognizing its own inferiority, Hovevei Zion made an effort to match its positions and strategies with those of the baron. This was dramatically illustrated during the settlers' revolts in the Rothschild colonies, when Hovevei Zion supported a compromise that was akin to surrender from the rebels' point of view. The deferential attitude of Hovevei Zion reached a peak in 1887 when its leaders, Pinsker and Lilienblum, exhorted the instigators of the uprising in Rishon le-Zion to "abandon their evil ways" and leave the colony.

Hovevei Zion's decision to follow Rothschild's lead, which was also evident, albeit more muted, in other spheres, was founded on genuine admiration for his accomplishments, but was pragmatic as well. Rothschild was actively engaged in Jewish colonization all over the country, and not least in the colonies of Hovevei Zion.[14] His purse was opened not once or twice, but repeatedly, and provided an important impetus in many different sectors of rural life.[15] In general, Rothschild's

---

13 In Yesud ha-Ma'ala nearly 1,000 dunams were owned by the settlers. On the early 1890s, see Barzilai, *Beit Halevi*, p. 45.
14 See, for example, Gordon to Shefer, 15 January 1884, in Druyanow, *Documents*, III, p. 589; Levontin to M.b.H. Hacohen, 15 November 1884, ibid., p. 594, n. 2.
15 More details in Aaronsohn, *Jewish Colonies*, pp. 406a–406c (maps 23, 24, table 25).

support was extended on two levels: private aid to individual settlers and aid to the community as a whole. On the one hand, he granted stipends, provided production resources and took on colonists as salaried employees, while on the other, he sponsored public services such as health care, development projects — especially in connection with the water supply — and legal aid, mainly to solve land registry problems.

Rothschild's involvement also had a visible impact outside the colonies. He helped private farms remain viable by granting loans on convenient terms. On the public service level, the facilities he developed in Rishon le-Zion, for example, strengthened the private farms in the vicinity whereas those in remote locations without access to such facilities found it impossible to survive.[16]

The dependence of the non-Rothschild sector increased further in 1890 as the autonomous farmers and colonies organized under other auspices began to plant vineyards and sell their produce to the Rothschild wineries. The only profitable crop and chief source of revenue in Rehovot in the 1890s were the grapes purchased by the Rishon le-Zion winery and subsidized by the baron.

It should be emphasized once again that Rothschild's involvement in Jewish settlement extended throughout the country. In the 1880s, the list included nine colonies and seven other rural settlements, as well as nine urban communities. In the colonies, he gained control through his ownership of land and operation of public services. Outside the colonies, his control was assured by two additional factors, namely monetary assistance or the equivalent, and technical expertise provided by his officials. On the negative side, Rothschild's dominion in the sphere of Jewish settlement had a very definite and stifling influence on the work of Hovevei Zion and other colonizing agencies.

Rothschild was willing to buy more costly land than other settlement societies operating in the region. Whereas certain tracts of land purchased by these other societies averaged around ten francs per dunam, the value of those acquired by Rothschild was closer to fourteen.[17] Notwithstanding the extravagance, which was roundly criticized by his contemporaries, by inflating real-estate prices he prevented those with fewer resources,

16 See Aaronsohn and Kark, pp. 55–57.
17 Aaronsohn, Jewish Colonies, pp. 407–408, nn. 21–22.

i.e., private farmers and Hovevei Zion, from expanding their holdings. This added a subjective difficulty to the objective ones encountered by those operating in the sphere of colonization. Nevertheless, Rothschild succeeded where others failed. Hovevei Zion's ambitious plans and enthusiasm dwindled in the face of adversity, but Rothschild persisted until his modest scheme became a vibrant undertaking of epic proportions.

Strategic Principles

Over the course of the 1880s, Rothschild's activity in the realm of Jewish colonization developed along five major lines:

Institutionalization: Rothschild's spontaneous, personal approach was abandoned in the course of time in favor of centralized decision-making and systematic implementation. The organ for carrying out this approach was the Rothschild administration, a centralized hierarchy that was essentially a form of government.

Intensification: Rothschild's involvement achieved greater depth by moving from the general to the particular. He began with public services and general assistance to the entire colony, and progressed to direct personal aid to each colonist. He also gained control of the so-called autonomous farmers.

Diversification: Rothschild's efforts in the colonies became more diversified as he began to take an interest in social and cultural affairs in addition to administration and economy. The focus of his bureaucratic mechanism shifted from administrators and agricultural instructors to civil servants, especially teachers, medical personnel and religious functionaries.

Territorial Expansion: Rothschild was originally active in two colonies. The number grew to four during his second stage of involvement, and nine during the third stage. From the middle of the decade, these colonies served as cores for further expansion, either through the purchase of adjacent tracts (and occasionally the establishment of a daughter colony), or as a springboard for settlement in a new site, not contiguous with the old one.

Predominance: Rothschild was involved in settlement activity beyond the borders of his own colonies, for the most part in the rural arena but to some extent in the urban sector as well. Usually this intervention was at the urging of the local population and not initiated by the baron himself. With the blessing of Hovevei Zion, he officially undertook the administration of Yesud ha-Ma'ala and Petah Tikva towards the end of the decade, by which time he was sponsoring projects in nearly every Jewish community and geographical region in the country and operating behind the scenes in a total of twenty-five sites of Jewish settlement.

Within these five categories, it is possible to discern other important trends. As we have seen, Rothschild's dominance was achieved through land ownership, capital investment and his staff of administrators. Land and money were used in combination in the colonies, and money alone, outside them. Yet the omnipresent element in every case were the administrators; without them, Rothschild's ideas could not be put into practice. This explains their peerless importance in his eyes and his unwavering support even when their presence infuriated the colonists. Given Rothschild's personal background as the scion of a patriarchal family whose financial empire in France was run according to hierarchic and centralistic principles in an era of burgeoning colonialism, there were also psychological reasons for his adoption of an approach that gave precedence to standard procedures and discipline, and put the agents of settlement before the settlers.

The notion that Rothschild and his officials did not see eye to eye, as was claimed by the colonists and Hovevei Zion at the time and often repeated by scholars, is refuted by the evidence.[18] Specific references to the operational methods of the administration and Rothschild's response to the settlers' uprisings indicate a fundamental agreement between them. Of course, there were occasions when an official acted contrary to Rothschild's instructions, but the exception only serves to prove the rule.[19] The centralization inherent in the system and the practice of reporting to superiors enabled Rothschild to monitor the work of his officials and assure a high level of correspondence. Each branch of the administration had a chief representative in Paris, and each sub-branch reported to Elie Schied, as the chief inspector. The hierarchy of agronomists was perhaps not as inflexible as the others, with the top man, Ermens, briefing Rothschild directly. But in the final analysis, the

---

18   Rokeah, Matters, Hacohen, Individual, p. 302; *Mi-Yerushalayim* I (1891), pp. 3–7 (Hebrew); Gvati, I, pp. 72–76.
19   Rothschild to Hirsch, 19 October 1885 (French), in Margalith, p. 205.

entire bureaucracy was subordinate to Rothschild, and the work of his staff was crosschecked through the "regular channels" (reports submitted by the chief executive of each branch) and personal correspondence with many regional and local officials.[20]

The work of these officials, who were stationed throughout the country and placed in charge of all spheres of development, was made possible through the transfer of funds from Baron de Rothschild. Capital was brought into the country in one of two ways: a) Via couriers from Paris, especially Scheid, who visited at least once or twice a year; b) Through the exchange of promissory notes. Rothschild's chief administrators would receive cash from local merchants who doubled as bankers and moneychangers (Breisch and Moyal in Jaffa, Valero in Jerusalem, Dick in Haifa, Franck in Beirut) in exchange for promissory notes that were redeemed in Istanbul.

The person in charge of distributing these funds was Samuel Hirsch, the AIU inspector in Palestine and headmaster of Mikve Israel. Using the local exchange method described above, Hirsch paid out tens of thousands of francs to Rothschild's administrators and sent the promissory notes to Paris, where Rothschild reimbursed the AIU. Sometimes Hirsch submitted the promissory notes to the administrators, who received their face value less commission from the moneychanger. The latter then sent the notes to Paris via Istanbul for payment.

It was true that enormous sums of money were injected into the colonization enterprise by Baron de Rothschild, but let us not overlook their productiveness. Unlike the *halukka* (charity distributed in the "Old Yishuv" by country of origin), which many scholars claim was similar to the financial aid provided by Rothschild, these funds were utilized largely for the benefit of the community: public construction and services, producton resources, land purchase, and development programs. Only a fraction of them was spent on direct aid to the colonists, and careful records were kept of all such grants on the assumption that they would later be repaid. These funds were not perceived as a permanent, legitimate

---

20 On Rothschhild's request for ongoing reports from his regional adminsitrators, see letters of 17 August 1884, 19 October 1885 (manuscript, French), CZA J41/72. From other letters of Rothschild and Hirsch it may be inferred that this request was complied with.

source of income. Newspapers and personal correspondence throughout the decade testify to the hope of all concerned that the colonies would one day attain economic independence and no longer require aid from Rothschild.[21]

The dynamic quality of Rothschild's efforts, which was crucial in setting the pace of development described above, owed much to the large network of officials and the generous flow of capital. No less important was the introduction of modern European knowhow. Rothschild's administrators were agents of change who brought with them new ideas in the realms of agriculture, administration, technology and communal services (especially medicine). Much of the knowledge was disseminated by European experts who were sent to the colonies and by colonists who completed specialized training overseas. Information was also gleaned from professional literature brought over from France and correspondence with French experts. Modern farming techniques were taught at the Mikve Israel agricultural school, while various tools and machinery from Paris were circulated among the colonies.

The water drilling projects sponsored by Rothschild were carried out with the help of Mikve Israel graduates who had undergone advanced training in France, sophisticated drills and pumps (including an experimental small-bit drill for dry digging), and a hydraulic engineering consultant in France who corresponded regulariy with the workmen. Modern technology was employed in other areas, too, such as soil testing prior to purchasing a new tract of land (six different tests were done in addition to laboratory chemical analysis) and new techniques in viticulture.

The drilling team moved among the colonies, as did nearly all the Rothschild officials, creating a constant interchange of manpower, knowhow and equipment that was enriched not only by foreign sources but by local input as well. As Rothschild's involvement entered its final stage, a growing number of native-born colonists were employed by the administration, and the farmers were better able to adapt the

---

21 On the fundamental difference between support of the "Old Yishuv" and support of the colonies, see Friedman, *Society*, pp. 2–3, 12. Erroneous statements on the imminence of economic independence in the "Zera Avraham" society charter, 17 Sivan, in Schub, *Memories*, p. 126.

techniques they learned to local conditions. The small-scale agricultural experimentation of the first half of the decade was expanded towards its end, and whole tracts of land (*champs d'expérience*) were set aside for experiments with new or improved crops.

In the course of this study, we have discussed land ownership as a key factor in Rothschild's achievements in the colonies and his policies in this regard have indeed attracted attention. Some researchers have concluded that "Rothschild had in mind two geo-political goals: penetrating and establishing a presence in various parts of the country, and merging Jewish lands into blocs as large as possible."[22] Without detracting from the significance of the issue, we would argue that Rothschild's land policy was not altogether coherent. Gaining control of the land was one of three tactics he employed in the colonies, and not necessarily the most important one. This is a conclusion we have reached after carefully examining Rothschild's actions in the colonies and rural sector, and reflecting on the scope of his efforts over time from an economic perspective.

Rothschild's domestic policies in the colonies did not accentuate land ownership. As we have seen, he allowed individual farmers to retain their property, and even sold tracts of land acquired by the administration to private settlers. The extent of Rothschild's land holdings in the 1880s also raises questions about the importance he attached to land ownership. Of the 57,000 dunams of land belonging to the Rothschild colonies in 1890, some 30,000 dunams, i.e., slightly more than half, were purchased by him from their Arab owners (see Table 8). The remainder were acquired by Hovevei Zion or the colonists themselves before being signed over to Rothschild under the patronage agreement. These included the lands of Petah Tikva acquired in the 1870s, and those of Rishon le-Zion, Rosh Pinna, Zikhron Ya'akov and Yesud ha-Ma'ala, acquired in the 1880s.

Comparing statistics for the Rothschild colonies and other rural settlements in the years 1890 and 1900 (Table 8), we find that the one noticeable increase among all the items examined was in the proportion of land owned by Baron de Rothschild. Even in absolute terms, Rothschild's acquisition of real estate was far greater in the 1890s than in the 1880s. Whereas the number of settlements under his auspices remained virtually

---

22   Hadas, p. 7. Also compare with Reichman, Geographical.

unchanged and the population slightly more than doubled, Rothschild controlled three and a half times more land in 1900 than he did in 1890.

Rothschild's land policy in the 1880s was thus less ambitious than the image it had engendered in the historiography of the period. The focus was not on expansion but on development of infrastructure in the broad sense: advances in housing, transportation, water supply; training of manpower in health-care, education and cultural services, and amassing of agricultural knowhow and technology. All this was done within circumscribed limits, on lands that were Jewish-owned. Rothschild's officials did engage in the purchase of more land and even founded new colonies, but as a relatively minor pursuit in contrast to the sum total of his work. Only in the 1890s did the accent shift from infrastructure to territorial expansion, a transition that was marked by the establishment of the Palestine Committee in July 1891. The goal of this committee was to increase Jewish land holdings in the wake of the frantic tide of Jewish immigration and new Ottoman land laws during 1890/91.[23] The year 1890 thus marked a change in the nature of Rothschild's involvement in Eretz Israel.

---

23   Kark, pp. 182, 192; Klausner, *Kattowitz*, II, pp. 69–72, 180–181.

Table 8
Rothschild colonies and other rural Jewish settlements 1890 and 1900 (rounded figures)

	No. of colonies	Population	Total area	Cereals	Vineyards	Plantation	Buildings[1]
Rothschild colonies 1890	9	1,900	59,000	22,740	9,010	2,450	525
Other Settlements 1890[2]	4	220[3]	26,000	3,160	1,090	180	40
Total 1890	13	2,120	85,000	25,900	10,100	2,630	565
Rothschild colonies 1900	10	3,880	200,900	111,050	18,620	11,940	780
Other Settlements 1900	11	1,310	75,500	28,330	9,320	2,210	330
Total 1900	21	5,190	276,400	139,380	27,940	14,150	1,110
Rothschild's share 1890[4]	65%	90%	69%	88%	89%	93%	93%
Rothschild's share 1900[4]	48%	75%	73%	80%	67%	84%	71%
Change in share 1890–1900	–30%	–17%	+6%	–9%	–25%	–10%	–24%

Sources: 1890 — adopted primarily from Gurevitz and Gretz, Table 30; 1900 — Margalith, Table C, pp. 210–211

1   The figure for buildings in Mazkeret Batya, Zikhron Ya'akov and daughter colonies in 1890, were supplemented on the basis of Klein, p. 35.
2   Gedera, Bnei Yehuda, Mikve Israel, Ness Ziona as well as other rural land purchased in the 1880s and not settled then (such as Shoshanat ha-Yarden and Duran — later Rehovot).
3   Including 130 residents of Mikve Israel (76 of them were students).
4   The autonomous farmers in the Rothschild colonies should be subtracted, but they accounted for a very small percentage.

Rothschild favored the transition to viticulture and the necessary agrarian reforms because it fitted in with his land policies and also because he perceived the colonization scheme as a social experiment. In principle, the colonists were not regarded as equal partners in the experiment, and their relations with the controlling body (i.e., Rothschild and his administration) were asymmetrical. The development of the colonies was not of the grassroots type; it was imposed from above, by the baron. Similarly, decisions concerning the shift from consumer to market-based agriculture and the agrarian reforms that were involved were made at the top echolons rather than evolving naturally from internal developments in the colonies themselves.[24]

In Rothschild's case, the dividing line between land policy and social experimentation was very narrow. Ideologically, if we weigh his contribution to the physical development of the country against his contribution to the development of human resources, we discern a movement in the direction of a nationalist approach towards the end of the 1880s — a trend that apparently gained strength in the 1890s. This brings us to the fundamental question of what prompted Rothschild to become actively involved in the country and what he sought to accomplish. Was it philanthropy or was it nationalism? Numerous attempts have been made to answer this question, but we can only guess at the truth owing to the paucity of sources, Rothschild's characteristic reticence, and his deliberately secretive mode of operation.[25]

---

24 These ideas were discussed with the late Prof. D. Weintraub. Also see Kellner, *Zion's Sake*, pp. 172–174.
25 Rothschild was wary of the political sensitivity of the Turks (see letters in Yavne'eli, II, pp. 73, 75). His motto was "Pensons-y toujour n'en parlons jamais." A first-hand source claims that he regularly destroyed letters pertaining to colonization in Eretz

Evaluating Rothschild's Contribution

By now, the long-standing debate over Rothschild and his administrators and their role in modern Jewish colonization has attained a solid footing in the historiography of Eretz Israel. Among the well-known basic weaknesses in Rothschild's scheme were the complex bureaucracy that ran the colonies and the funding upon which they became reliant. Criticism of the moral depravity caused by patronage was not unfounded. Indeed, the financial support extended by Rothschild created communities of dependents and sometimes indentured farmers who stopped working in the 1890s and lived off philanthropy. Lacking a genuine attachment to the land, numerous second-generation colonists left the country at the turn of the century, and others had no qualms about employing cheap Arab laborers in preference to Jews. This last issue, Arab versus Jewish labor, developed into a head-on confrontation between the pioneers of the First Aliya and those who came later, and hung over the colonies like a dark shadow for many years to come. Not surprisingly, criticism of Rothschild's work reached a peak after the First Aliya.

Disparaging remarks about the patronage system, the actions of the administrators and the baron were voiced even in the 1880s by various individuals. But public opinion, which was largely shaped by Hovevei Zion, was generally positive and admiring, sometimes to the point of awe and self-belittlement. Criticism of Rothschild and his administration was thus overshadowed and the system of patronage remained intact.[26]

Lately, after dozens of years of dwelling on the faults of the Rothschild administration and downplaying its positive side, researchers are adopting a more favorable stance. In a return to the views common in the 1880s, Rothschild's work is being reevaluated on the basis of his awesome financial contribution, acquisition of land, establishment of colonies, support of struggling farm settlements, and felicitous timing.[27]

In general, this reassessment corresponds with our current findings except for two important points that require correction and clarification.

Israel (oral testimony of James de Rothschild to A. Bein in 1964). I am grateful to Dr. Bein and Mr. Y. Mayorek for bringing this to my attention.

26 See note 14, above for positive evaluation of Rothschild's ideological goals; also see Wissotsky, *Ha-havazzelet* 15 (1885), p. 298; and Kressel, *Father*, pp. 31–24.

27 Four points cited by Giladi, Baron, pp. 59–61.

One pertains to Rothschild's role in land acquisition, which was less significant in the 1880s than his role in developing infrastructure and public services. While both were central to his work in the colonies during the First Aliya period, the latter, with its intensive, qualitative orientation, was probably the more important.

The intensity with which Rothschild devoted himself to consolidating services and infrastructure can be evaluated from two vantage points. On the negative side, it led to an overdevelopment of the productive sector at the expense of economic efficiency, which kept the colonies from achieving independence (as was the case later, when Jewish settlement came under the auspices of the World Zionist Organization and the Government of Israel). In addition, these public services were exploited by Rothschild and his officials as a means of manipulating the population.

On the positive side are the infrastructure and services developed in response to basic needs. Like all pioneering settlements, the Jewish colonies began in a void insofar as physical infrastructure was concerned, and extensive construction was necessary. The problem was compounded by the demographic composition of the population with its large proportion of young people (consumers of health and educational services). Normally, all disposable income would be spent on consumption, causing stagnation in the productive sector. Indeed, this was the case in the early settlements established by Hovevei Zion before Rothschild stepped in. Only the massive injection of capital of which Rothschild was capable could satisfy the colonists' many personal needs and at the same time further agricultural and industrial development.

In this respect, Rothschild fulfilled the duties of a quasi-governmental institution, which brings us to our second point. The literature to date has not defined the Rothschild enterprise in a manner that presents the sum total of its parts and illuminates its overall significance. Our contention is that Baron de Rothschild was akin to the "national institutions" — an empirical-historical term for the Jewish Agency and World Zionist Organization as the organs of self-government under the British occupation and Mandate of Palestine (1918–1948).[28] Despite his reservations, Rothschild committed himself, step by step, to carrying out all the

---

28 Gvati, I, pp. 173–315 (especially pp. 197–200, 216–220, 232–239, 281–284), 339–342.

functions of a government vis-à-vis the colonies. The work of Rothschild and the national institutions was remarkably similar in organization and substance. Both provided frameworks for a unique form of settlement under foreign rule, and as the term "national institutions" suggests, took charge of all institutional activities and imparted to them a national character.

The Jewish Agency–World Zionist Organization maintained various departments that were responsible, like Rothschild's officials, for agricultural development (including cadastral mapping and land registration), housing and road construction, health, education, cultural affairs, and religion. There were also departments for administration, domestic security, public works, and other issues indirectly related to settlement. In terms of operational policy, both Rothschild and the Jewish Agency–World Zionist Organization were characterized by a systematic, centralistic approach, emphasis on planning (functional-economic and political-social), and perception of modernization as the key to advancement. To achieve this end, they drew upon local and foreign resources, and conducted numerous experiments. Rothschild and his administration were invaluable in that they stepped in at mid-point and kept the young colonization enterprise going until it was capable of maintaining itself — which is precisely the goal of government-supported settlement, then and today.

With slight differences in emphasis, the similarity continued in such areas as commerce and industry, and relations with the government authorities and the Arabs (handled by the Jewish Agency's Political Department). In some spheres, such as the acquisition and reclamation of land for cultivation, the list of duties of the Jewish National Fund might have been lifted from the assignment book of some Rothschild official. This body was appointed to seek out land for purchase, handle negotiations, obtain official permits from the authorities, reclaim barren land, drain swamps, and plant trees. The policy of supplying settlers with initiated jobs during the first years of settlement was reminiscent of Rothschild's employment of the pioneers and their families as day laborers in his nurseries and plantations.

On the other hand, the Rothschild administration did not handle some important issues such as immigration, whereas the national institutions had special departments for overseas promotion, organization and absorption. This had more to do with political circumstances in the 1880s and the innovative and experimental character of Rothschild's work than with the final goals. Rothschild, too, spoke privately of the "ingathering of the exiles" as a future possibility, but he recognized that the time was not ripe, settling in the meanwhile for a modest scheme involving selective, controlled immigration — what the national institutions would later hail as "dunam after dunam," and Herzl would scorn as "retail settlement" or "settlement by the back door." Likewise, most of the other differences between Rothschild and the national institutions in terms of spheres of activity and methods were a product of the changing times.

In summary, without declaration and fanfare, Baron de Rothschild assumed responsibility for a major portion of the settlement activities later undertaken by the national institutions. If we review Rothschild's accomplishments in this light, we find that the patronage system and the actions of the administrators have been criticized unfairly. The bureaucratic ills and rebellions were not entirely the fault of the officials. Contrary to widespread opinion, the administration was not overstaffed in the 1880s; as we have shown, the figures incorporated all employees working in the colonies, including those of minor importance.

The negative reputation of the officials themselves was also unjustified. Most were experts in various branches of farming and community services and did highly important work. While they were often accused of overspending and extravagance, the fact remains that the colonies received no services from the government, and the novelty of the colonization enterprise sometimes led to errors in judgment. On the whole, they were not the menacing brutes depicted in the literature; they constituted a buffer between the colonists and Rothschild, who really pulled the strings, and as such they were the ones who came under attack when the colonists rebelled. In fact, the officials were merely following orders, but behind these orders was a basic conflict between an administrative body that could not succeed without comprehensive planning and conformity, and a band of settlers who were forced to stifle their own desires to ensure that the planner did not fail.[29]

The fundamental nature of Rothschild's efforts did not change in the 1890s, even when other settlement agencies began to operate in the region. Like the national institutions in later years, he was involved in

29   Kellner, *Zion's Sake*, p. 174.

every aspect of Jewish life, in all areas of Jewish settlement. He assisted the independent colonies of Rehovot and Hadera by arranging for land ownership and building permits, purchasing Rehovot's grape harvests at subsidized rates, and draining Hadera's swamps; he extended financial support to the Hovevei Zion colonies of Gedera and Be'er Tuviya; he aided the Jewish communities of small towns such as Jericho; he sponsored the publication of Hebrew textbooks; and he negotiated for Eliezer Ben-Yehuda's release from prison. Even Dr. Hillel Jaffe, the chairman of the Hovevei Zion committee in Palestine and a sworn opponent of the Rothschild administration during the 1890s, admitted privately that "without the baron, there would be nothing in this country."[30]

By this time, Rothschild and his officials no longer played an exclusive role in the sphere of colonization. Hovevei Zion, local settlement societies and the Jewish Colonisation Association were active, too, especially Hovevei Zion, which was given legal status by the Russian government in 1890. Through its new headquarters in Jaffa and various branches, Hovevei Zion resumed its work in Palestine, resettling Jewish emigrés who fled Europe in panic over the next year and a half.

A totally new element was the Jewish Colonisation Association (JCA), founded in 1891 by Baron Maurice de Hirsch, a renowned Jewish philanthropist. This organization sponsored Jewish settlement in other countries, particularly Argentina, but it became active in Palestine, too, towards the end of 1896. The JCA acquired land, provided financial support to colonies that were not receiving aid from Rothschild, and in 1899 even established a settlement of its own.[31]

Rothschild was still responsible for much of the development in the colonies in the late 1890s, but with the exception of land acquisition, his primacy was less obvious than in the 1880s. The bulk of his work was in the older colonies, on projects that had already been launched. Even the new colonies founded in the 1890s were in many respects a continuation, given the fact that much of the land was purchased in the previous decade.[32] Indeed, some colonies were a direct outgrowth of development activities sponsored by another party on the same site. But the Hovevei Zion colonies of the 1890s encompassed land that had formerly belonged

---

30 Letters of 20 August 1894 and 23 February 1895 in Jaffe, pp. 101, 112.
31 Margalith, Table 3, pp. 210–21; Schama, throughout. Also see Table 8.
32 The lands of Tantura and Shefeya, Be'er Tuviya, Nes Ziona and Mishmar ha-Yarden,

to Rothschild and, furthermore, quite a few of the founders had worked for Rothschild and acquired their agricultural training in his colonies.[33]

From an economic perspective, too, Rothschild's actions in the 1880s were directly related to developments in the late nineteenth century. His fundamental decision to promote land-intensive fruit farming, whose products were marked for industry and foreign markets, was well-chosen from many standpoints. It was consonant with the limited amount of land suitable for dry farming, the need for a high per-unit income to assure reasonable living standards, the necessity for an agricultural branch to which urbanites-turned-farmers could easily adapt, the development of a solidly based modern economy, the expansion of the agricultural work force, and local conditions in Palestine. Mixed farming, for instance, lent itself to all the above, but the produce could not be effectively marketed under prevailing local conditions. Historically, there is no doubt that plantations presented the best alternative.

Rothschild's decision was to have an impact that continued into the next decade. As Scheid pointed out, much of the independent settlement in the 1890s hinged on the baron's promotion of viticulture and establishment of wine cellars. He argued that the colonies of Gedera, Nes Ziona and Rehovot "would have long ceased to exist or never been founded at all," if not for their vineyards and the sale of grapes to the Rishon le-Zion winery.[34] The same held true for Ein Zeitim and Mishmar ha-Yarden, which were planned as winegrowing colonies associated with a wine cellar in Rosh Pinna. The founders of Hadera hoped to market grapes to the Rothschild winery in Zikhron Ya'akov. All these were independent colonies that emerged in the first half of the 1890s, and represented a majority among the second-decade colonies that survived into the twentieth century. Thus we find that Rothschild's introduction of vineyards in the agricultural colonies of the 1880s influenced not only the

---

Rehovot, Mahanayim, and perhaps Ein Zeitim and Sejera. The lands of the last three were acquired some time in 1890.

33 The lands of Be'er Tuviya, Mahanayim, Sejera and Ein Zeitim, and the settlers of Mishmar ha-Yarden, Nes Ziona and Be'er Tuviya. All the pioneers of Metulla (and the majority of those who settler in the Lower Galilee at the turn of the century) hailed from the early Rothschild colonies.

34 E. Scheid, "The Baron's Generosity," in Eliav, *First Aliyah*, II, pp. 334–335.

baron's colonies of the next decade, but also the independent settlements that developed alongside them.

Early Settlement in Palestine as Colonization

The Rothschild Colonies Compared
In what measure were the first years of Jewish settlement in Palestine, and especially the activities of Baron de Rothschild and his officials, another example of colonization? Earlier in this work, we discussed two main types of colonization: *colonisation de peuplement* or *d'enracinement*, in which the conditions in a foreign country pave the way for permanent European settlement, and *colonisation d'exploitation*, in which the central motive for settlement is financial gain.[35] Can Jewish settlement in Palestine during its first decade be defined in these terms?

The Jews brought an immense sum of money into the country during this period. Individual settlers invested all their savings in the establishment of family farms, and thousands of Hovevei Zion adherents throughout Europe contributed towards the support of the colonies. But far above them all, in a category of his own, was Baron Edmond de Rothschild, who enriched the country during the period in question by at least eight million francs, i.e., an average of one million francs a year. Albeit considerably less than the sum derived from the commonly-cited estimate of Rothschild's total financial support ($1.6 million or 40 million francs until the beginning of January 1900), which is more than 2 million francs a year, this was a sum far greater than that contributed by all other Jews throughout world. The funds collected by all the Hovevei Zion societies in Europe for Jewish settlement in Palestine totalled less than an average of 50 thousand francs per year.[36] In both national and global terms, it was a contribution of awesome proportions. For the sake

---

35 Compare with Arlosoroff, who claims that the only important achievement of the typology is to differentiate the "colonization of immigrants" from other categories (Arlosoroff, p. 13); also see Wilkansky, who says there are only two types of colonization — foreign, which is motivated by the desire for conquest, privately funded and reliant on military strength; and domestic, which is the product of national initiative and reliant on agricultural manpower.

36 Ahad Ha-am, Yishuv, p. 233; Bein, p. 10, n.1 and many others.

of comparison, the leading philanthropist of the time, George Peabody, donated less than half a million francs a year to his most important project; and the value of cargo entering and leaving Palestine in the 1880s reached about 5–6 million francs a year.[37]

Is it possible that this was only a profit-seeking venture on the part of a wealthy developer, in the manner of Leopold II in the Congo or Menier on the Canadian island of Anti-Costi?[38] A researcher who would answer that question in the positive describes Rothschild's involvement in the Jewish settlement of Palestine as a traditional colonialist takeover by an experienced capitalist with vested interests. The reconstruction of facts and events in the current work, to my best understanding, proves that nothing was further from the truth. There is no substantiation for the claims that Rothschild was the sole owner, that the lands were used solely for his own benefit, that his goal was quick, guaranteed profit, and that he developed monoculture farms styled after the huge estates in Algeria in order to maximize his profits.[39]

To set the record straight, Edmond de Rothschild was not an experienced capitalist; his brothers, to whom this appellation was much more suited, were openly opposed to his involvement in the colonies. Secondly, Rothschild was not the sole proprietor of the land, even in the colonies where he exercised full control; private farms continued to operate alongside those managed by the administration, and at least on one occasion Rothschild encouraged their expansion. Thirdly, Rothschild avoided acquiring land that was already in Jewish hands, which would have facilitated registry of ownership and lowered investment costs.

---

37 Avni, *Argentina*, p. 26 (on Peabody); Avitsur, *Jaffa Port*, Table 11, and Ledoulx report, 1888, Archives of French Ministry of Foreign Affairs, Consular and Commercial Correspondence, Jerusalem 5, pp. 101–113 (on commercial activity in 1885–1887).

38 See: Lichtervelde; Hamelin, pp. 157–177; Leschem, pp. 53, 59, 63, 93 (the author does not cite primary sources in support of these claims or examine a variety of secondary sources).

39 The literature on Rothschild dwells frequently on the skepticism of some of his closest advisors and their sense that his investments in Palestine were akin to 'building castles on the sand'. The misgivings of his family and the solitary nature of his activities are also accentuated (see Bouvrier, p. 280). Nevertheless, he was accused of operating for profit even in the 1880s, by a contemporary who lists the sums contributed to Petah Tikva and wonders what other motive Rothschild might have for assisting a colony not under his patronage (Diskin, fol. 6 a–b).

Some of the land was divided up and expenses for registration and parcellation were not added on. Finally, Rothschild was very far from being a profit-seeker. A large proportion of his investment was directed not toward production or preparatory infrastructure, but toward the development and management of public services. He consistently avoided the acquisition of urban land, commercial ventures, or any other lucrative offers that came his way. Not only was he uninterested in maximum profit, but he willingly entered into projects that were guaranteed to generate losses.[40]

It is true that Rothschild recorded the sums he paid out to the settlers and reminded them from time to time of their repayment obligations; but direct aid accounted for a tiny fraction of his investment in the colonies. These loans were nearly interest-free and whatever monies were recouped — at a much later date, and in some cases only in the 1940s — were reinvested entirely in colonization. When Rothschild turned over his vast property holdings and financial assets in Palestine to the Jewish Colonisation Association in 1900, the transaction was free of stipulations or a desire for profit.[41] Rothschild even provided JCA with an additional grant of 15 million francs to be used for the benefit of the colonies.

In short, none of this colossal investment in the colonization enterprise was motivated by personal gain. The actions of Rothschild, like others devoted to the cause of Jewish colonization, were financially one-sided; the resources flowed from overseas to Palestine and not vice versa, as was typical of exploitative colonization. Hence, settlement in Eretz Israel was not a case of *colonisation d'exploitation*. But was it *colonisation de peuplement*? As noted in the introductory chapter, this form of settlement was assisted in many ways by governments. The colonists benefited from legislation that facilitated land purchase, from infrastructure and services supplied by the government, and from financial support, both

---

40 Gvati, I, p. 85; farmers' debts listed in the administration records for Rosh Pinna (CZA J15/6359) and Zikhron Ya'akov (CZA J15/5956); IOUs of farmers of Rishon le-Zion (CZA J15/6089); compare with massive profits of Leopold II and his partners in Congo, amounting to an average of 4 million francs a year — seven times more than they invested!

41 Schama, pp. 137–189; Aaronsohn, Building, pp. 268–272.

direct and indirect, that enabled the establishment and development of their colonies.

In many instances of European colonization in countries under direct foreign rule, government and settlement were so intertwined that it was difficult to separate colonization from colonialism.[42] Thus it is not surprising that Leroy-Beaulieu's monumental work on colonization devotes only one paragraph to emigration and resettlement in a lengthy discussion of the governmental, commercial, economic and social aspects of French colonization in Algeria.[43]

Even in cases of indirect government, such as the French protectorate in Tunisia in 1881, legislative action (like the passage of the Enzel Law) paved the way for the settlement of Europeans and eliminated the need for direct intervention.[44]

Government also played a critical role in domestic colonization, which was not discussed here, but nevertheless should be noted. It served as the major dispenser of loans to small farms in Western Europe and Scandinavia (Germany, Denmark, Sweden, Norway and England) in the late nineteenth century; as the source of discounts and rebates to settlers in Western Canada after three years of settlement (a provision of the Land Law of 1872) and concessions to development companies that brought thousands of families to the region beginning in 1884; and as the financing body behind the committees that resettled hundreds of thousands of people in Posen and Siberia in the mid-1880s (providing free land, loans, development of infrastructure and public building).[45]

In Palestine, on the other hand, government and colonization were totally separate. The Ottoman authorities not only failed to supply the Jewish colonies (as all other inhabitants in fact) with basic services, but there was a strong conflict of interest between them. The Turks were apprehensive about another national minority agitating in the Ottoman

---

42   See, for example, the passage of land ownership and taxation regulations that openly and directly facilitated European settlement in North and Central Africa at the expense of the natives, in Yacono, I, pp. 283–285; Julien, p. 648; Church, pp. 57–60. Even intellectuals like Albert Memmi and Jean-Paul Sartre used colonialism and colonization interchangeably. See Memmi, pp. XXV, 3.

43   Leroy-Beaulieu, I, pp. 371–395 (pp. 367–525).

44   Sethom, p. 112; Ficaya, p. 34.

45   Ettinger, pp. 95–99; England, pp. 46–53, 59.

Empire (friction with the Balkan peoples led to the Balkan War in 1878), while simultaneously fearing the growing influence of the European powers through the presence of communities holding foreign citizenship.

These fears generated a negative attitude that persisted throughout the First Aliya period. As a result, the local authorities in Palestine adopted a hard line against the Jews, and the central government in Istanbul passed a series of stiff immigration laws (in 1881/2, 1883, 1884, 1887/8, and 1889) that created inequality between the local inhabitants and newcomers, and discriminated against Europeans.[46] The Jewish settlers were prohibited from purchasing land and holding deeds in their name, and thus could not obtain building permits. The restrictions imposed by the Turkish authorities influenced the geography of the early colonies in the following ways:

a) Temporary Sites

Certain colonies were not founded on the site that was originally chosen for them but in a temporary location where offical permission was unnecessary. Sometimes settlement began on the outskirts of the purchased land beside an Arab village, as in the case of Rosh Pinna and the neighboring village of Ja'una; sometimes the early camping site was not on the land at all but inside an Arab village, as in the case of the early settlers of Ekron who took up residence in Akir, and the settlers of Bnei Yehuda who resided in Rumthaniyya and Bir esh-Shkūm. Building on the permanent site commenced much later after the land was properly registered and permits were finally obtained from the authorities. In Ekron, the original plans were implemented in stages throughout the 1880s; in Rosh Pinna, full-scale development took place only at the turn of the century.

b) Temporary Housing

Many of the pioneers lived at first in prefabricated cabins that could be put up within a day and did not require building permits. Occasionally, others renovated adobe structures such as the hushot (primitive mud huts) in Zikhron Ya'akov, or rehabilitated old buildings such as those acquired with the land in Nahalat Reuven and Yesud ha-Ma'ala. Settlers of Rishon le-Zion and Yesud ha-Ma'ala also lived in thatched booths,

---

46 Mandel, pp. 1–9; Eliav, Diplomatic, pp. 117–132.

those of Gedera in Bedouin-style tents, and the settlers of Ekron and Gedera in barns and farm shelters.

c) Nearby Operational Bases
Until housing was complete, each colony maintained an operational base in a nearby urban community. The circumstances in some colonies dictated a separation between the pioneers and their families for a period of two to three years. The women and children stayed in town, while the men lived and worked in the colonies.

d) Dissolution
So much time passed before title deeds were issued that orderly settlement and economic development were seriously hindered. Even wells could not be dug until the paperwork was complete. In the 1880s this caused the dissolution of two colonies, one directly and the other indirectly. In the first case, the pioneers became impatient and withdrew their plans; in the other, so many settlers left that the colony could no longer function.

Unlike many settlers in other parts of the world, the Jewish pioneers in Eretz Isarel paid for their land in full. In addition to the negotiated price, they paid exorbitant registration fees that virtually doubled the outlay.[47] The investment was so high that it acted as a filter, keeping out the adventurers and speculators who were frequently attracted to colonization schemes in other regions by the concessions and special privileges offered by the government.

In the face of government opposition, Rothschild was wary of assisting colonization openly. He opposed the creation of an independent political entity or even hinting at such intentions. He kept his activities within the realm of the Jewish community, and cautioned against flaunting the Jewish presence in the rural sector. He even demanded that the buildings in his colonies not be visible from the highways.[48]

---

47 Ben Levi (Frumkin), "Against Destroyers," *Ha-havazzelet* 19, no. 23 (1889) pp. 179–188 (Hebrew); Diskin, fol. 6a.
48 Rothschild's letters to Hirsch on 3 January and 1 February 1883, Yavne'eli, II, pp. 73 and 75 respectively, and letter of 21 January 1886 (manuscript, French), CZA J41/72.

Studies linking early Jewish colonization with colonialism have addressed the problem of the detachment and opposition of the Ottoman government in three ways. Through the selective use of sources (i.e., sources from a later date, quoted out of context), some researchers have tried to create the impression of tacit cooperation between the government and the settlers which culminated in the expropriation of land from Arab residents and its sale to Jews. Others admit that the Ottomans were opposed to colonization, but were incapable of defying the European powers, especially Germany and Russia, who intervened on behalf of their "Zionist settlers." The implication is that Jewish colonization was used by the countries of Europe to promote their colonial interests, which, of course, is totally unfounded.[49] The third and most subtle argument, is that Rothschild himself was a colonialist, and through his dominance, transformed the entire enterprise into a colonial venture.

Leschem, for example, defines Jewish colonization as the "third stage in the intervention of European colonial powers." She claims that their actions in 1860–1870 led to large sectors of land being transferred to Arab absentee landlords. In the second stage, the peasants were dispossessed and turned into a body of unemployed manpower, and in the third stage, they became an agricultural proletariat that supplied Rothschild's plantations with cheap labor. Leschem sees a direct parallel in the land laws in Algeria which pared the way for French colonization.[50] On the one hand, this says nothing about the alleged positive approach of the Ottomans and the colonial powers; on the other, we know that Rothschild opposed the employment of Arabs in his colonies and favored Jewish labor despite the higher cost. Furthermore, Rothschild had no intention of altering the demographic structure of the country and supported selective immigration, where as one of the goals of colonialism, also in cases of domestic colonization such as the resettlement of Germans in the eastern provinces, was the establishment of a demographic majority.

Jewish settlement in Palestine was to some extent also unique in the relationship that existed between the pioneers and the local inhabitants during the era under discussion. The theme of conqueror versus conquered or settlers versus natives is often presented in the literature as central to

---

49 Kayyali, p. 16; Öke, pp. 329–341.
50 Leschem, pp. 44–46.

colonization. This is true both for generalized studies on the theory of colonization and for case studies (see Introduction). It has been shown that all colonizing efforts bearing a colonial stamp encounter resistance and opposition from the native population. In Palestine, however, the relationship between newcomers and local inhabitants was of marginal importance. Obviously, presence of foreigners and cultural differences created some tension and conflict, but during the first decade of Jewish colonization, and for at least thirty years more, it did not escalate to national proportions.[51]

The normalcy of relations between the Jewish settlers and the Arabs were attested to by the lack of tension on a national scale. French colonization in Algeria was a direct consequence of military occupation, and the Italians settled in Libya after a turbulent period of conquest, uprising and anarchy. By contrast, the arrival of the colonists (whether Jews or Christians) in Palestine was at first nearly uneventful and did not incite organized protest for the time being. While security left much to be desired — highway robbery, theft and murder were common — the Jews suffered no more than the German Templers or the rest of the population. The attacks on the colonies of Petah Tikva and Gedera in the 1880s were not triggered by nationalism but by economic grievances; actually they should be considered as local disputes between neighbors.[52]

Violence in Palestine was on an entirely different scale than incidents such as the 1839 Mitijda massacre in Algeria when all European settlers in the valley were slaughtered. Only two Jewish colonies established in the second half of the 1880s took visible precautions to secure their inhabitants. Both were built in a rectangle and surrounded by a "protective wall." However, this wall was of simple construction and less than two meters high. It joined up the rear walls of the farm buildings and enclosed the yards, and was mainly designed to keep out cattle rustlers. It was perforated throughout by wickets (one per farm) that were large enough

---

51 Ro'i, pp. 245–268; Mandel, pp. 34–38.
52 Ibid., loc. cit., Avneri, pp. 68–77. The first indication of popular national opposition was in mid-1890 when a group of Arab intellectuals from Jaffa protested that the Jews were taking over the country. For those who consider this the start of organized Arab resistance to Jewish settlement, 1890 marked the beginning of a new era.

for a person to pass through, but not livestock.[53] This could hardly compare with the defensive network of thick walls, embankments and fortifications that the French colonists in Algeria erected to ward off attack.

In sum, the early Jewish colonies were not an example of *colonisation d'exploitation*. Neither Rothschild nor anyone else involved in the settlement of Palestine was a profit-seeking capitalist. The government extended no aid whatsoever, either directly or indirectly. However, if we take this network and peel away the political and economic layers, we find all the features central to *colonisation de peuplement* in the narrow sense of European settlement in an underdeveloped foreign country.

The question to which we now address ourselves is how this form of colonization affected the landscape.

Colonization, Colonialism and Geography

The work of D. Meinig, one of the world's leading historical geographers, sheds important light on Jewish colonization in Palestine despite the fact that his essay purports to study imperialist expansion.[54] Meinig belongs to that category of researchers described in the introduction as making no distinction between imperialism, colonialism and colonization. In his inquiry into settlement geography he frequently uses the terms "colonization" and "imperialism" synonymously, which narrows the gap between his study and ours. Furthermore, although his approach is extremely broad-based from the persectives of time and place, his theories are no less applicable to case studies.[55] In Meining's view, imperialism is a phenomenon that manifests itself in five spheres: politics, society, culture, economy and psychology.

1) From a political perspective, imperialism and colonialism are defined as the takeover of another country by an occupying political entity that sends in agents (governor, military commander, officials) backed up by armed forces (police, army).

---

53 The wickets were generally 160 cm. high and 60–70 cm. wide (Ben-Artzi, *Documents*, p. 141).
54 See bibliography for Meinig.
55 Meinig agreed with me on this point in a conversation that took place in Oxford in August 1983.

2) In society, occupation precipitates the creation of a new social order led by the imperial agents as the "ethical aristocracy." Beneath them is a new class of local residents who are intermediaries between the imperial agents and the other native population.

3) The outcome of this process is cultural change that is expected to affect both sides, though not in equal measure. Most of the pressure is exerted on the natives, through schools, religious institutions, courts, and daily contact.

4) New economic relations are established, such as direct taxation of the natives, takeover of industry and resources, and initiation of economic programs by the occupying government. The government may intervene in less obvious ways, by imposing indirect taxes, penetrating commercial markets, manipulating the laws, and reinterpreting property rights. At the same time, it may contribute positively through capital investment, purchase of services and goods, and payment of wages, i.e., creating an economic flow from mother country to colony that transforms the relationship into an economic partnership.

5) On a psychological level, the occupying government tries to inspire reverence among the natives in order to minimize costs and maintain control with the least possible interference. This requires a change in the psyche of the natives regarding the symbols of authority, power and prestige.

If Jewish settlement in Palestine were an example of colonial expansion according to Meinig's definition, these five categories would have the following geographical implications:

1) On a political level, the imperial agents would be positioned strategically throughout the occupied region and a network of roads would be developed to establish links between them and between the colony and the imperial homeland. This did not occur in Palestine. Rothschild avoided stationing his officials in strategic locations although he had hundreds of them working for him in the 1880s (we have names, professions, dates, and places of assignment for at least 170). All of them resided and operated in the colonies alone. In negotiations with the government, Rothschild relied as much as possible on intermediaries who maintained close contact with the local authorities rather than sending in his own officials. The relations between his immediate associates and the government were kept to a minimum. Neither did Rothschild build

a network of roadways that connected the colonies or linked them up to the ports (aside from short access sections leading from the colonies to the nearest highways). There was a constant flow of manpower, commodities, knowhow and directives between Paris and Eretz Israel, but this was accomplished through existing channels (established by the authorities or parties operating in the region before Rothschild), without the takeover or creation of new channels. All of this, of course, was a consequence of the basic political divergence between the Ottoman government and Jewish settlement.

2) No socio-geographical changes, such as the emergence of segregated districts or bi-cultural communities, were noted in Palestine as a result of Rothschild's efforts. Certain regions were considered preferable for settlement, but within these areas one found an intermingling of old and new Arab villages (constituting the majority) side by side with new outposts of Jewish settlement. There is no evidence that the social hierarchy was altered by the contact between Arabs and Jewish settlers, and the Jews did not enjoy a higher social status than their Arab neighbors.

3) According to Meinig, one could expect widespread cultural influences affecting both institutions and lifestyle (language, dress, modern vs. traditional occupations). No such cultural diffusion was evident in Palestine. The Jewish settlers did not impose their culture on the Arabs either hierarchically (beginning with those aspects of Arab life that were more susceptible to influence) or gradationally (beginning with those spheres in which contact between the settlers and Arabs was most intensive). No cultural pressure was exerted on local inhabitants, and if there were mutual influences, they were spontaneous and sporadic. For every Arab who spoke Yiddish, Hebrew or French, there was a Jew who spoke Arabic. Even in the second decade of Jewish colonization, when Rothschild was a major employer of Arabs and hence a facilitator of daily contact between the settlers and the local inhabitants, it is difficult to discern the kind of cultural interchange envisaged by Meinig.

4) The dominion over assets and natural resources, as well as the inauguration or expansion of commercial and other economic ties between mother country and colony, are unmistakable signs of imperialism. In economic relations that are less perceptible and straightforward, tracing the source of decision-making with regard to investment and employment can be highly revealing. In our case, Rothschild made no attempt to gain

control of national assets or resources. On the contrary, he came to the aid of the colonies when they were in the midst of an economic crisis brought on chiefly by the lack of such resources. His agronomists spent much of their time in the 1880s experimenting with crops that would thrive under local conditions, and in doing so, physically changed the landscape (through the introduction of *champs d'expérience* and irrigated fields). This possibility is not considered by Meinig. As he suggests, decision-making with regard to some of the investments carried out in the 1890s (Zikhron Ya'akov wine cellar, perfume and silk refineries) can be traced to the previous decade. Yet Rothschild's economic activity was restricted to the "New Yishuv." There were no efforts to expand, commerically or otherwise, outside the colonies, and needless to say, no taxes were imposed by the baron or any other body involved in Jewish settlement. It was heavy Ottoman taxation that was so often described in the sources as a major stumbling block for the early pioneers.[56] Financial transactions did take place between the colonists and the local inhabitants, either on a one-time basis (purchase of land) or continuously (payment of wages to Arab laborers), both of which left their mark on the Arab sector in the 1880s.[57] However, these commercial relations were far from constituting a broad national phenomenon, and any foreign contacts through Rothschild were totally one-sided, involving transfers from France to Palestine but not vice versa.

5) Finally, none of Rothschild's actions were deliberately geared to alter the psyche of the inhabitants. From a geographical perspective, he did his best to downplay the presence of his officials and the modification of the landscape. He exercised no control over the provincial capital (Jerusalem), the mosques or the holy places, and he studiously avoided building in conspicious places such as crossroads or regional centers. Every effort was made to avoid involvement outside the Jewish

---

56 On the oppressive Ottoman taxation, see Diskin, fol. 6; 23b; figures for the high taxes on wheat in Barzilai, *Beit Halevi*, pp. 31, 38–39 (see also: Aaronsohn, Baron, Table 6, p. 240).

57 On the improved living standards of Arab villages near the colonies, see "Within the Country, *Ha-zvi* 2 (1886), no. 29 (Hebrew). On the settlement of 400 Arab families in the vicinity of Rishon le-Zion in the 1880s, see Grazovsky's letter of 18 December 1889, Druyanow, *Documents*, III, p. 66. On a house built on the lands of Gedera, see Hissin, *Diary*, p. 76.

community, and this policy was verbalized on various occasions, both in a general context and pertaining specifically to geography.[58]

The geographical features theoretically associated with colonialism did not materialize in the Jewish colonization enterprise in Eretz Israel, and for good reason: two basic conditions of the colonial process were conspicuously missing — forceful occupation and exploitation. Jewish settlement in the 1880s was colonization in the narrow, purely geographic sense in which the term was originally used. In this respect, it had certain features in common with colonization in other regions of the world. Yet there were some components, described below, that were patently unique to Palestine.

Uniqueness of Jewish Colonization

The uniqueness of the Jewish colonization enterprise on a univeral, regional and local scale is undeniable, despite the points of similarity with other such ventures. During its early years, colonization in the Holy Land was the undertaking of an externally sustained foreign body that brought in manpower, capital and knowhow to promote its own interests, independent of local factors. It was thus colonization of the type defined in our introduction as "the reshaping of the landscape following the migration and settlement of a foreign entity," as distinct from colonialism with its political-economic orientation. In terms of general structure, it was akin to *colonisation de peuplement sans drapeaux*.[59]

The Jewish colonies, like others we have described, faced seven major hurdles: purchasing land and securing ownership rights, developing a water supply, mobilizing funds and credit, choosing proper farming methods, adapting to life in a new land, organizing socially, and safeguarding person and property.

Those actively involved in settlement in Palestine, especially Rothschild and his administration, were clearly influenced by prevailing trends in the realm of colonization. The French colonies, with their

---

58   See note 45, above. He maintained his anonymity through the appellation *Ha-nadiv ha-yadua* (the well-known benefactor) and attempted to visit the country incognito in the spring of 1887. He and his wife left their luxurious yacht at Port Said and appeared in Jaffa port one day aboard an ordinary ship carrying Christian pilgrims.
59   Definition in Arlosoroff, p. 12.

centralistic management, minimal input from the settlers, reliance on Parisian supervisors (*intendents*), and "contracts of sale" (*contract pact*), should have been an obvious model.[60] Many ideas and modes of operation were borrowed from them, including general approaches to settlement, experimentation with new crops, and updating technology through the use of imported machinery and foreign expertise.[61] Shifting the plane of discussion from positivistic to humanistic, we find that colonial terminology influenced the thinking of Rothschild and his officials even subconsciously. Thus the metropolis or main city, serving as the seat of power and government, was noticeably absent from the settlement hierarchy in Palestine; in this respect, one could speak of the whole country as a colony administered from Paris.

It should be borne in mind that some aspects of Jewish colonization overlapped with independent local trends emerging in nineteenth-century Palestine and the Levant. Among them were the establishment of colonies by both groups of Muslims (such as Egyptians and Circassians) along the lines of the traditional Arab village, and groups of Christians (Americans and Germans); the injection of foreign capital and knowhow by European powers and Christian churches; and the development of agriculture and technology, both by the Ottomans, who built telegraph lines and carriage roads, and by wealthy Arab landowners who began to introduce modern farming on their estates.[62]

All these trends, and others, too, received a boost from Jewish colonization, but they were set in motion before its onset and were viable without it. If we look at the period critically, we see that even the First Aliya, which produced the early colonies, was more successful in increasing Jewish population in the cities rather than the countryside. The flow of urban immigration was bi-directional, contributing on the

---

60 Compare with the Rothschild administration and the contracts signed by settlers of the JCA in Argentina. These contracts were binding for twenty years until the repayment of the settlement loan, and stipulated that the settler could not lease his land or employ foreign laborers.
61 Aaronsohn, Settlement; Avitsur, Agriculture, pp. 229–236; also compare with agricultural experiments and introduction of new branches of farming on the island of Anti-Costi (see Hamelin; Aaronsohn, Jewish Colonies, 5, pp. 32–33). The use of advanced technologies was not always successful. See Avitsur, *Plow*, pp. 90–92.
62 Avitsur, *Daily Life*, pp. 311–340; Gross, pp. 24–63.

one hand to the development of the "New Yishuv" in Jaffa, Haifa, and Jerusalem, and on the other to the strengthening of the "Old Yishuv" based in the holy cities. In Jerusalem, the Jewish community doubled in size during this period.[63]

Jewish settlement in Eretz Israel was thus firmly anchored in global and local processes, but it differed from other colonization in two striking and interrelated ways. First of all, the colonies owed their entire existence to the human component rather than to natural attributes. From a geographical standpoint, Jewish colonization spearheaded landscape change in defiance of physiography. In the light of humanism no less than positivism, it was man who was victorious. Whereas the target country of other colonizing ventures was chosen after carefully considering the pros and cons, i.e., through a logical process of deduction, such factors had no bearing on colonization in Eretz Israel for the simple freason that it was motivated not by pragmatism and economics but by ideology.[64]

The debate over the natural potential of the country taken up by Jews like Carl Netter and Christians like Claude R. Conder prior to the onset of Jewish colonization, was thus totally irrelevant.[65] Man was the overriding factor. Just as the human component counterbalanced the regional advantages of the Jaffa region and steered nearly half of all settlement in the 1880s northwards, cancelled out the relative advantages enjoyed by Petah Tikva over Rishon le-Zion and Rishon le-Zion over Zikhron Ya'akov in the 1880s, and had an effect on every other sphere of inquiry related to Jewish settlement, human determination and willpower consistently came out ahead against the forces of nature.[66]

The establishment of the Jewish colonies was an example of the human component imposing itself upon the environment. Rothschild,

---

63   Ben-Arieh, Jerusalem, pp. 172–174.
64   Hardy, pp. 25–26. Also see introduction, pp. 33–34 on the physiographic and economic advantages that attracted Baron Hirsch to Argentina (cheap arable land, plentiful rainfall, convenient transportation).
65   For a fascimile of Netter's letter and responses to it, and Conder's treatises in 1878 and 1891, see Kark and Aaronsohn, pp. 1–17.
66   The contemporary sources are not very informative on climatic conditions in the country. While Rothschild's aid to the settlers was similar to "insurance," it is surprising that natural disasters as serious as the drought in 1889/90 were not mentioned in their letters. Also see Hacohen, Land of Israel, p. 28.

Hovevei Zion and the pioneers pitched themselves against adverse topographical-geological and economic-agricultural conditions — and were victorious.[67] It is thus impossible to understand Jewish settlement in Palestine or the willing participation of Baron de Rothschild from a purely pragmatic perspective, in terms of profit and loss. This is just as true on the micro level as on the macro. It was as applicable to the baron's insistence on developing Zikhron Ya'akov on its original site rather than moving to a fertile area requiring less investment, as it was to the decision of individual Jews to resettle in a land that lacked the attractions of other countries then accepting immigrants.[68]

This brings us to another dimension, related to ideology, that made Jewish colonization in Eretz Israel unique: the return of a people to its ancestral homeland. Behind all the settlement activity depicted here were the ideological, historical, national and religious aspirations of the Jewish people. It was this special circumstance that made Jewish settlement so different in substance from colonization in other parts of the world, despite the similarities. It also colored Rothschild's relationship with the pioneers, which was the inverse of that normally found between a capitalist settlement agent and settlers. Rothschild was not the prime mover but only a facilitator; he provided support for a colonization movement that had come into the world prior to his involvement.

Notwithstanding his unparalleled contribution and the indelible imprint of those in his employ, Rothschild was not an organic and inseparable part of the colonization enterprise. He was attracted to it and took it up as a cause; he did his best to shape and influence it, and left a deep and lasting mark. Yet for all the timeliness of his intervention and the paths he carved, which were followed for years to come, when in 1900 he withdrew from personal responsibility and transferred the helm to the Jewish Colonisation Association, no major harm was done. The transition period was not free of problems but it was no more than the end of one chapter and the beginning of another. The baron stepped aside, yet the colonization of Eretz Israel continued.

---

67 Scheid, p. 73.
68 For the baron's decision in principle concerning the site of Zikhron Ya'akov, which was obviously not economically worthwhile, see Scheid, p. 73.

BIBLIOGRAPHY

Archival Sources

Israel

Central Zionist Archives, Jerusalem (CZA)

Institutional Archives
  J15: Mikve Israel Archives
  J41: PICA Archives (including JCA and Rothschild Archives)

Personal Papers
  A9: Alter Druyanow (collection)
  A25: Yehoshua Barzilai-Eisenstadt
  A32: Menashé Meerovitch
  A34: Zalman David Levontin
  A51: Zadoc Kahn
  A109: Yehi'el Michel Pines
  A164: Amnon Hourvitz
  A192: David Idelovitch
  A302: Aharon Ever-Hadani (Feldman)

Photo Collection

Jewish National and University Library, Jerusalem (JNUL)
  Department of Manuscripts and Archives

Yad Izhak Ben-Zvi, Jerusalem
  Archives

Department of Geography, Hebrew University of Jerusalem
  Aerial Photo Collection
  Map Collection

Rishon le-Zion Museum
Historical Archives
Zikhron Ya'akov Library and Archives

France

Archives de Ministère des Affaires Étrangères, Paris and Nantes
Correspondance Consulaire et Commercial — Turquie
Correspondance Politique — Turquie
Archives Diplomatique rapatriés de Beyrouth

Archives Nationales Françaises, Paris
132 AQ: Les Archives de Maison de Rothschild
F10: Les Archives de Ministère d'Agriculture
F12: Les Archives de Ministère de Commerce et d'Industrie

Archives d'Alliance Israélite Universelle, Paris
Israel XXXVIII E120

Bibliographical Abbreviations
Books and Articles[1]

Aaronsohn, Agriculture = R. Aaronsohn, "The Beginnings of Modern Jewish Agriculture in Palestine: Indigenous versus Imported," *Agricultural History* 69 (1995), pp. 438–453.
Aaronsohn, Baron = R. Aaronsohn, *Baron Rothschild and the Colonies: The Beginnings of Jewish Colonization in Eretz Israel*, Jerusalem 1990 (Hebrew).
Aaronsohn, Building = R. Aaronsohn, "Building the Land: Stages in First Aliya Colonization (1882–1904)," *Jerusalem Cathedra* 3 (1983), pp. 236–279.
Aaronsohn, Colonisation = A. Aaronsohn, "La colonisation juive en Palestine," *Bulletin de Société Botanique de France* 56 (1909), pp. 353–359.
Aaronsohn, Colonization = R. Aaronsohn, "Baron Rothschild and the Initial

---

[1] Hebrew titles are given in English translation. Whenever the publisher has supplied a translation, this is generally used, even if it involves some inconsistency in spelling.

Stage of Jewish Settlement in Palestine (1882–1890): A Different Type of Colonization," *Journal of Historical Geography* 19 (1993), pp. 142–156.

Aaronsohn, Cultural = R. Aaronsohn, "The Cultural Landscape of Pre-Zionist Settlements," in R. Kark (ed.), *The Land that Became Israel: Studies in Historical Geography*, New Haven, London and Jerusalem 1989, pp. 147–166.

Aaronsohn, Establishment = R. Aaronsohn, "The Establishment and Initial Development of Zikhron Ya'akov and Rishon le-Zion as Two of the First Jewish Colonies in Palestine," M.A. thesis, The Hebrew University of Jerusalem, 1979 (Hebrew).

Aaronsohn, Jewish Colonies = R. Aaronsohn, "The Jewish Colonies at their Inception and the Contribution of Baron Rothschild to their Development," I–II, Ph.D. dissertation, The Hebrew University of Jerusalem, 1985 (Hebrew).

Aaronsohn, Officials = R. Aaronsohn, "Baron Rothschild's Officials, 1882–1890," *Cathedra,* 74 (December 1994), pp. 157–178 (Hebrew).

Aaronsohn, Settlement = R. Aaronsohn, "The Settlement Ideologies of the Founders of the First Colonies in Eretz Yisrael," in A. Shinan (ed.), *Emigration and Settlement in Jewish and General History*, Jerusalem 1982, pp. 225–232 (Hebrew).

Aaronsohn, Vines = R. Aaronsohn, "Vines and Wineries in the Jewish Colonies: Introducing Modern Viticulture into Nineteenth-Century Palestine," *Studies in Zionism* 14 (1993), pp. 31–51.

Aaronsohn and Kark = R. Aaronsohn and R. Kark, "Shoshanat Ha-yarden," *Teva-Va-aretz* 24, no. 2 (1982), pp. 55–57 (Hebrew).

Admiralty = Great Britain. Admiralty Naval Staff, Intelligence Department, *The Jewish Colonies in Palestine, 1882–1914*, London 1909.

Ahad Ha-am, This = Ahad Ha-am, "This is not the Way," *Ha-melitz* 29, no. 53 (1889) (Hebrew).

Ahad Ha-am, Truth = Ahad Ha-am, "Truth from Eretz Israel," *Ha-melitz* 31, nos. 125–134 (1891) (Hebrew).

Ahad Ha-am, Yishuv = Ahad Ha-am, "The Yishuv and its Guardians," *Collected Works*, Tel Aviv 1950, pp. 211–245 (Hebrew).

Altschuler = A. M. Altschuler, "Diary" (manuscript, no pagination), CZA A9/79–3 (Hebrew).

Ariel = D. Ariel (Leibowitz), *The Moshava of Gedera: Its Development and History*, Jerusalem 1979 (Hebrew).

Arlosoroff = C. Arlosoroff, *A World History of Colonization (Collected Works,* IV), Tel Aviv 1934 (Hebrew).
Avitsur, Agriculture = S. Avitsur, "Agriculture, Handicrafts and Light Industry during the Period of the First Aliya," in M. Eliav (ed.), *The First Aliyah,* Jerusalem 1981, I, pp. 225–244 (Hebrew).
Avitsur, *Daily Life* = S. Avitsur, *Daily Life in Eretz Israel in the Nineteenth Century,* Tel Aviv 1972 (Hebrew).
Avitsur, *Inventors* = S. Avitsur, *Inventors and Adopters,* Jerusalem and Tel Aviv 1985 (Hebrew).
Avitsur, *Jaffa Port* = S. Avitsur, *Jaffa Port at its Zenith and in Decline,* Tel Aviv 1972 (Hebrew).
Avitsur, *Plow* = S. Avitsur, *The Plow in Palestine: History and Development,* Tel Aviv 1965 (Hebrew).
Avitsur, Watermelons = S. Avitsur, "Watermelons in the Eretz Israel Economy," *Merhavim* 1 (1974), pp. 80–91 (Hebrew).
Avneri = A. L. Avneri, *The Claim of Dispossession: Jewish Land Settlement and the Arabs, 1878–1948,* New York 1984.
Avni, Argentina = H. Avni, *Argentina and the Jews: A History of Jewish Immigration,* Tuscaloosa 1991.
Avni, Jewish Agriculture = H. Avni, "Jewish Agriculture in Argentina: The Project that Failed?" in A. Shinan (ed.), *Emigration and Settlement in Jewish and General History,* Jerusalem 1982, pp. 313–334 (Hebrew).
Avni, *Promised Land* = H. Avni, *Argentina, the "Promised Land": Baron de Hirsch's Colonization Project in the Argentine Republic,* Jerusalem 1973 (Hebrew).
Barnett = Z. Barnett, *Memoirs,* Jerusalem 1929 (Hebrew).
Barzilai, *Beit Halevi* = Y. Barzilai (Eisenstadt), *Beit Halevi: Letters from Eretz Israel,* Jerusalem 1892–1895 (Hebrew).
Barzilai, *Colonies* = Y. Barzilai (Eisenstadt), *The Colonies of Eretz Israel in 1891,* St. Petersberg 1892 (Hebrew).
Barzilai, Memories = Y. Barzilai (Eisenstadt), "Memories of the First Days," *Ha-olam* 7, no. 41 (1913), pp. 2–8; 8, no. 17 (1914), pp. 2–5; 8, no. 21 (1914), pp. 2–6 (Hebrew).
Bassin, *Jewish Yishuv* = G. Bassin, *The Jewish Yishuv in Eretz Israel during the First Aliya Period: Annotated Bibliography,* Tel Aviv 1975 (Hebrew).
Bassin, Selected = G. Bassin, "Selected Hebrew Bibliography," in M. Eliav (ed.), *The First Aliyah,* Jerusalem 1981, II, pp. 429–445 (Hebrew).

Beaudicour = L. Beaudicour, *La colonisation de l'Algérie: ses elements*, Paris 1956.

Bein = A. Bein, *A History of Zionist Settlement from the Herzl Period to Our Days*, Ramat Gan 1976 (Hebrew).

Belkind = I. Belkind, *In the Path of the Biluim*, Tel Aviv 1983 (Hebrew).

Ben-Arieh, Aspects = Y. Ben-Arieh, "Geographic Aspects of the Development of the first Jewish Settlements in Palestine," in M. Eliav (ed.), *The First Aliyah*, I, Jerusalem 1981, pp. 85–96 (Hebrew).

Ben-Arieh, *Jerusalem* = Y. Ben-Arieh, *Jerusalem in the Nineteenth-Century*, II: *The New City*, Jerusalem and New York 1986.

Ben-Arieh, Settlements = Y. Ben-Arieh, "The Development of Twelve Major Settlements in Nineteenth Century Palestine," *Cathedra* 19 (April 1981), pp. 83–143 (Hebrew).

Ben-Artzi, Changes = Y. Ben-Artzi, "Changes in the Agricultural Sector of the Moshavot, 1882–1914," in G. G. Gilbar (ed.), *Ottoman Palestine 1800–1914*, Leiden 1990, pp. 131–158.

Ben-Artzi, Documents = Y. Ben-Artzi, "Documents Regarding the Construction of Buildings and Stables in Zichron-Ya'akov (1883–1885)," *Cathedra* 29 (September 1983), pp. 45–62 (Hebrew).

Ben-Artzi, Galilee Colonies = Y. Ben-Artzi, "The Galilee Colonies in 1882–1914 from a Geographical-Settlement Perspective," in A. Shmueli, A. Soffer and N. Kliot (eds.), *In the Lands of Galilee*, I, Haifa 1983, pp. 405–426 (Hebrew).

Ben-Artzi, Hartuv = Y. Ben-Artzi, "Hartuv — A Forgotten Colony in the Judean Mountains," *Ofakim Be-geografia* 3 (1977), pp. 123–139 (Hebrew).

Ben-Artzi, *Jewish* = Y. Ben-Artzi, *Jewish Moshava Settlements in Eretz Israel (1882–1914)*, Jerusalem 1988 (Hebrew).

Ben-Yehuda, Fickle = E. Ben-Yehuda, "Fickle Nation," *Ha-zvi* 3, nos. 20, 22 (1887) (Hebrew).

Ben-Yehuda, Settlement = E. Ben-Yehuda, "The Settlement of Eretz Israel," *Ha-levanon* 20, no. 2 (1888), p. 16 (Hebrew).

Bendel = Y. Bendel, "Memories of Rosh Pinna," *Bustenai* 3, no. 34 (9 December 1931), pp. 14–15; no. 35 (16 December 1931), pp. 14–15 (Hebrew).

Bouvier = J. Bouvier, *Les Rothschilds*, Paris 1967.

Braslavsky = M. Braslavsky, *Laborers and Labor Organizations of the First Aliya: History and Sources*, Tel Aviv 1961 (Hebrew).

Brill = Y. Brill, *Yesud Hama'ala: The Immigration of Eleven Farmers from Russia in 1883,* Jerusalem 1978 (Hebrew).
Bronstein = Y. Bronstein, "One of the Students of Zikhron Ya'akov," *Ha-melitz* 29, no. 185 (1889) (Hebrew).
Carmel = A. Carmel, *German Settlement in Palestine at the End of Turkish Rule: Political, Local and International Problems,* Jerusalem 1973 (Hebrew).
Cassuto = D. Cassuto, "Construction in Eretz Israel from Mishkenot Sha'ananim to the Establishment of Tel Aviv," in *Craftsmanship and Art in Nineteenth-Century Eretz-Israel,* Jerusalem 1979, pp. 217–259 (Hebrew).
Church = H. R. J. Church, *Modern Colonization,* New York 1951.
Citron = S. L. Citron, *History of Hibbat Zion,* Odessa 1914 (Hebrew).
Cohen = E. Cohen, "Man as the Initiatior of Arid Zone Development," in Y. Mindlak and S. F. Singer (eds.), *Arid Zone Development,* Cambridge 1977, pp. 234–243.
Cohen, Be'er Tuviya = Sh. Cohen, "Reminiscences of Be'er Tuviya," *Bustenai* 9 (1938), pp. 17–19 (Hebrew).
Colonisation en Algérie = Algérie: Direction de l'Agriculture, de Commerce et de la Colonisation, *La colonisation en Algérie, 1830–1921,* Alger 1922.
D'arbela = I. G. D'arbela, "Health Conditions in the Colonies near Jaffa," *Yerushalayim* 3 (1890), pp. 90–92 (Hebrew).
Delmaire = J. M. Delmaire, "1891 — Vers le sionisme politique," *Yod* 2, no. 2 (1976), pp. 51–66.
Despois = J. Despois, "La colonisation italienne en Libya," Ph.D. dissertation, Paris 1935.
Diskin = M. Diskin, *The History of Mordechai,* Jerusalem 1889 (Hebrew).
Doucet = R. Doucet, *Commentaires sur la colonisation,* Paris 1926.
Druck = D. Druck, *Baron Edmond de Rothschild,* New York 1928.
Druyanow, *Documents* = A. Druyanow (ed.), *Documents on the History of Hibbat-Zion and the Settlement of Eretz Israel,* I–III, Odessa and Tel Aviv 1925–1932 (Hebrew and other languages).
Druyanow, *First Days* = A. Druyanow (ed.), *From the First Days: Journal of the History of the Rebirth of Eretz Israel* (supplements to *Bustenai*), I–II, Tel Aviv 1934–1936 (Hebrew).
Druyanow and Laskov = A. Druyanow (ed.), *Documents on the History of Hibbat-Zion and the Settlement of Eretz Israel,* new rev. ed. by S. Laskov, I–VII, Tel Aviv 1982–1993 (Hebrew).

Elboim-Dror = R. Elboim-Dror, *Hebrew Education in Eretz Israel*, I: *1854–1914*, Jerusalem 1986 (Hebrew).

Eliav, Diplomatic = M. Eliav, "Diplomatic Intervention Concerning Restrictions on Jewish Immigration and Purchase of Land at the End of the Nineteenth Century," *Cathedra* 26 (December 1982), pp. 117–132 (Hebrew).

Eliav, Eretz Israel = M. Eliav, *Eretz Israel and its Yishuv in the 19th Century*, Jerusalem 1978 (Hebrew).

Eliav, First Aliyah = M. Eliav (ed.), *The First Aliyah*, I–II, Jerusalem 1981 (Hebrew).

England = R. England, *The Colonization of Western Canada*, London 1936.

Epstein, History = Y. Epstein, "The History of the Colony of Shimron or Zikhron Ya'akov," *Knesset Yisrael* 1 (1886), pp. 966–967 (Hebrew).

Epstein, Question = Y. Epstein, "Unanswered Question," *Ha-shiloah* 17 (1917), pp. 193–206 (Hebrew).

Ettinger = A. Ettinger, "Settlement Methods in Other Countries," in *Ba'avoda [At Work]: A Pamphlet for Members*, Jaffa 1918, pp. 95–100 (Hebrew).

Ever-Hadani, Fifty = A. Ever-Hadani (Feldman), *Fifty Years of Settlement in Lower Galilee*, Ramat Gan [1956?] (Hebrew).

Ever-Hadani, PICA = A. Ever-Hadani, "From Foundation to Statehood — PICA Volume, I: The Pioneers and the Well-Known Philanthropist, 1882–1900," CZA A302/46 (typescript, Hebrew).

Ever-Hadani, Vinegrowers = A. Ever-Hadani, *The History of the Vinegrowers' Association, 1906–1966*, Rishon le-Zion and Zikhron Ya'akov 1966 (Hebrew).

Fellman = J. Fellman, *The Revival of a Classical Tongue*, Hague and Paris 1973.

Ficaya = P. Ficaya, "Le peuplement italienne en Tunisie," Ph.D. dissertation, Paris 1931.

Fishman = J. L. Fishman (Maimon) (ed.), *Rabbi Samuel Mohilever Memorial Volume*, Jerusalem 1923 (Hebrew).

Franc = J. Franc, *La colonisation de la Mitidja (Collection du centenaire de l'Algérié)*, Paris 1928.

Freiman = A. M. Freiman, *Anniversary Volume of the Colony of Rishon le-Zion*, I–II, Jerusalem and Jaffa 1907–1913 (Hebrew).

Friedenstein = S. I. Friedenstein, "The Cry of Samaria," *Ha-melitz* 19, no. 70 (1883), pp. 1120–1122 (Hebrew).

Friedman, Social = M. Friedman, "On the Social Significance of the Polemic on *Shemita*," *Shalem* 1 (1974), pp. 455–479 (Hebrew).

Friedman, *Society* = M. Friedman, *Society and Religion: The Non-Zionist Orthodox in Eretz-Israel, 1918–1936*, Jerusalem 1977 (Hebrew).

Frumkin = I. D. Frumkin, "Four Colonies," in G. Kressel (ed.), *Selected Works of I. D. Frumkin*, Jerusalem 1954, pp. 174–183 (Hebrew).

Gaon = M. D. Gaon, *Oriental Jews in Eretz Israel*, I–II, Jerusalem 1928–1938 (Hebrew).

Gartner = A. Gartner, "Mass Immigration of European Jewry, 1881–1914," in A. Shinan (ed.), *Emigration and Settlement in Jewish and General History*, Jerusalem 1982, pp. 343–383 (Hebrew).

Gautier = E. F. Gautier, *Un siècle de colonisation: études au microscope*, Paris 1930.

Gera = G. Gera, *Ancestral Volition*, Tel Aviv 1982 (Hebrew).

Giladi, Agricultural = D. Giladi, "Agricultural Branches in Rishon le-Zion in the Years 1882–1900," *Nofim* 1 (1975), pp. 7–21 (Hebrew).

Giladi, Agronomic = D. Giladi, "The Agronomic Development of the Old Colonies in Palestine, 1882–1914," in M. Maoz (ed.), *Studies on Palestine during the Ottoman Period*, Jerusalem 1975, pp. 175–189.

Giladi, Baron = D. Giladi, "The Baron, his Administration and the First Colonies in Eretz Israel: A Re-Evaluation," *Cathedra* 2 (November 1976), pp. 59–68 (Hebrew).

Giladi, Be'er Tuviya = D. Giladi, "Be'er Tuviya: The Failure of a Settlement," *Zionism* 1 (1980), pp. 9–47.

Giladi, Citizens = D. Giladi, "Citizens vs Residents in Rishon le-Zion (1900–1914)," *Keshet* 23 (1974), pp. 148–163.

Giladi, Rishon le-Zion = D. Giladi, "Rishon le-Zion under the Tutelage of Baron Rothschild (1882–1900)," *Cathedra* 9 (October 1978), pp. 127–152 (Hebrew).

Giladi, Rothschild = D. Giladi, "Baron Rothschild and the Patronage System of his Administration," in M. Eliav (ed.), *The First Aliyah*, Jerusalem 1981, I, pp. 179–206 (Hebrew).

Giladi and Naor = D. Giladi and M. Naor, *Rothschild, "Founder of the Yishuv," and his Activities in Eretz Israel*, Jerusalem 1982 (Hebrew).

Ginsberg and Zussman = A. Ginsberg (Ahad Ha-am) and A. Zussman, *Critical Remarks on the Colonies of the Holy Land*, Odessa 1900 (Hebrew).

Goldberg and Zweibner = J. Goldberg and A. Zweibner, *Souvenir von Jerusalem* [n. p, n.d.] c. 1898(?).

Goldman, Be'er Tuviya = Y. Goldman, "She'ar Yashuv — Be'er Tuviya (Castina)," *Geon Ha-aretz* 2 (1894), pp. 15–23 (Hebrew).
Goldman, General View = Y. Goldman, "A General View of the State of the Jews in the Holy Land," *He-asif* 1 (1884), pp. 121–154; ibid. 3 (1887), pp. 69–98 (Hebrew).
Goldman, Overview = Y. Goldman, "An Overview of Settlement and Colonies in Eretz Israel over the Last Three Years (1885–1887)," *He-asif* 4 (1888), p. 17; ibid. 5 (1889), p. 13 (Hebrew).
Gordon = D. Gordon, "On the Settlement of Eretz Israel," *Ha-maggid* 27, nos. 24, 27, 29 (1883), (Hebrew).
Grandadir = G. Grandadir (ed.), *Atlas des colonies françaises*, Paris 1934.
Granovsky = A. Granovsky (Granott), *The Landholding System of Eretz Israel*, Tel Aviv 1949 (Hebrew).
Grayewski = P. Grayewski (ed.), *Memorial Stones*, vols. 8–10, 14, 15, 17 [Jaffa, Petah Tikva, Rishon le-Zion, Jerusalem, Ekron, Zikhron Ya'akov], Jerusalem 1931–1932 (Hebrew).
Griffin = A. P. C. Griffin (ed.), *List of Books...Periodicals.. Colonization*, Washington 1900.
Gross = N. Gross, "The Economy of Eretz Israel at the End of the Nineteenth Century," in *Banker to a Nation Reborn: The History of Bank Leumi Le-israel*, Ramat Gan 1977, pp. 24–63 (Hebrew).
Grünwald = K. Grünwald, *Tuerkenhirsch: A Study of Baron Maurice de Hirsch*, Jerusalem 1966.
Gurevich and Gertz = D. Gurevich and A. Gertz, *Jewish Agricultural Settlement in Eretz Israel (General Survey and Statistical Summaries)*, Jerusalem 1938 (Hebrew).
Gvati = H. Gvati, *A Hundred Years of Settlement*, I–II, Jerusalem 1985 (Hebrew).
Hacohen, Hasty = M. ben H. Hacohen, "Hasty Settlement," in idem, *From Evening to Evening: Collection of Essays by Mordechai ben Hillel Hacohen*, II, Vilna 1904, pp. 55–119 (Hebrew).
Hacohen, Individual = M. ben H. Hacohen, "Individual Opinion," in idem, *From Evening to Evening: Collection of Essays by Mordechai ben Hillel*, II, Vilna 1904, pp. 300–308.
Hacohen, Land of Israel = M. ben H. Hacohen, "On the Land of Israel," in idem, *From Evening to Evening: Collection of Essays by Mordechai ben Hillel*, II, Vilna 1904, pp. 3–54 (Hebrew).

Hada Hu = Hada Hu [pseud.], "Rosh Pinna," *Knesset Yisrael* 2 (1887), pp. 217–224 (Hebrew).

Hadas = E. Hadas, "The Baron's Political Objectives in Purchasing Land in Eretz Israel," *Nofim*, 7 (1977), pp. 7–11 (Hebrew).

Hamelin = L. E. Hamelin, "L'ère française Menier de 1895 à 1926 à l'ile d'Anti-Costi (Canada)," *Annales de Géographie* 89 (1980), pp. 157–177.

Hanauer = E. Hanauer, "Notes on the History of Modern Colonisation in Palestine," *Quarterly Statement of the Palestine Exploration Fund* (1900), pp. 128–132.

Haramati, *Beginnings* = S. Haramati, *The Beginnings of Hebrew Education in Eretz Israel and its Contribution to the Revival of the Hebrew Language, 1883–1914*, Jerusalem 1979 (Hebrew).

Haramati, Revival = S. Haramati, "The Revival of Hebrew as a Spoken Language in the Settlements," in M. Eliav (ed.), *The First Aliyah*, Jerusalem 1981, I, pp. 426–446 (Hebrew).

Hardy = G. Hardy, *Géographie et colonisation*, Paris 1933.

Harisman = A. M. Harisman, *The Vanguard of the Hula: The History of Yesud Hama'ala and its Founders*, Jerusalem 1958 (Hebrew).

Harosen = J. Harosen, *The Vision of Settlement in the Galilee*, Jerusalem 1971 (Hebrew).

Harris and Warkentin = C. Harris and J. Warkentin, *Canada before Confederation: A Study in Historical Geography*, Toronto 1974.

Herschberg, *Oriental Lands* = A. S. Herschberg, *In Oriental Lands*, Jerusalem 1978 (Hebrew).

Herschberg, *Way* = A. S. Herschberg, *The Way of the New Yishuv in Eretz Israel*, Jerusalem 1979 (Hebrew).

Hissin, *Diary* = C. Hissin, *Diary of a Biluite*, Tel Aviv 1928 (Hebrew; first published in Russian in 1887).

Hissin, *Journey* = C. Hissin, *Journey in the Promised Land*, Tel Aviv 1982 (Hebrew).

Horowitz, Diary = Z. Horowitz, "The Diary of Zvi Horowitz, 1883–1890," CZA A164/16/1 (typescript; no pagination; Hebrew).

Horowitz, Gedera = Y. Horowitz, "Inquirer from Zion — Gedera," *Knesset Yisrael* 1 (1886), pp. 992–997 (Hebrew).

Horowitz, Yesud ha-Ma'ala = G. L. Horowitz, "Inquirer from Zion: Two Days at the Colony of Yesud ha-Ma'ala," *Knesset Yisrael* 3 (1888), pp. 247–258 (Hebrew).

Idelovitch = D. Idelovitch (ed.), *Rishon le-Zion 1882–1941*, Rishon le-Zion 1941 (Hebrew).
Ilan = Z. Ilan, *Attempts at Jewish Settlement in Transjordan, 1871–1947*, Jerusalem 1984 (Hebrew).
Izraelit = E. Izraelit, "The History of the Colony of Castina and a Few Reminiscences, Part I," JNUL V797/29 (manuscript, Hebrew).
Jaffe = H. Jaffe, *Generation of Pioneers*, Jerusalem 1971 (Hebrew).
Jardeni = G. Jardeni, *The Hebrew Press in Eretz Israel 1863–1904*, Tel Aviv 1969 (Hebrew).
Jawitz, *Dew* = Z. Jawitz, *The Dew of Childhood: Teaching the Children of Bnei Yehuda the Rudiments of Learning*, Warsaw 1893 (Hebrew).
Jawitz, Education = Z. Jawitz, "On the Matter of the Education of the Children of the Farmers of Eretz Israel...Yahud 1888," *Ha-aretz* 2 (1891), pp. 57–63 (Hebrew).
Jawitz, *Letter* = *Letter from the Vistas of the Land*, Warsaw 1892 (Hebrew).
Julien = C. A. Julien, *Histoire de l'Afrique du Nord*, Paris 1931.
Kaniel = Y. Kaniel, *Continuity and Change: Old Yishuv and New Yishuv during the First and Second Aliyah*, Jerusalem 1981 (Hebrew).
Kantor, Basic = "Basic Necessities...: [letter of 17 Adar 1888]," quoted in "Falsehood Shall be Silenced," *Ha-melitz* 28, no. 112 (1888), pp. 1187–1188; ibid. no. 113 (1888), pp. 1196–1198 (Hebrew original in CZA A9/101/11).
Kantor, Through = (Mrs.) Kantor, "Through the Eyes of a Settler's Wife: Letters from the Moshava, edited and annotated by Ran Aaronsohn," in D. Bernstein (ed.), *Pioneers and Homemakers: Jewish Women in the Prestate Israeli Society*, Albany 1992, pp. 29–47.
Kark = R. Kark, "Land Acquisition and New Agricultural Settlements in Palestine during the Tyomkin Period, 1890–1892," *Ha-zionut* 9 (1984), pp. 179–194 (Hebrew).
Karpat = K. Karpat, "Ottoman Immigration Policies and Settlement in Palestine," in I. Abu Lughod and B. Abu Laban (eds.), *Settlers Regimes in Africa and the Arab World*, Wilmette 1974, pp. 58–72.
Katz, Development = S. Katz, "The Development of Orange-Growing during the Early Years of Zionist Settlement," *Nofim* 5 (1977), pp. 8–26 (Hebrew).
Katz, First Furrow = S. Katz, "The First Furrow: Ideology, Settlement and Agriculture in Petah Tiqva in its First Decade (1878–1888)," *Cathedra* 23 (April 1982), pp. 57–124 (Hebrew).
Kayyali = A. Kayyali, *Palestine — A Modern History*, London 1978.

Kellner, *First* = J. Kellner, *The First Aliyot: Myth and Reality*, Jerusalem 1982 (Hebrew).

Kellner, *Revolt* = J. Kellner, "The Revolt of the Settlers of Rishon le-Zion in 1887 and the Uprising of the Jewish Immigrant in New York in 1882," *Cathedra* 5 (October 1977), pp. 3–29 (Hebrew).

Kellner, *Zion's Sake* = J. Kellner, *For Zion's Sake: World Jewry's Efforts to Relieve Distress in the Yishuv, 1869–1882*, Jerusalem 1976 (Hebrew).

Kimhi = D. Kimhi (ed.), *Anniversary Volume of the Teachers' Association, 1903–1928*, Jerusalem 1929 (Hebrew).

Kimmerling = B. Kimmerling, "The Influence of Land and Territorial Factors in the Jewish-Arab Dispute on the Building of Jewish Society in Eretz Israel (from the Beginning of Settlement to 1955)," Ph.D. dissertation, The Hebrew University of Jerusalem, 1971 (Hebrew).

Klausner, Ascending = I. Klausner, "Ascending the Golan," *Ha-umma* 25 (1968), pp. 57–69 (Hebrew).

Klausner, *Hibbat Zion* = I. Klausner, *Hibbat Zion in Rumania*, Jerusalem 1958 (Hebrew).

Klausner, *Kattowitz* = I. Klausner, *From Kattowitz to Basel*, I–II (*The Zionist Movement in Russia*, II-III), Jerusalem 1965 (Hebrew).

Klausner, *Nation* = I. Klausner, *A Nation Awakens (The Zionist Movement in Russia*, I), Jerusalem 1966 (Hebrew).

Klein = M. Klein, *Migdal Zophim: The Jewish Problem and Agriculture as its Solution*, Philadelphia 1889.

Kolatt = I. Kolatt, "Jewish Laborers of the First Aliyah," in M. Eliav (ed.), *The First Aliyah*, I, Jerusalem 1981, pp. 427–446.

Kostitsky = A. Kostitsky, *Before the Morning Dawned: Stories Told by the Pioneers of the Galilee*, Tel Aviv 1982 (Hebrew).

Kressel, *Father* = G. Kressel, *The Achievement of the Father of the Yishuv, Baron Edmond de Rothschild*, Haifa 1954 (Hebrew).

Kressel, *Petah Tikva* = G. Kressel, *Petah Tikva: Mother of the Colonies*, Petah Tikva 1953 (Hebrew).

Laskov = S. Laskov, *The Biluim*, Jerusalem 1979 (Hebrew).

Lemon and Pollack = A. Lemon and M. Pollack (eds.), *Studies in Overseas Settlement and Population*, London 1980.

Leroy-Beaulieu = P. Leroy-Beaulieu, *De la colonisation chez les peuples modernes*, I–III, Paris 1908.

Leschem = L. Leschem, "Rothschild et la colonisation juive en Palestine," M.A. Thesis, Université de Paris, 1978.

Levontin = Z. D. Levontin, *To the Land of Our Forefathers*, Tel Aviv 1964 (Hebrew).

Lichtervelde = L. de Lichtervelde, *Leopold II*, Bruxelles 1935.

Lilienblum = M. L. Lilienblum, *Path Traversed by the Exiled*, Warsaw 1899 (Hebrew).

Livingstone = W. P. Livingstone, *A Galilee Doctor*, London 1925.

Loth = G. Loth, *Le peuplement italien en Tunisie*, Paris 1905.

Lubman-Haviv = Y. Lubman-Haviv (ed.), *Mordechai Lubman: The Man and his Work*, Tel Aviv 1968 (Hebrew).

Luncz, Guide = A. M. Luncz, *Guide to Palestine and Syria*, Jerusalem 1891 (Hebrew).

Luncz, Look = A. M. Luncz, "A Look at the Holy Land over the Past Five Years," *Yerushalayim* 2 (1887), pp. 167–184 (Hebrew).

Luncz, Rothschild = A. M. Luncz, "The House of Rothschild and Jerusalem," *Luah Eretz Israel*, 1906, pp. 169–203 (Hebrew).

Mandel = N. Mandel, *The Arabs and Zionism before World War I*, Los Angeles 1976.

Manheim = C. Manheim, *Colonisation: principes et realisations*, Paris and Envers 1937.

Margalith = I. Margalith, *Le Baron Edmond de Rothschild et la colonisation juive en Palestine*, Paris 1954.

Margalith and Goldstein = I. Margalith and Y. Goldstein, "The Baron's Settlement Scheme 1882–1899," in I. Kollat (ed.), *The History of the Jewish Community in Eretz Israel since 1882, Part I: The Ottoman Period*, Jerusalem 1989, pp. 419–537 (Hebrew).

McKay = D. V. McKay, "The French in Tunisia," *Geographical Review* 35 (1945), pp. 368–390.

Meerovitch, *Advice* = M. Meerovitch, *Advice and Insight*, Warsaw 1885 (Hebrew).

Meerovitch, *Bilu* = M. Meerovitch, *In the Days of Bilu*, Jerusalem 1942 (Hebrew).

Meerovitch, *Birth Pangs* = M. Meerovitch, *Birth Pangs of Revival: A Collection of Essays*, ed. Y. Avneri, Tel Aviv 1931 (Hebrew).

Meerovitch, Castina = M. Meerovitch, "The Colony of Castina or Decisive Proof of the the Ability of Farmers in Eretz Israel to Live Off Grain," *Ha-ikar* 5 (1891), pp. 1–11 (Hebrew).

Meerovitch, *Description* = M. Meerovitch, *Description of the Colonies*, Odessa 1900 (Russian).
Meerovitch, Planting = M. Meerovitch, "Planting in Rishon Le-Zion," in D. Idelovitch (ed.), *Rishon Le-Zion 1882–1941*, Rishon Le-Zion 1941, pp. 240–255 (Hebrew).
Meinig = D. Meinig, "Geographical Analysis of Imperial Expansion," in A. R. H. Baker and M. Billinge (eds.), *Period and Place*, Cambridge 1982, pp. 72–78.
Memmi = A. Memmi, *The Colonizer and the Colonized*, New York 1965.
Monheim = C. Monhein, *Colonisation: Principes et realisation*, Paris and Anvers 1947.
Morris = H. C. Morris, *History of Colonization*, London 1900.
Na'aman = S. Na'aman, "Bilu: An Emancipatory Movement and a Settlement Group," *Ha-tzionut* 8 (1983), pp. 11–56 (Hebrew).
Neiman = D. Neiman (ed.), *Mazkeret Batya (formerly Ekron), 1883–1967*, Tel Aviv 1968 (Hebrew).
Niv = D. Niv (ed.), *Rosh Pinna One Hundred Years Old (1882–1982)*, Rosh Pinna 1983 (Hebrew).
Ofek = U. Ofek, "'And Ye Were Unto Hebrew People': The Growth of an Innate Children's Literature in Eretz-Israel," *Cathedra* 3 (February 1977), pp. 73–116 (Hebrew).
Öke = M. K. Öke, "The Ottoman Empire, Zionism and the Question of Palestine (1880–1908)," *International Journal of Middle East Studies* 14 (1983), pp. 329–341.
Oliphant = L. Oliphant, *Haifa, or Life in Modern Palestine*, London 1887 (Hebrew version: Jerusalem, 1976).
Passron = R. E. Passron, "Les grandes sociétés de la colonisation dans l'Afrique de Nord," Ph.D. dissertation [Algeria], 1925.
Pelman = A. Pelman (ed.), *The Pioneers of Jewish Citriculture in Eretz Israel*, Tel Aviv 1940 (Hebrew).
Penslar = D. J. Penslar, *Zionism and Technocracy: The Engineering of Jewish Settlement in Palestine, 1870–1918*, Bloomington 1991.
Personalities = Y. Shavit, Y. Goldstein and H. Be'er, *Personalities in Eretz-Israel 1799–1948: A Biographical Dictionary*, Tel Aviv 1983 (Hebrew).
Pioneer Settlement = *Pioneer Settlement*, New York 1932 [publication of the American Geographical Society].
Pines = Y. M. Pines, *Building the Land*, I–II, Tel Aviv 1938–1939 (Hebrew).

Piquet = V. Piquet, *L'Algérie française: un siècle de colonisation, 1830–1930*, Paris 1930.

Poncet = J. Poncet, *La colonisation et l'agriculture européene en Tunisie depuis 1881: étude de géographie historique et économique*, Paris 1962.

Pukhachewsky, Feuilleton = M. Pukhachewsky, "Feuilleton: Letter from the Holy Land," *Ha-melitz* 26, no. 29 (1886), p. 452 (Hebrew).

Pukhachewsky, Founders = M. Pukhachewsky, "The Founders: Selected Memoirs," *Bustenai* 1, nos. 6–34, 37–38, 40–44 (1929) (Hebrew).

Pukhachewsky, Viniculture = M. Pukhachewsky, "History of Viniculture in Rishon Le-Zion," in D. Idelovitch (ed.), *Rishon Le-Zion 1882–1941*, Rishon Le-Zion 1941, pp. 263–269 (Hebrew).

Raab = Y. Raab (Ben-Ezer), *The First Furrow*, Tel Aviv 1956 (Hebrew).

Rabinowitz, Foundation Stone = S. P. Rabinowitz, "Inquirer from Zion: Foundation Stone: Rishon le-Zion, Rosh Pinna, Ekron, Petah Tikva, Yesud Ha-ma'ala," *Knesset Yisrael* 1 (1886), pp. 978–992, 997–1000 (Hebrew).

Rabinowitz, Review = S. P. Rabinowitz, "Inquirer from Zion: A Review of Life in the Settlements of the Holy Land at the End of 1887," *Knesset Yisrael* 2 (1887), pp. 203–216 (Hebrew).

Raffalovich, 1887 = S. Raffalovich, "From Time to Time, Individual Cases...from the Month of Tishrei 1885 to the Month of Nissan 1886...," *He-asif* 3 (1887), pp. 61–68 (Hebrew).

Raffalovich, 1888 = S. Raffalovich, "From Time to Time, a Reminder of All the Events...from the Month of Nissan 1887 to the Month of Tevet 1888...," *Knesset Yisrael* 3 (1888), pp. 231–236 (Hebrew).

Raffalovich and Sachs = I. Raffalovich and M. E. Sachs, *The Appearance of Eretz Israel and the Colonies*, Jerusalem 1899 [album of photos].

Reichman, *Foothold* = S. Reichman, *From Foothold to Settled Territory — The Jewish Settlement 1918–1948: A Geographical Interpretation and Documentation*, Jerusalem 1979 (Hebrew).

Reichman, Geographical = S. Reichman, "Geographical Elements in the Zionist Colonization Method in Late Turkish Times," *Eretz Israel* 17 (1984), pp. 117–127 (Hebrew).

Reichman and Hasson = S. Reichman and S. Hasson, "A Cross-Cultural Diffusion of Colonisation: From Posen to Palestine," *Annals of Association of American Geographers* 71, 1 (1984), pp. 57–70.

Rogel = N. Rogel, "The 'Deed of Purchase' of Rosh Pinah," *Cathedra* 65 (September 1992), pp. 117–136 (Hebrew).

Ro'i = Y. Ro'i, "Jewish-Arab Relations in the First Aliyah Settlements," in M. Eliav (ed.), *The First Aliyah,* Jerusalem 1981, I, pp. 245–286 (Hebrew).

Rokeah, Basin = A. Rokeah, "And You Constructed a Basin between the Two Walls," *Ha-havazzelet* 19 (1888), pp. 113–115, 121–123 (Hebrew).

Rokeah, Between = A. Rokeah, "Between Hall and Altar," *Ha-havazzelet* 18 (1888), pp. 154–158, 193–196, 204–207 (Hebrew).

Rokeah, Colonies 1888 = A. Rokeah, "From the Colonies," *Ha-havazzelet* 18 (1888), pp. 244, 249–253, 261–262, 268–271, 281–287; ibid. 19 (1889), pp. 27–31, 47–53, 59–62, 73–77 (Hebrew).

Rokeah, Colonies 1889 = A. Rokeah, "From the Colonies and the Small Towns," *Ha-havazzelet* 19 (1889), pp. 147–150 (Hebrew).

Rokeah, Colony = A. Rokeah, "A Colony Floating in the Air," *Ha-havazzelet* 19 (1889), pp. 85–87 (Hebrew).

Rokeah, Evil Writs = A. Rokeah, "Those Who Write Out Evil Writs," *Ha-havazzelet* 19 (1889), pp. 34–37 (Hebrew).

Rokeah, Lament = A. Rokeah, "A Lament to Those Who Leave," *Ha-havazzelet* 19 (1889), pp. 143–145 (Hebrew).

Rokeah, Matters = A. Rokeah, "Matters will Become Clearer," *Ha-havazzelet* 18 (1888), pp. 89–91, 97–100 (Hebrew).

Rosen = S. P. Rosen, "Jaffa," *Ha-maggid* 32 (1888), pp. 333–334 (Hebrew).

Salmon, Bilu = Y. Salmon, "The Bilu Movement," in M. Eliav (ed.), *The First Aliyah,* Jerusalem 1981, I, pp. 117–140 (Hebrew).

Salmon, Confrontation = Y. Salmon, "The Confrontation between *Haredim* and *Maskilim* in the Hibbat Zion Movement in the 1880's," *Ha-tzionut* 5 (1978), pp. 43–77 (Hebrew).

Samsonov = A. Samsonov, *Zikhron Ya'akov: A Historical Chronicle, 1882–1942,* Tel Aviv 1947 (Hebrew).

Sauer = P. Sauer, *The Holy Land Called: The Story of the Temple Society,* Melbourne 1991.

Schama = S. Schama, *Two Rothschilds and the Land of Israel,* New York 1978.

Scheid = E. Scheid, *Memoirs of the Jewish Colonies and Travels in Palestine,* Jerusalem 1983 (Hebrew).

Schub, Memories = M. D. Schub, *Memories of the House of David,* Jerusalem 1973² (Hebrew).

Schub, Private Farms = M. D. Schub, *The History of the Private Farms in the Upper Galilee,* Warsaw 1893 (Hebrew).

Schub, Yesud = M.D. Schub, *Yesud ha-Ma'alah,* Tel Aviv 1931 (Hebrew).

Sethom = H. Sethom, *Les Fellahs de la Presqu'île du Cap Bon*, I–III, Paris 1947.
Shafir = G. Shafir, *Land, Labor and the Origins of the Israeli-Palestinian Conflict, 1882–1914*, Cambridge 1989.
Shapiro = Y. Shapiro, *A Century of Mikveh Israel*, Tel Aviv 1970 (Hebrew).
Shapiro, Petah Tikva = N. Shapiro, "Outlines to the Urbanic Development of Petach-Tiqva During its First Jubilee," M.A. Thesis, Tel Aviv University, 1976 (Hebrew).
Shilo = M. Shilo, "The Transformation of the Role of Women in the First Aliya, 1882–1903," *Jewish Social Studies* n.s. 2, no. 2 (1994), pp. 64–86.
Shmulichansky = M. V. Shmulichansky, "Everyday Life — Holy Land," *Ha-melitz* 28 (1888), pp. 1211–1212, 1341 (Hebrew).
Smilansky, *Chapters* = M. Smilansky, *Chapters in the History of the Yishuv*, I–III, Tel Aviv 1939–1945 (Hebrew).
Smilansky, *Family* = M. Smilansky, *Family of the Land*, I–II, Tel Aviv 1943–1944 (Hebrew).
Smilansky, History = M. Smilansky, "On the History of the Yishuv in Eretz Israel," *Luah Ahiasaf* 12 (1905), pp. 131–146 [republished in *Ha-shiloah* 17 (1906), nos. 97–98; 18 (1907), nos. 99–100; 19 (1908), nos. 101–102] (Hebrew).
Smilansky, *Memoirs* = M. Smilansky, *Memoirs*, I–II (*Collected Works of M. Smilansky, VIII–IX*), Tel Aviv 1935 (Hebrew).
Smilansky, *Nes Ziona* = M. Smilansky, *Nes Ziona at Seventy*, Tel Aviv 1953 (Hebrew).
Smilansky, Uncle = M. Smilansky, "House of the 'Uncle'," *Bustenai* 1, no. 1 (April 3, 1929), pp. 13–15 (Hebrew).
Sokolow = N. Sokolow, *Precious Land*, Warsaw 1885 (Hebrew).
Stewart = N. R. Stewart, "Foreign Agricultural Colonization as a Study in Cultural Geography," *Professional Geographer* 15 (1963), pp. 1–5.
Straus = R. Straus, "Palestine as a Colonial Enterprise," *Jewish Social Studies* 5 (1943), pp. 327–354.
Tartakower = A. Tartakower, *The Scroll of Settlement, I: The History of Settlement and its Major Problems in Our Day*, Tel Aviv 1957 (Hebrew).
Taubenhaus = E. Taubenhaus, *On a Lonely Path: The Life of a Dreamer and Soldier in the City of the Kabbalists*, Jerusalem 1959 (Hebrew).
Tidhar = D. Tidhar, *Encyclopedia of the Pioneers and Builders of the Yishuv*, I–XIX., Tel Aviv 1947–1971 (Hebrew).
Townsend = M. E. Townsend, *European Colonial Expansion since 1871*, New York 1941.

Trager = H. Trager, *Pioneers in Palestine: Stories of One of the First Settlers in Petach Tikvah*, London 1923.
Triwaks and Steinman = I. Triwaks and E. Steinman, *Book of a Hundred Years*, Tel Aviv 1938 (Hebrew).
Tropeh, *Basic* = E. Tropeh, *A Basic History of Petah Tikva*, Petah Tikva 1949 (Hebrew).
Tropeh, *Beginning* = E. Tropeh (ed.), *The Beginning: Marking Seventy Years since the Founding of Petah Tikva, 1878–1948*, Petah Tikva 1948 (Hebrew).
Tsoibner and Goldberg = A. Tsoibner and Y. Goldberg, *The Holy City of Jerusalem...and the Colonies*, [n.p. 1899?] (An album of photos).
Ussishkin = M. Ussishkin, *Commemorative Volume on the Seventieth Birthday of Menachem Ussishkin*, Jerusalem 1934 (Hebrew).
Vital = D. Vital, *The Origins of Zionism*, Oxford 1975.
Wack = H. W. Wack, *The Story of the Congo Free State*, New York 1905.
Waibel = L. Waibel, "European Colonization in Southern Brazil," *Geographical Review* 40 (1950), pp. 529–547.
Walk = Z. Walk, "The Development of National Education in the Settlements," in M. Eliav (ed.), *The First Aliyah*, I, Jerusalem 1981, pp. 407–425 (Hebrew).
Weil = J. Weil, *Zadoc Kahn 1839–1905*, Paris 1912.
Weintraub = D. Weintraub, M. Lissak and Y. Azmon, *Moshava, Kibbutz and Moshav: Patterns of Jewish Rural Settlement and Development in Palestine*, Ithaca and London 1969.
Wilkansky = Y. Wilkansky (Elazari-Volcani), "Waiting for Capital," *Ha-poel Ha-tzair* 3, no. 1 (June 20, 1913), pp. 4–7 (Hebrew).
Winsberg = M. D. Winsberg, "Jewish Agricultural Colonization in Entre Rios, Argentina: Some Social and Economic Aspects of a Venture in Resettlement," *The American Journal of Economics and Sociology* 27 (1968), pp. 285–295, 423–428; 28 (1969), pp. 179–192.
Wissotzky = K. Z. Wissotzky, *Letters Concerning the Settlement of Eretz Israel*, Jerusalem 1980 (Hebrew).
Yaari-Poleskin, *Dreamers* = Y. Yaari-Poleskin, *Dreamers and Fighters*, Tel Aviv 1920 (Hebrew).
Yaari-Poleskin, *Rothschild* = Y. Yaari-Poleskin, *Baron Edmond de Rothschild (The Well-Known Philanthropist)*, I–II, Tel Aviv 1930–1931 (Hebrew).
Yaari-Poleskin and Harisman = A. Yaari-Poleskin and A. M. Harisman (eds.), *Petah Tikva Fiftieth Anniversary Volume, 1878–1928*, Petah Tikva 1929 (Hebrew).
Yacono = X. Yacono, *La colonisation des pleines de Chèlif*, I–II [Algeria], 1955–1956.

Yavne'eli = S. Yavne'eli, *The Book of Zionism,* I: *The Hibbat Zion Period*, I–II, Jerusalem and Tel Aviv 1961 (Hebrew).

Yellin = D. Yellin, *From Dan to Beersheba (Collected Works,* III), Jerusalem 1973 (Hebrew).

Yver = G. Yver, "La conquête et la colonisation de l'Algérie," *Histoire et historiens de l'Algérie*, Paris 1931, pp. 267–306.

Zemach = S. Zemach, *Labor and Labor*, Jerusalem 1946 (Hebrew).

Zussman = A. Zussman, "A History of Orchards in Rishon Le-Zion," in D. Idelovitch (ed.), *Rishon Le-Zion 1882–1941*, Rishon Le-Zion 1941, pp. 256–263 (Hebrew).

INDEX

The index includes names of places and persons and a selection of topics, mentioned in the text and the titles of the illustrations (but not in the illustrations themselves and the notes). Topics mentioned throughout the book, such as colonies, settlement and colonization, Eretz Israel/Palestine, Jews, Edmond de Rothschild (and his nick-names) or the baron's administration (Officials, Agents and so on), are omitted from the index.

Aboulafia, M.   128, 132
Abu family   84
Acre   39, 74, 262, 264
Africa   15, 42
   North Africa   20, 21, 22, 25, 30, 31, 70, 132, 225
Agricultural Machinery, *See* Farm equipment
Agronomists (or Agricultural instructor or Gardener or Jardiniers)   56, 60, 62, 65, 78, 80, 81, 93, 104, 110, 119, 194, 211-213, 121-124, 128, 130, 134-136, 138-141, 144, 149, 159, 216, 224-227, 229, 232, 249, 252, 271, 295
Akir. *See* Ekron
Alexandria   222
Algiers   21
Algeria   17, 21-27, 29, 31, 43, 44, 95, 96, 134, 135, 138, 140, 232, 285, 287, 290-292.
Balkan   289
Alliance Israélite Universelle (or AIU)   54-56, 59, 68, 71, 74, 97, 119, 122-124, 130, 136, 142, 151, 154-159, 267, 272
Alsace   68, 124, 126-128, 130, 154, 157, 158
America (or Americans)   15, 36, 66, 297
Animals   57, 189, 195, 199, 200, 215, 222, 233, 248, 252
   Work (or Draft) animals   24, 26, 57, 58, 60, 62, 70, 71, 105, 160, 168, 196, 200, 223, 226, 228, 248.
   See also Cattle; Livestock; Sheep
Anti-costi island   119, 285
Arabs   22, 49, 56, 57, 73, 78, 81, 84, 85, 88, 96, 98, 100, 102, 104, 106, 108, 119, 120, 134, 136, 139-141, 147, 148, 153, 160-163, 165, 177, 189, 195, 206-208, 210, 213, 216, 223-225, 227, 228, 232, 238, 251, 258, 259, 264, 274, 278, 280, 288, 290, 291, 294, 295, 297.

See also Bedouin
Arabic   101, 128, 134, 149, 294
Argentina   20, 35, 36, 37, 282
Arieh, D.   158
Arlosoroff, C.   16, 20
Asia   15
Atlit   252
Australia (or Australian)   15, 215
Ayūn Qāra   78, 79, 83, 96, 99, 268

Bat Shlomo (or Umm el-Jamal)
   97, 99-101, 106, 107, 130, 160,
   176, 180, 201, 202, 207, 223
Bedouin   34, 109, 163, 181, 189,
   289
Be'er Tuviya (or Castina)   97-99,
   101-105, 107, 110, 127, 130,
   145, 158, 176, 179, 180, 201,
   207, 218, 227, 282
Behar, N.   88, 158
Beirut   74, 119, 130, 140, 157,
   216, 262, 272
Benschimol, J.   122-125, 127, 128,
   132
Ben-Yehuda, E.   246, 247, 282
Berlin   59, 119
Bessarabia   98, 101, 106, 111
Bialystok   51, 84, 142
Bilu (or Biluim)   51, 59-62, 79, 83,
   85, 164, 247
Bir esh-Shkūm   98, 288
Bloch, A.   104, 128, 132
Bnei Yehuda   83, 98, 267, 288
Bon, cap   33, 34, 35
Bordeaux   142, 159
Boufarik   23, 29
Brazil   20, 44

Breisch   272
Brill, A.   132
Brill, S.   119
Brill, Y.   56
Britain (or England)   287
   British colonies   19
   British Mandate   42, 264, 279
Brody   124
Buenos Aires   36

Cairo   135
Canada   19, 20, 119, 285
Capital (or Funds)   26, 28, 29, 31,
   33, 39, 40, 42, 44, 45, 49-52, 56,
   58, 60, 92, 109, 121-123, 148,
   157, 167-169, 178, 233-235, 243,
   260, 261, 265-267, 269-273, 275,
   278, 279, 284, 285, 289, 293,
   295-297
   Private capital   22, 24, 25, 32,
   35, 52, 76, 85, 101, 261, 267.
   See also Credit
Capitalists (or Capitalistic)   21, 22,
   25, 26, 28, 34, 232, 285, 292,
   299
Carmel   264
Castina. *See* Be'er Tuviya
Cattle (or Beef or Cows or Calves)
   37, 57, 71, 222, 223, 291
Cavelan, F. G.   134, 135
Cellars. *See* Wine cellars
Central Committee of Hovevei Zion
   in Galatz   69, 73, 119, 157
Centralization (or Centralism)   80,
   90, 114, 132, 166, 205, 207, 209,
   261, 270, 271, 280, 297
Cereals. *See* Grain crops

Château Lafite   94, 159
Chèlif   17, 27, 29
Children (or Boys or Girls)   51, 96, 99, 101, 124, 149-151, 168, 216, 221, 224, 233, 238, 243-245, 247, 250, 253, 261, 289
China (or Chinese)   20
Christians   130, 134, 135, 138-140, 142, 153, 159, 160, 291, 297, 298
Church, H.   17, 43
Ciracassians   297
Citrus (or Citriculture or Citrons or Lemons)   34, 62, 80, 95, 96, 111, 119, 214, 215, 232.
   See also Oranges
Classes   24-26, 28, 99, 124, 175, 204, 238, 253, 293, 294.
   See also Capitalists; Craftsmen; Laborers
Climate   20, 31, 36, 44, 95, 140, 142, 215
Clinics. See Hospitals
Cohn, A., Dr.   54, 155
Colonialism   15, 17, 18, 19, 285, 287, 290, 292, 296
Comité de Bienfaisance Israélite de Paris   53, 68, 75, 124, 125
Companies. *See* Societies
Concession (or Land concession)   21, 22, 24, 25, 289
Conder, C. R.   298
Consistoire Central   53, 154
Contacts (or Agreements)   56, 69, 74, 82, 104, 120, 160, 161, 211, 225, 271, 274, 297
Congo   43, 119, 285

Constantinople (or Istanbul)   74, 88, 92, 93, 128, 159, 272, 288
Consuls   35, 74
Cooperatives   29, 33, 37, 41, 170, 205
Craftsmen (or Artisans)   24, 25, 141, 154, 159, 176, 238, 252, 261
Credit (or Loans)   22, 25, 28, 31, 33, 34, 56, 59-61, 65, 76, 101, 108, 114, 121, 122, 170, 221, 228, 267, 269, 286, 287, 296

Dairy farming   37, 220, 222, 223.
   See also Cattle; Sheep
Damascus   88, 93, 128
Deshays, J.   130, 132, 134, 135
Doctors (or Physicians)   40, 70, 80, 121, 146-148, 151-153, 193, 194
Druskieniki Conference   87, 91, 92
Dugourd, J.   59-62, 65, 78, 106, 122-124, 128, 130, 132, 134, 135, 142, 220, 221

Education (or Schooling)   38, 51, 52, 54, 71, 81, 96, 121, 124, 126, 149-151, 168, 175, 236, 243, 245-247, 249, 250, 253, 254, 258, 275, 279, 280.
   See also Schools
Egypt (or Egyptians)   134, 138, 140, 222, 297
Ein Zeitim   130, 132, 283
Ekron (or Akir or Mazkeret Batia)   55-58, 65, 67, 69, 73, 76, 80-82, 88, 100, 101, 123-125, 127, 128,

130, 132, 138, 155, 158, 176, 179, 189, 192, 193, 201, 202, 204, 218, 221, 288, 289
Ellrichshausen, J. F., Baron von 41, 42
England. See Britain
Environment 16, 31, 44, 175, 298
Erlanger, M. 56, 58, 59, 64, 74, 86, 90-92, 94, 123, 132, 133, 154-156, 221
Ermens, G. 94, 109, 111, 134, 135, 139, 159, 271
Ettinger, E. 102, 127, 132
Europe (or Europeans) 15-17, 20, 22-24, 29-35, 39, 40, 50-52, 74, 81, 83, 88, 146, 160, 161, 171, 189, 193, 205, 213, 215, 223, 224, 226-229, 235, 258, 260, 262, 264, 267, 273, 282, 284, 287, 288, 290, 292, 297
Eastern Europe 20, 49, 66, 83, 130, 209, 243, 249, 253, 256, 262
Experimental fields (or Agricultural experiments) 95, 109, 111, 121, 204, 210, 215, 216, 218-221, 231, 233, 235, 258, 259, 273, 295, 297

Farms 22-26, 32-34, 36, 41, 95, 105, 221, 257, 268, 269, 285, 287
Farm buildings (or Farm structures) 26, 70, 73, 81, 101, 111, 121, 176, 179-181, 183, 188, 189, 195, 205, 289, 291
Farm equipment (or Agricultural machinery) 56, 58, 64, 81, 102, 121, 195, 202, 226, 227, 258, 265, 273, 297.
See also Plows
Feinberg, J. 52, 58-60, 155
Fernandez, I. 74, 159
Field crops. *See* Grains
Forey, P. 134, 135
France (or French government or Frenchmen) 22, 24-35, 53, 54, 56, 61, 62, 69, 74, 78, 81, 94-96, 119, 125-130, 132-136, 138-140, 142, 144, 154, 155, 159, 209, 212, 226-228, 231, 232, 244, 271, 273, 291, 295
French colonies (or French colonization) 17, 19-27, 30-33, 43, 44, 70, 132, 225, 287, 290, 292, 296. *See also* Algeria, Morocco, Tunisia
French 70, 71, 123, 127-130, 149, 150, 157, 158, 210-213, 245, 245, 294
Franck, E. 119, 130, 132, 133, 154, 156-158, 272
Frutiger 63

Galilee 80, 84, 107, 125, 202, 264, 265
Gayon, Prof. 94, 159
Gaza 102, 108
Gedera 50, 51, 85, 86, 91-94, 102, 119, 164, 176, 182, 183, 187, 190, 192, 204, 205, 207, 214, 247, 267, 282, 283, 289, 291
Germany (or Germans) 20, 22, 38-42, 44, 144, 160, 207, 222,

226, 258, 287, 290, 291
German colonization   290, 297
Golan   83, 98, 264
Grains (or Field crops or Cereals)
   33, 37, 39, 57, 71, 78, 94-96,
   101, 138, 210, 211, 217-219,
   231, 232, 233.
   See also Wheat

Hadera   144, 282, 283
Haifa   39-41, 50, 69, 71, 74, 84,
   119, 124, 160, 177, 178, 202,
   206, 221, 232, 264
Hardegg, G. D.   38, 39, 40
Hardy, G.   16, 17, 44
Hayim, D.   127, 132
Health (or Medical care)   28, 52,
   54, 64, 70, 71, 81, 96, 121, 135-
   137, 146-148, 151, 168, 258,
   268, 269, 273, 275, 279, 280.
   See also Illness, Hospitals, Pharmacies, Sanitation
Hebrew   71, 149, 175, 193, 242,
   245, 246, 252, 254, 255, 258,
   294
   Hebrew publications (Hebrew books or Hebrew newspapers)
   56, 245-247, 267, 282
Hebron   259, 265
Hirsch M., Baron de   35, 36, 37,
   267, 282
Hirsch, S.   55, 56, 58, 59, 61, 68,
   74, 78, 86, 91, 92, 122-124, 126,
   127, 130, 132, 133, 154-158, 272
Hoffmann, C.   38, 40
Horowitz, G. L.   132
Hospitals (or Clinics)   28, 39, 40,
   108, 146, 147, 193, 268
Housing   23, 24, 26, , 50, 52, 56,
   60, 62, 64, 70, 73, 76, 81, 85, 93,
   99-102, 106, 109-111, 121, 151,
   164, 176, 177, 179-181, 183,
   185, 187, 189, 195, 200, 201,
   205, 206, 208, 258, 267, 275,
   280, 288, 289
Hovevei Zion   49, 51, 52, 55, 56,
   74, 83-87, 91, 92, 97-99, 101,
   106, 108-111, 113, 115, 135,
   149, 155-157, 160, 164, 169,
   176, 180, 187, 190, 192, 193,
   195, 201, 204, 228, 231, 233,
   247, 253, 260, 261, 266-271,
   274, 278, 279, 282, 284, 299.
   See also Odessa Committee;
   Central Committee of Galatz
Hungary (or Hungarian)   51, 226

Illness (or Diseases or Epidemics or
   Plagues)   23, 33, 40, 126, 135,
   233, 242.
   See also Malaria
India   135, 136, 213.
   See also Kashmir
Industries (or Factories)   144, 165,
   175, 195, 196, 198, 203, 204,
   215, 216, 231, 232, 235, 258,
   279, 280, 283, 293, 295
   Industrial crops (or Industrial plantations)   26, 94, 95, 109,
   111, 114, 121, 136, 215, 216,
   218, 231
Infrastracture   24, 25, 31, 55, 60,
   81, 121, 124, 134, 136, 144, 175,
   181, 199, 209, 235, 275, 279,

286, 287.
See also Railways, Roads, Water supply
Institutions 20, 29, 88, 184, 188, 279-281, 293, 294
Irrigation 25, 79-81, 104, 136, 199, 215, 218, 220, 221, 232, 235, 258, 295
Istanbul. *See* Constantinople
Italy (or Italian government or Italians) 30-35, 44, 136, 291
Italian colonies (or Italian colonization) 20, 30, 35, 43, 44

Jaffa 39, 40, 41, 50, 58, 60, 61, 85-88, 91, 102, 104, 123, 128, 158, 202, 221, 222, 243, 264, 266, 272, 282, 298
Jaffe, H. 282
Ja'una 219, 288
Jericho 88, 282
Jerusalem (or Jerusalemites) 38, 40, 41, 51, 56, 63, 74, 83, 87, 93, 102, 136, 142, 144, 148, 158, 183, 242, 243, 246, 252, 259, 262, 264-266, 272, 295, 298
Jewish Charity Committee of Paris. *See* Comité de Bienfaisance de Paris
Jewish Colonisation Association (or JCA) 20, 35-37, 139, 144, 282, 286, 299
Jordan 83, 88, 202
Judea (or Judean) 80, 124, 128, 142, 202, 264

Kahn, Z. 59, 94, 132, 133, 154-156
Kashmir 135, 140
Kattowitz convention 83, 86

Laborers (or Workers) 22, 24-26, 29, 30, 32, 33, 60-62, 76, 84, 88, 90, 96, 99-102, 104, 105, 114, 134, 136, 141, 143, 148, 149, 154, 160-166, 168-170, 216, 223-226, 229, 231, 233, 236, 238, 242, 247, 253, 261, 278, 280, 290, 295
Lachman, E. 119, 204
Land 18, 21-24, 26-28, 30, 31, 34-37, 39, 41, 43, 50, 64, 74, 77, 81, 94, 98-100, 105, 113, 114, 121, 162, 168, 183, 202, 210, 219, 221, 225, 228, 231, 233, 235, 250, 262, 265, 268, 273-275, 285, 287
Land acquisition 22, 23, 25, 27, 32-34, 36, 39, 40, 42, 52, 56, 58, 63, 64, 73, 74, 76-79, 82-86, 88, 92, 93, 97, 98, 100-102, 106, 108, 109, 111, 121, 158, 211, 219, 233, 238, 242, 243, 254, 261, 262, 265, 266, 269, 270, 272-275, 278-280, 282, 286, 288, 295, 297
Land allocation (or Land distribution) 24-26, 61, 71, 76, 78, 92, 109, 177, 181, 187, 196, 211, 216, 219, 220, 242, 286
Land parcels (or Land quotas or Plots) 23-25, 31-33, 40, 77, 78, 94, 95, 101, 109, 111, 136, 164,

176, 177, 181-183, 185, 204, 228, 229, 232
Land ownership (or Land registration)   22, 25, 27, 28, 32-34, 49, 56, 61, 64, 69, 73-76, 79, 84, 85, 92, 104, 108-111, 113, 114, 119, 120, 155, 158, 161, 169, 170, 177, 183, 264, 265, 267-269, 271, 274, 275, 280, 282, 285, 286, 288, 290
Land uses   26, 28, 29, 79, 94, 95, 108, 163, 168, 203, 204, 209, 217-221, 231, 258, 259, 283
Laws (or Legislation or Regulations or Rules)   22, 28, 33, 34, 43, 69, 70, 74, 75, 90, 93, 102, 169, 183, 192, 212, 248, 250, 264, 275, 286-290, 293
Lebanon   119, 157, 216, 225
Lehrer family   99, 223
Leopold II   43, 119, 285
Leroy-Beaulieu, P.   159, 287
Levant   74, 125, 297
Levontin, D. Z.   60
Libya   30, 31, 43, 44, 291
Lilienblum, M. L   268
Lippman   61, 159
Lituania   51, 84, 85
Livestock (or Herds)   23, 26, 34, 51, 70, 73, 101, 111, 161, 205, 210, 220, 222, 223, 232, 292. *See also* Cattle; Dairy farming; Sheep
Local governance (or Local committee)   29, 39, 60, 61, 64, 69, 71, 83, 85, 90, 113, 114, 169, 240, 241, 253

Location   21, 22, 27, 28, 33, 35, 36, 39, 44, 50, 51, 74, 76, 85, 98, 99, 105, 106, 113, 193, 196, 204, 205, 220, 221, 262, 264, 265, 269, 288, 293, 295
London   36
Lubman, M.   144, 160
Lubovsky, M.   99
Lustgarten, H. C.   132
Lyon, M.   127, 132

Malaria   28, 29, 38, 40, 105, 125, 135, 142
Markets (or Marketing or Shipping)   22, 29, 31, 33, 35-37, 41, 64, 94, 121, 201, 204, 221, 222, 231, 232, 277, 283, 293
Marseilles   188
Mazkeret Batya.   *See* Ekron
Mediterranean (or Mediterraneans)   21, 27, 35, 95, 130, 138, 140, 156, 214, 215, 226, 228, 258
Medoc   213
Meerovitch, M.   79
Meinig, D.   293-295
Meir Shefeya.   *See* Shefeya
Metulla   107, 128, 130, 132
Mezhirech   84, 85
Mikve Israel   54-56, 60, 67, 78, 85, 87, 96, 113, 122-124, 126, 127, 130, 136-140, 142, 156, 164, 215, 224, 225, 232, 257, 272, 273
Mishmar ha-Yarden (or Shoshanat ha-Yarden)   99, 100, 267, 283
Mitidja valley   21-23, 26, 29, 291
Mohilewer, S.   52, 55, 58, 155

Montefiore, M., Sir 83
Montpellier 136
Morocco (or Moroccan) 123, 125, 127
Mortier, C., Prof. 94, 159
Moyal, A. 58, 123, 130, 154, 156, 158, 272
Mulberry 23, 62, 80, 95, 96, 104, 164, 200, 215, 216, 231
Muslims 21, 161, 297

Nablus 108, 264
Nahalat Reuven. *See* Nes Ziona
Nationalism 277, 279-281, 287, 291, 299
Natives 17, 22, 27, 29, 45, 134, 136, 139, 140, 158, 273, 290, 291, 293
Nazareth 39
Nes Ziona (or Nahalat Reuven or Wadi el-Hanin) 88, 99, 100, 113, 222, 223, 268, 283, 288
Netter, C. 53-55, 58, 59, 123, 126, 142, 156, 298

Odessa Committee 109, 267
Old Yishuv 54, 98, 113, 260, 264, 272, 298
Oliphant, L. 222, 267
Olives 23, 31, 34, 73, 79, 80, 96, 114, 196, 215, 216, 231, 232
Oranges 41, 62, 80, 215, 232
Orchards. *See* Plantations
Oschri, I. 126, 127, 130, 132
Ossowetzky, B. 128, 130, 132
Ossowetzky, J. 79, 86-88, 102. 109, 111, 122-128, 132

Ottoman empire (or Ottoman authorities) 42, 52, 70, 73-75, 84, 93, 102, 120, 159, 169, 177, 209, 213, 236, 260, 262, 265, 275, 287-290, 294, 297.
See also Turkia

Papo, J. 61, 142
Paris (or Parisians) , 24, 52, 53, 56, 59, 61, 69, 80, 88, 90, 91, 93, 97, 109, 123-127, 130, 132, 134, 135, 139, 151, 154-158, 169, 245, 247, 250, 266, 271-273, 294, 297
Patronage 60, 61, 64, 66, 71, 83, 108, 111-113, 123, 132, 187, 220, 273, 277, 278, 281
Pelman, S. I. 221
Petah Tikva 49, 51, 68, 83, 84, 86, 88, 91, 92, 102, 108, 110, 111, 119, 125, 127, 128, 130, 132, 144, 152, 176, 183-187, 190, 192, 196, 201, 204, 207, 218, 219, 221, 223, 239, 267, 268, 271, 274, 291, 298
Pharmacies (or Pharmacists) 29, 111, 146, 147, 177, 181, 191-193, 259, 285
Philanthropy (or Philantropists) 37, 52, 53, 60, 66, 162, 267, 277, 278, 282
Phyloxera 22, 26, 35, 213
Pines, Y. M. 83, 85
Pinsker, L. 87, 91, 92, 268
Plantations (or Orchards) 34, 39, 55, 78-81, 83, 91, 94-96, 104, 106, 107, 114, 135, 136, 140,

163, 204, 210, 212, 214-216, 218-220, 227, 229, 231-233, 235, 248, 258, 280, 283, 290. *See also* Citrus; Mulberry; Oranges; Vines

Plots. *See* Land parcels

Plow (or Plowing)   33, 57, 60, 70, 81, 199, 212, 219, 226, 227

Poland   84

Posen   287

Protestants (or Evangelists)   20, 38, 41

Pukhachewsky, M.   132

Qatra   83, 85

Radom   56, 58, 74

Railways (or Railroads)   25, 28, 29, 33

Rain   31, 36, 71, 105

Ramla   56, 108

Reforms (or Reorganizations)   30, 69, 82, 91, 93, 94, 106, 114, 219, 229, 242, 277

Rehovot   204, 269, 283

Reichman, S.   20

Revolts (or Rebellions)   23, 24, 37, 80, 87, 88, 90-92, 104, 125, 126, 165, 166, 169, 170, 268, 271, 281, 291

Rishon le-Zion   49-52, 58-69, 73, 76, 78-80, 83, 87, 88, 90-92, 94-99, 102, 104, 114, 119. 122, 123, 125, 127, 128, 130, 132, 135, 139, 142-144, 148, 149, 152, 155, 164, 167, 176, 179, 183, 185-187, 191, 193, 194, 196-199, 201, 204-207, 211, 216, 217, 219, 220, 222, 223, 225, 226, 233, 242, 244, 245, 247, 250, 252, 258, 264, 266-269, 274, 283, 298

Roads (or Routes or Streets or Ways)   24-26, 28, 31, 33, 39, 50, 71, 73, 74, 81, 104, 110, 120, 126, 135, 164, 177, 179-183, 185, 187, 194, 199-204, 206-208, 216, 228, 235, 25x, 258, 266, 280, 289, 291, 293-295, 297

Rosh Pinna   49, 50, 68-71, 73, 76, 80, 81, 88, 96-98, 109, 110, 124-127, 130, 132, 135, 138, 139, 144, 150, 161, 176, 183, 186, 187, 191, 192, 194, 196, 199, 201, 202, 204-208, 219, 222, 225, 240, 242, 259, 264, 266, 274, 283, 288

Rothshild family (or House of Rothschild)   53, 54, 76, 113, 155

Rumania (or Rumanian)   49, 69, 73, 74, 76, 119, 144, 157, 177, 226

Rumthaniyya   83, 98, 288

Russia (or Russian)   20, 49, 54, 55, 56, 66, 91, 98, 119, 124, 126, 130, 134, 135, 149, 155, 160, 226, 267, 282, 290

Sahel plains   22, 23

Safed   50, 70, 71, 83, 84, 98, 108, 202, 216, 225, 259, 264

Samaria   202, 264, 265

Sanitation (or Hygienic Conditions)

23, 28, 121, 242
Sarona 40-42
Scandinavia (or Denmark or Norway or Sweden) 39, 285, 287
Scheid, E. 68, 69, 74, 75, 79, 80, 90, 92-94, 100, 122, 124-126, 128-130, 132, 140, 141, 157, 158, 166, 212, 266, 271, 272, 283
Schools 29, 39, 40, 64, 70, 81, 88, 97, 108, 142, 149-152, 156, 158, 168, 177, 179-181, 191-193, 196, 204, 216, 236, 243-247, 249, 250, 254, 258, 268, 293
Farming schools (or Agriculture schools) 54, 56, 88, 96-98, 100, 106, 122, 134, 136, 138, 149, 164, 179, 193, 224, 225, 257, 273.
See also Graignon; Mikve Israel; Montpellier; Ruaiba; Versailles
Security 23, 28, 29, 39, 98, 153, 265, 280, 291, 296
Senegal 135, 140
Services (or Public/Community services) 40, 52, 64, 70, 81, 82, 97, 101, 106, 110-112, 114, 120, 121, 132, 146, 149, 168-170, 175, 180, 190-193, 203, 204, 233-235, 268-270, 272, 273, 279, 281, 286, 287.
See also Education; Health
Shawiye. See Shefeya
Sheep 71, 211, 222
Shefeya (or Meir Shefeya or Shawiya) 97-99, 106, 107, 130, 176, 180, 201, 202, 207

Shoshanat ha-Yarden. *See* Mishmar ha-Yarden
Shub, M. D. 71
Siberia 20, 287
Sicily (or Sicilians) 30, 32
Site 49, 50, 56, 75, 76, 84, 85, 98, 99, 119, 177, 179, 180, 183, 198, 201, 204, 206, 220, 251, 262, 265, 270, 271, 282, 288, 293, 299
Historical sites 252, 255
Slor, H. M. 144
Soils (or Rocks or Sands) 44, 211-213, 216, 219, 221, 227, 229, 232, 265, 273
Societies (or Companies) 23, 25, 26, 33, 34, 38, 41, 42, 49, 52, 83, 85, 98, 240-242, 253, 254, 267, 269, 282, 284.
See also Comite Central de Bienfaisance; Hovevei Zion
Spain 135, 136, 138, 140
Spatial distribution (or Spatial pattern) 35, 205, 208, 261, 264, 265
Strassendorf 176, 179-182, 187, 201
Sumeil 221, 267
Swamps 28, 216, 280, 282
Switzerland 22, 40, 125
Synagogues 70, 76, 81, 101, 108, 149, 152, 177, 179-181, 191-193, 196, 204, 206, 236, 248, 249, 258

Tantura 144, 202
Taxes (or Fees) 30, 4X, 52, 169,

233, 293, 295
Technology (or Technics or Tools) 17, 25, 44, 53, 61, 81, 82, 136, 138, 144, 163, 196, 209, 210, 223, 226-229, 231, 258, 265, 269, 273, 275, 297
Templers (or Temple Society) 20, 38-42, 160, 177, 206, 221, 232, 258, 259, 291
Tenancy (or Tenant farmers) 30, 32, 33, 49, 84, 85, 99, 100, 104, 106, 108, 225
Tiberias 150, 259, 264
Transjordan 98, 99, 113, 264. *See also* Golan
Transportation 28, 36, 39-41, 56, 275. *See also* Roads
Trees 28, 62, 95, 164, 200, 212, 214- 216, 220, 229, 231, 235, 250, 280
Fruit trees 23, 84, 96, 104, 106, 210, 211, 215, 216, 220, 221, 231, 235. *See also* Citrus; Mulberry; Olives
Tripoli 30, 31
Tunisia 30-35, 43, 44, 287
Turkia (or Turkish authorities or Turks) 70, 74, 84, 88, 125, 148, 155, 161, 190, 213, 251, 262, 287, 288. *See also* Ottoman empire

Ukraine 54
United States 66
Umm el-Jamal. *See* Bat Shlomo

Valero, H. 272
Vienna 59
Vines (or Vineyards or Grapes or Viticulture) 22, 23, 26, 31, 33, 35, 39, 41, 51, 62, 63, 78-81, 88, 95, 97, 99, 106, 111, 114, 127, 135-137, 139, 140, 164, 168, 196, 208, 210, 211, 212-216, 218-220, 227-229, 231-235, 248, 252, 258, 269, 273, 282, 283. *See also* Phylloxera; Wines
Vegetables 33, 51, 62, 71, 135, 210, 220-223, 231, 235
Versailles 96, 134-136

Wadi el-Hanin. *See* Nes Ziona
Wage (or Salary or Pay) 104, 110, 111, 120, 121, 123, 125, 132, 134, 136, 137, 139-141, 146, 149-154, 157, 158, 160, 161, 166-168, 170, 233, 246, 268, 293, 295
Water (or Water supply) 28, 29, 31, 50, 55, 59-62, 81, 85, 105, 121, 142, 168, 170, 179, 192, 199-201, 220, 221, 228, 231, 232, 268, 269, 273, 275, 296
Water conduits (or Water channels or Pipes) 28, 200, 221, 228
Water towers 141, 198, 200, 205. *See also* Irrigation; Wells
Wells 28, 59-61, 73, 80, 92, 93, 104, 108, 109, 159, 164, 169, 198-200, 221, 228, 232, 289
Wheat 23, 26, 60, 63, 71, 78-82,

85, 104, 106, 108, 114, 140, 161, 210, 211, 217-219, 228, 231, 233, 258
Wines 136, 142, 159, 212, 213, 231, 248
Wine cellars (or Wineries or Cellars) 41, 79, 94, 95, 114, 121, 128, 142-144, 152, 159, 165, 168, 169, 196-199, 204, 212, 216, 228, 231, 233, 234, 248, 258, 269, 277, 283, 295
Women (or Wives) 70, 96, 146, 147, 151, 161, 168, 191-193, 195, 221, 224, 289
Workers. *See* Laborers
Wormser, J. L. 109, 124, 126, 127, 129
Wurttemberg 38, 42

Yahud 84, 86, 88, 111, 144, 267
Yacono, X. 17, 27, 29
Yesud ha-Ma'ala 50, 83, 84, 86, 91, 92, 98, 108-110, 130, 132, 144, 158, 176, 181, 192, 201, 202, 204, 207, 218, 267, 271, 274, 288
Yiddish 97, 149, 243, 245, 294

Zammarin. *See* Zikhron Ya'akov
Zikhron Ya'akov 49, 50, 68, 69, 71-77, 80, 88, 95-101, 106, 107, 119, 124, 125, 127-130, 132, 135, 136, 138, 139, 141, 142, 144, 149, 151, 153, 157, 159, 160, 162, 164, 167, 176-180, 182, 183, 190, 192-194, 196, 198, 199, 201-204, 206, 207, 215, 21x, 221-224, 228, 234, 242, 249, 251, 252, 264, 266, 274, 283, 288, 295, 298, 299
Zionism (or Zionists) 19, 175, 243, 260, 279, 280, 290